Microsoft®
SQL Server® 2012
Step by Step

Patrick LeBlanc

ISBN: 978-0-7356-6386-2

Fourth Printing: September 2015

Printed and bound in the United States of America.

Microsoft Press books are available through booksellers and distributors worldwide. If you need support related to this book, email Microsoft Press Book Support at mspinput@microsoft.com. Please tell us what you think of this book at *http://www.microsoft.com/learning/booksurvey*.

Microsoft and the trademarks listed at *http://www.microsoft.com/about/legal/en/us/IntellectualProperty/Trademarks/EN-US.aspx* are trademarks of the Microsoft group of companies. All other marks are property of their respective owners.

The example companies, organizations, products, domain names, email addresses, logos, people, places, and events depicted herein are fictitious. No association with any real company, organization, product, domain name, email address, logo, person, place, or event is intended or should be inferred.

Acquisitions Editor: Ken Jones

Developmental Editor: Box Twelve Communications

Production Editor: Melanie Yarbrough

Editorial Production: Box Twelve Communications

Technical Reviewer: William Assaf

Copyeditor: Zyg Group, LLC

Indexer: BIM Publishing Services

Cover Design: Twist Creative • Seattle

Cover Composition: Zyg Group, LLC

Illustrator: Rebecca Demarest

I would like to dedicate this book to my wife. When I am frustrated and just want to quit, she finds a way to motivate me and drive me to get back on track. During the writing of this book, she never complained once about the long nights of typing. Instead she encouraged and supported me the whole time. Thank you sweetheart for all that you do for our family. I could not have done this without you.

—PATRICK LEBLANC

Contents at a Glance

Contents

Chapter 3   **Using SQL Server 2012 administration and**
                  development tools   **21**

PART II   **DESIGNING DATABASES**

Chapter 4   **Designing SQL Server databases**   **35**

Chapter 5   Creating your first table   49

Chapter 6   Building and maintaining indexes   73

PART III   ADVANCED DATABASE DESIGN TOPICS

Chapter 7   Table compression   95

Chapter 8   Table partitioning   105

Chapter 9   Database snapshots   117

Introduction

SQL Server is Microsoft's core database platform. Microsoft SQL Server has matured from supporting small departmental tasks to hosting some of the largest databases deployed in the world today. More recent releases of SQL Server boast capabilities and features that surpass those of most of its competitors.

SQL Server 2012 continues the trend by adding hundreds of new capabilities and features to an already robust toolkit. These features include more advanced and scalable high-availability and disaster recovery solutions, streamlined development and deployment processes, advanced and resilient auditing capabilities, and several new Transact-SQL (T-SQL) enhancements, to mention a few.

This book provides a comprehensive tour of the vast majority of the tools and features available within the Microsoft SQL Server Database Engine. Each chapter provides an overview and explanation of the feature, followed by steps that demonstrate how to implement, deploy, or use that feature in your environment. As you progress through each section and chapter, you will build on the knowledge you gained in previous chapters.

Who should read this book

This book teaches the fundamentals of the SQL Server 2012 Database Engine platform. It is intended for information technology (IT) professionals who are new to SQL Server, those who are new to SQL Server 2012, or those who are moving from another relational database engine to SQL Server. IT professionals who are experienced with SQL Server may find useful information here; however, most of the content is introductory and focused on teaching the fundamental concepts.

This book assumes that you have at least a minimal understanding of relational databases. Beyond that, a basic knowledge of Microsoft technologies such as Windows will assist in some areas.

Who should not read this book

This book is not for experienced SQL Server database administrators (DBAs)—it is aimed at teaching the fundamentals of SQL Server.

Organization of this book

This book is divided into nine parts, each of which focuses on a different aspect or technology of SQL Server 2012.

- Part I, "Getting started with Microsoft SQL Server 2012," provides an overview of SQL Server 2012, and then details how to install SQL Server and use the administrative and development tools.

- Part II, "Designing databases," focuses on creating databases and tables, with a small emphasis on indexing.

- Part III, "Advanced database design topics," focuses on advanced techniques such as compression and partitioning. In addition, you will be introduced to the topic of database snapshots.

- Part IV, "Using Transact-SQL (T-SQL)," delves into the details of using T-SQL to manipulate data in your SQL Server databases and tables.

- Part V, "Creating other database objects," continues the introduction of T-SQL, but this time the focus is on creating other database objects that you can use for data retrieval.

- Part VI, "SQL Server replication," provides an overview of each replication type available in SQL Server 2012.

- Part VII, "Database maintenance," includes several chapters that explain how to build a comprehensive maintenance solution that ensures the availability and performance of your SQL Server environment.

- Part VIII, "Database management," covers several aspects of the technology that assist you as the DBA in proactively monitoring and managing a single or multiserver SQL Server topology.

- Finally, Part IX, "High-availability solutions," focuses on the features of SQL Server that ensure that your servers are available should a catastrophic event occur.

Conventions and features in this book

This book presents information using conventions designed to make the information readable and easy to follow.

- Each exercise consists of a series of tasks, presented as numbered steps (1, 2, and so on) listing each action you must take to complete the exercise.

- Boxed elements with labels such as "Note" provide additional information or alternative methods for completing a step successfully.

- Text that you type (apart from code blocks) appears in bold.

- A plus sign (+) between two key names means that you must press those keys at the same time. For example, "Press Alt+Tab" means that you hold down the Alt key while you press the Tab key.

- A vertical bar between two or more menu items (for example, File | Close) means that you should select the first menu or menu item, then the next, and so on.

System requirements

You will need the following hardware and software to complete the practice exercises in this book:

- Windows 7 SP1 32-bit or higher, or Windows Server 2008 Standard SP2 32-bit or higher

- Microsoft SQL Server 2012 Evaluation edition, SQL Server 2012 Developer edition, or SQL Server 2012 Enterprise edition

> **Note** You can use other editions of SQL Server 2012, but you will be limited by the feature set supported by the SQL Server edition that you have installed.

- 2.0 GHz Pentium III+ (or faster) processor

- 1 GB of available, physical RAM

- 2 GB of available disk space

- Video (800 × 600 or higher resolution) monitor with at least 256 colors

- CD-ROM or DVD-ROM drive

- Microsoft mouse or compatible pointing device

You will also need to have administrator access to your computer to configure SQL Server 2012.

Code samples

Most of the chapters in this book include exercises that let you interactively try out new material learned in the main text. All sample projects, in both their pre-exercise and postexercise formats, can be downloaded from the following page:

http://go.microsoft.com/FWLink/?Linkid=263543

Follow the instructions to download the <yoursamplefile.zip> file.

> **Note** In addition to the code samples, your system should have Microsoft Visual Studio 2010 and SQL Server 2008 installed. The following instructions use SQL Server Management Studio 2008 to set up the sample database used with the practice examples. Install the latest service packs for each product, if they are available.

Installing the code samples

Follow these steps to install the code samples on your computer so that you can use them with the exercises in this book.

1. Unzip the 9780735663862_files.zip file that you downloaded from the book's website (name a specific directory along with directions to create it, if necessary).

2. If prompted, review the displayed end user license agreement. If you accept the terms, select the accept option, and then click Next.

> **Note** If the license agreement doesn't appear, you can access it from the same webpage from which you downloaded the 9780735663862_files.zip file.

Using the code samples

The folder created by the Setup.exe program contains three subfolders.

- **Sample Database**   This folder contains the SQL script used to build the sample database.

- **Exercises**   The main example projects referenced in each chapter appear in this folder. Many of these projects are incomplete and will not run without following the steps indicated in the associated chapter. Separate folders indicate each chapter's sample code, and there are distinct folders for the C# and Visual Basic versions of each example.

- **Completed Exercises**   This folder contains all content from the Exercises folder, but with chapter-specific instructions applied.

To complete an exercise, access the appropriate chapter-and-language folder in the Exercises folder, and open the project file. If your system is configured to display file extensions, Visual Basic project files use a .vbproj extension; C# project files use .csproj as the file extension.

Acknowledgments

I would like to first start by thanking God for giving me the knowledge and dedication to complete this book. Next, I would like to thank my wife Karlyn and two children, PJ and Kalyn, for supporting me in this project. There were many long nights and many days when I just did not want to write, and they would provide the motivation that I needed to get it done. Thanks to each of them for lighting a fire in me to complete this book. I would like to especially thank my wife for her continued and ongoing commitment to me and my career. She exemplifies what a good mother, wife, and role model should be, and I just want to say thanks for everything.

To my technical editor, William Assaf, I say thanks for all the great comments and corrections. Without you, none of this would have been possible. During the long nights spent writing, I made so many mistakes, and unfortunately you had to read and find them. Thanks for that. I would also like to thank you for stepping in and writing Chapter 24, "Extended Events," and Chapter 30, "Dynamic management objects," probably two of the best chapters in the book.

I would also like to thank the two people who helped me write Chapter 31, "AlwaysOn," and Chapter 32, "Log shipping," Chad Churchwell and Mindy Curnutt. I wrangled them at the PASS Summit in 2012, and a month later I had complete chapters from both. Thanks for all your help on this project.

Finally, I would like to thank the editing team who worked on my book. They were the most patient group of editors that I have worked with: Jeff Riley, Melanie Yarbrough, and Nicole LeClerc. Thanks, everyone, for working so hard on this book.

Errata & book support

We've made every effort to ensure the accuracy of this book and its companion content. Any errors that have been reported since this book was published are listed on our Microsoft Press site:

http://go.microsoft.com/FWLink/?Linkid=263544

If you find an error that is not already listed, you can report it to us through the same page.

If you need additional support, email Microsoft Press Book Support at *mspinput@microsoft.com*.

Please note that product support for Microsoft software is not offered through the addresses above.

We want to hear from you

At Microsoft Press, your satisfaction is our top priority, and your feedback our most valuable asset. Please tell us what you think of this book at

http://www.microsoft.com/learning/booksurvey

The survey is short, and we read every one of your comments and ideas. Thanks in advance for your input!

Stay in touch

Let's keep the conversation going! We're on Twitter: *http://twitter.com/MicrosoftPress*

PART I

Getting started with Microsoft SQL Server 2012

CHAPTER 1

Overview of Microsoft SQL Server 2012

After completing this chapter, you will be able to

- Explain SQL Server components and features and their uses.

- Identify SQL Server features vital to your environment.

- Define and scope your SQL Server installation topology from a high level.

The process of learning a new technology can be daunting and sometimes involves a tremendous amount of time and effort. Each step of the process, from installing and configuring the software to deploying the first project, introduces new challenges. These challenges often grow when the technology includes several components and features, so the first step, especially with a multicomponent technology, is to identify the components your environment requires and gain a good understanding of the functionality of each component. To that end, in this chapter, you will examine the components and features of Microsoft SQL Server 2012 and determine how they fit into your installation.

Like most relational database management systems (RDBMS), SQL Server 2012 includes several components. The product itself, however, is often divided into two distinct categories: business intelligence (BI) and the Database Engine.

Business intelligence

Business intelligence (BI) refers to data transformed into knowledge that can then be used to make more informed business decisions. For example, a company whose primary purpose is to sell bikes could use its data to identify sales trends and the purchasing patterns of its customers. From that analysis, the company could decide to focus sales efforts on a particular area or region, which in turn could lead to better opportunities and offer the company competitive advantages in its industry.

While the BI features of SQL Server 2012 can add highly visible and effective value to business users and data consumers, in this book you'll focus primarily on the features specific to the Database Engine.

Database Engine

The Database Engine sits at the core of the SQL Server components. The engine operates as a service on a machine, which is often referred to as an *instance* of SQL Server. You can run multiple instances of SQL Server on a given server. When you connect to SQL Server, the instance is the target of the connection. Once an application is connected, it sends Transact-SQL (T-SQL) statements to the instance. The instance in return sends data back to the client. Within the connection is a security layer that validates access to the data as specified by the database administrators (DBAs). The Database Engine enables you to leverage the full capabilities of all of the other components, such as accessing, storing, and securing the data.

The storage component of the Database Engine determines how the data is stored on disk. When designing your databases, you will specify various aspects that will dictate how your tables, indexes, and, in some cases, views are physically organized on your disk subsystem. You will examine the concepts of tables, indexes, and views in detail in later chapters. In SQL Server 2012, you can physically distribute data across disks by *partitioning* it, or dividing the data into distinct, independent parts. Partitioning not only improves query performance, but it also simplifies the process of managing and maintaining your data. With the release of SQL Server 2012, Microsoft increased the number of supported partitions to 15,000 per table.

Within the Database Engine itself, the storage engine is the primary component. Surrounding it are several additional components that depend on the engine. These components include the following:

- T-SQL programming interface (Microsoft's implementations of the SQL ANSI standard language)

- Security subsystem

- Replication

- SQL Server Agent

- High availability and disaster recovery tools

- SQL Server Integration Services

- SQL Server Management tools

The following sections provide a brief explanation of each component.

T-SQL programming interface

What is the value in storing data if you cannot access it? SQL Server provides a rich programming language that allows you to write simple and complex queries against the underlying storage structures. Using T-SQL, you can write data manipulation queries that enable you to modify and access the data on demand. You can create objects such as views, stored procedures, triggers, and user-defined functions that act as a means of surfacing that data. Applications written in programming languages such as Visual Basic and C# .NET can send T-SQL queries from applications to the Database Engine. The Database Engine will then resolve the queries and send the results back to the client.

In addition, you can write data definition queries to create and modify objects that act as mechanisms for surfacing the data. T-SQL also allows you to manage server configurations and security seamlessly. T-SQL is a *set-based* language, meaning that it performs optimally when interacting with data in sets as opposed to manipulating strings or iterating over rows of data. While T-SQL is capable of these *cursor-based* operations, these types of operations are less efficient than a properly designed set-based approach. If you find you are using T-SQL to perform cursor-based operations, consider leveraging a common language runtime (CLR) language. Using your favorite compiler (Visual Studio, for example), you can extend the functionality of T-SQL.

SQL Server 2012 introduces several new T-SQL programming enhancements, including a simpler form of paging, windowing functions, and error handling. A THROW statement is introduced that provides a way to elegantly handle errors by raising exceptions. You can now create a FileTable that builds on the FileStream technology introduced in SQL Server 2008. Coupling the FileTable with Full-TextSearch allows you to run complicated queries against massive amounts of text data (such as the complete text of this book). SQL Server 2012 also introduces several new conversion, string, logical, data, and time functions.

Security subsystem

In most organizations, data is the most valuable asset, and keeping that data secure is a major concern. Any vulnerability in an organization's security might end up triggering a series of events that could prove catastrophic to the business. This is why SQL Server 2012 consists of a robust security subsystem that allows you to control access via two modes of authentication, SQL and Windows. As an administrator, you are able to configure SQL Server security at multiple levels. Using T-SQL or SQL Server Management Studio, you can control access to a particular instance of SQL Server, to specific databases, to objects within those databases, and even to columns within a particular table.

SQL Server also includes native encryption. For example, if you want to secure employees' Social Security numbers, using column level encryption, you could encrypt a single column in a table. SQL Server also includes Transparent Data Encryption (TDE), which allows you to encrypt an entire database without affecting how clients and applications access the data. However, if someone were to breach your network security and obtain a copy of a data file or backup file, the only way that person could access the data is with an encryption key that you set and store.

Even with all of these security capabilities, SQL Server provides you with the ability to audit your server and databases proactively. In SQL Server 2012, you can filter audit events before they are written to the audit log. Chapter 26, "Security," describes how to plan and deploy your SQL Server security strategy. You will learn specific concepts around creating logins and users, and you will examine how to create a security approach and maintain security accounts.

Also in SQL Server 2012, you can create user-defined server roles, which can assist in providing a more secure method of allocating server-level access to server administrators. Microsoft has included the ability to create users within a database without requiring you to create a server login, known as *contained databases*. In past versions of SQL Server, prior to granting access at the database level, an administrator was required to create a server login. With the advent of SQL Server 2012, a user can be self-contained within a database.

Replication

SQL Server replication has been available in most releases of the product. Over time, replication types were introduced to ensure that users could configure replication architectures that satisfied a wide range of scenarios. Using SQL Server replication technology, you can distribute data locally, to different locations, using File Transfer Protocol (FTP), over the Internet, and to mobile users. Replication can be configured to push data, pull data, and merge data across local area networks (LANs) and wide area networks (WANs).

The simplest form of replication, *snapshot* replication, periodically takes a snapshot of the data and distributes it to servers that are subscribed to the publication. Snapshot replication is typically used to move data at longer intervals, such as daily or nightly. While this method is effective, it is often insufficient in satisfying the high demands of users for near real-time data. If higher throughput is required, users often leverage *transactional* replication. Instead of distributing snapshots of data, transactional replication continuously sends data changes as they happen to the subscribers. Transactional replication is typically used in a server-to-server topology where one server is the source of the data and the other server is used as a backup copy or for reporting.

Both replication types are one-way data movements. But what if you need bidirectional movement? For example, assume you have mobile users who work offline. While they are offline, they enter information into a database residing on an instance of SQL Server running on their laptops. What happens when they return to the office and connect to the network? In this scenario, the local instance will synchronize with the company's primary SQL Server database. Merge replication will move transactions between the publisher and subscriber since the last time synchronization occurred.

SQL Server professionals debate the use of replication as a high availability (HA) or disaster recovery (DR) technology. Could it be used for either? There is a possibility; however, replication moves only schema changes and data. To provide an effective HA or DR topology, every aspect of the instance should be included such as security, maintenance, jobs, and so on. Therefore, using replication in either case could pose potential problems in the event of hardware failure or a disaster.

See Also *Chapter 19, "Replication," discusses the replication in depth.*

SQL Server Agent

SQL Server Agent runs as a separate service on an instance of SQL Server. Each instance of SQL Server has an accompanying SQL Agent service. The primary use of SQL Server Agent is to execute scheduled tasks, such as rebuilding indexes, backing up databases, loading the data warehouse, and so on. It allows you to schedule the jobs to run at various intervals throughout the day or night.

To ensure that you are notified in the event of a job failure, SQL Server Agent allows you to configure operators and alerts. An operator is simply an individual and an email address. Once you configure an operator, you can send notifications or alerts to that person when a job succeeds, completes, or fails.

High Availability and Disaster Recovery Tools

With growing demands on server availability and uptime, it is vital that your RDBMS include several mechanisms that will ensure the consistency and availability of your data. SQL Server 2012 provides four technologies for high availability:

- **AlwaysOn Availability Groups** In SQL Server 2012, Microsoft introduces AlwaysOn Availability Groups. An Availability Group supports failover for a set of databases and leverages the existing database mirroring technology to maintain secondary replicas of the database on local or remote instances of SQL Server. This technology differs from traditional failover clustering in two ways:

  - You can configure automatic failover without the use of a Storage Area Network (SAN).

  - You can configure one or more of the secondary replicas to support read-only operations.

  Since a SAN is no longer required, you now have the ability to configure HA and DR using one technology. By leveraging the database mirroring capability to move data over distances using TCP/IP, you can have a copy of the database stored in a data center located in a different geographic area.

- **Failover clustering** SQL Server failover cluster instances provide high availability support at the server level. Prior to building an AlwaysOn SQL Server failover instance, you must create and configure a Windows Server failover cluster.

- **Database mirroring** A predecessor of AlwaysOn, database mirroring provides high availability at the database level. It maintains two copies of the database on instances of SQL Server running on separate servers. Typically, the servers are hosted in separate geographic locations, not only ensuring HA, but also providing DR. If you want to incorporate automatic failover, you must include a third server (witness) that will change which server is the owner of the database. Unlike with AlwaysOn, with database mirroring you cannot directly read the secondary copy of the database. You can, however, create a snapshot of the database for read-only purposes. The snapshot will have a different name, so any clients connecting to it must be aware of the name change. Please note that this feature has been deprecated and replaced by AlwaysOn; therefore, going forward, you should use AlwaysOn instead of database mirroring.

- **Log shipping** This is another technology that provides high availability at the database level, which is ideal for very low-latency networks. The transaction log for a specific database is sent to a secondary server from the primary server and restored. Just as with AlwaysOn and database mirroring, you can configure log shipping in a way that allows the secondary database to be read.

Note If you are familiar with SQL Server, you may be wondering why replication does not appear in the preceding list. This is because replication lacks a few key features, such as holistic database synchronization (as opposed to object-level movement).

SQL Server Integration Services

SQL Server Integration Services (SSIS) is a platform that allows you to build high-performance extraction, transformation, and loading (ETL) frameworks for data warehouses. So why is it included in here in a list of Database Engine components? In most cases SSIS is used for ETL; however, it offers a number of tasks and transformations that extend its usage well beyond ETL.

For example, if you are new to administering a SQL Server environment, SSIS provides you with the tools needed to perform several administrative tasks, including rebuilding indexes, updating statistics, and backing up databases, which make up the primary list of maintenance items that should be performed on any database. Without SSIS, as a new administrator you could spend a lot of time writing T-SQL just to get these activities running on a regular basis. But this is not the extent of the capabilities of SSIS for administrators. How often are you asked for an export of data to Microsoft Excel or to move data from one server to another? Using SSIS, you can quickly export or import data from various sources, including Excel, text files, Oracle, and DB2.

SQL Server Management Tools

SQL Server 2012 includes two graphical user interfaces that enable you to manage, monitor, maintain, and develop in a SQL Server environment. The first is SQL Server Management Studio (SSMS), which allows you to perform just about any action you can think of against an instance of SQL Server. It is an integrated environment where you can access many instances of SQL Server. It consists of a broad set of tools with a rich set of interfaces and script editors that simplify the process of developing and configuring SQL Server instances.

In addition to SSMS, SQL Server 2012 introduces SQL Server Data Tools (SSDT). SSDT is another integrated environment, but it was designed specifically for database developers. You can explore the database and database objects using the SQL Server Object Explorer. So far, some of the most talked-about features of SSDT are the ability to easily create or edit database objects and data, and run queries directly from the interface. Using the visual Table Designer, you can change table schemas for both database projects and online database instances.

Summary

SQL Server offers a robust set of components and tools to enable you to design an efficient, flexible, and highly available database topology for your organization. Each component either complements or supplements the capabilities and functionality of the others. Throughout the rest of this book, you will discover how the components work independently and together.

CHAPTER 2

Installing, Configuring, and Upgrading Microsoft SQL Server 2012

After completing this chapter, you will be able to

- Understand the differences between the various SQL Server editions.

- Select hardware for your SQL Server instance.

- Use the setup files to install an instance of SQL Server.

Editions of SQL Server 2012

It's now time to get your hands dirty and start working with SQL Server. However, before you run off and install an instance of SQL Server, you should first become familiar with the different editions of SQL Server that Microsoft offers. The SQL Server 2012 versions are offered in three categories: primary, specialized, and breadth. All editions come in 32-bit and 64-bit flavors, so don't worry if you don't have any 64-bit machines available; you can still get started with SQL Server. However, this book will cover the installation and configuration of a 64-bit version of SQL Server.

The first category, primary, contains what some consider the three core production editions of SQL Server. With this release of SQL Server, Microsoft has removed the Data Center edition and replaced it with the Business Intelligence edition. Table 2-1 provides a list of each of the primary editions, accompanied by a brief description.

TABLE 2-1 SQL Server 2012 Primary Editions

Edition	Description
Enterprise	This is considered the premium edition of SQL Server. This edition is all-inclusive, meaning that it contains all the features available in every edition. SQL Server Enterprise delivers a comprehensive data center solution that supports a high level of mission-critical workloads, blazing-fast performance, virtualization, and business intelligence (BI) capabilities.
Business Intelligence	This is a new addition to the SQL Server family. It is focused on delivering all-encompassing BI-focused solutions. The Business Intelligence edition enables organizations to build, deploy, and manage highly scalable solutions efficiently and effectively. When accessing data, end users will have a browser-based experience that allows them to slice and dice data in ways that they could previously only imagine.
Standard	While not as robust as the Enterprise or BI edition, the Standard edition does boast several intriguing capabilities. Most important, it encompasses basic data management and BI capabilities that are more in line with the needs of smaller-scale deployments of SQL Server. If you are looking at running a departmental application, or if you have a smaller organization, this is the version for you.

The next category is hard to call a category because it contains only one version, but it is still noteworthy. The specialized category contains the Web edition. This edition is optimally designed for those SQL Server instances that will support Internet-facing workloads and is intended for web hosting service providers. It allows organizations of any size to deploy web-based content such as webpages, applications, sites, and services.

The final category, breadth, was designed for specific scenarios and is offered for free or at a very low price. Table 2-2 describes the two editions in this category: Developer and Express.

TABLE 2-2 SQL Server 2012 Breadth Editions

Edition	Description
Developer	This is identical to the Enterprise edition, except that it is licensed only for development and test systems. You cannot use it for production purposes. Note, however, that you can easily upgrade it to the Enterprise license for production use if you need to.
Express	The Express version of SQL Server is a great entry-level product. It is perfect for learning and building small data-driven applications.

This book covers features of SQL Server that span the entire product line, so it will use the Developer edition. You can download an evaluation copy from *http://www.microsoft.com/sqlserver*.

Choosing hardware for SQL Server

Choosing the hardware to run your software is often a challenge. With SQL Server 2012, it's even more challenging because you must consider the disk subsystem along with the typical server specifications, such as CPU and memory, among others.

As with any relational database management system (RDBMS), memory is at the top of the resource list. This book doesn't delve too deeply into a hardware discussion, since the main purpose is to get you started with SQL Server, but note that hardware requirements vary across SQL Server editions. At a minimum, your server should meet the hardware specifications outlined in Table 2-3.

TABLE 2-3   SQL Server 2012 Recommended Hardware Specifications

Component	Requirement
Processor	Processor type: Intel Pentium IV or AMD Athlon Processor Speed: 2.0 GHz or faster
Memory	4 GB or more
Hard disk space	Database Engine, data files, and replication: 811 MB SSIS: 591 MB Client components: 1823 MB

The requirements provided are specific to an Enterprise, Business Intelligence, or Standard installation. The number of processors, size of your disk subsystem, and amount of memory are primarily dependent on the type of workload, your availability requirements, and I/O requirements. For more information on specific requirements for other editions, please refer to SQL Server 2012 Books Online. An exhaustive list is provided for every edition.

Software prerequisites

Once you've chosen your hardware, you must ensure that the proper software is installed before you set up your SQL Server instance. For the sake of brevity, this section will focus on those instances that are included in the primary category of SQL Server editions. Table 2-4 provides a list of the minimum software requirements for those editions.

TABLE 2-4 SQL Server 2012 Minimum Software Requirements

Software	Requirement
Operating system	Enterprise and BI versions operating system requirements: Windows Server 2008 R2 SP1 64-bit Datacenter Windows Server 2008 R2 SP1 64-bit Enterprise Windows Server 2008 R2 SP1 64-bit Standard Windows Server 2008 R2 SP1 64-bit Web Windows Server 2008 SP2 64-bit Datacenter Windows Server 2008 SP2 64-bit Enterprise Windows Server 2008 SP2 64-bit Standard Windows Server 2008 SP2 64-bit Web Standard and Developer versions operating system requirements: Windows 7 SP1 64-bit Ultimate Windows 7 SP1 64-bit Enterprise Windows 7 SP1 64-bit Professional Windows Server 2008 SP2 64-bit Datacenter Windows Server 2008 SP2 64-bit Foundation Windows Vista SP2 64-bit Ultimate Windows Vista SP2 64-bit Enterprise Windows Vista SP2 64-bit Business
.NET Framework	.NET 3.5 SP1
Internet software	Internet Explorer 7.0 or later

In addition to these requirements, SQL Server setup installs .NET 4.0, SQL Server Native Client, and SQL Server–specific support files.

Before installation

Prior to installing SQL Server, ensure that you have selected and configured hardware that will support the version of SQL Server you plan to use. Also, carefully consider the hardware and software requirements for that version. In addition, ensure that all the external needs, such as service accounts and service packs, have been created, configured, or downloaded.

SQL Server instances

SQL Server 2012 supports multiple Database Engine instances on the same computer. Typically, the initial install of SQL Server is the default instance, which assumes the name of the computer on which SQL Server is being installed. Any additional installed instances are referred to as *named instances*. SQL Server 2012 supports side-by-side installations of instances with earlier versions. For example, if a SQL Server 2005 default instance is currently installed, you can install a SQL Server 2012 named instance on the same machine.

The following is a list of all the SQL Server versions that can be installed side-by-side with SQL Server 2012:

- SQL Server 2005 (32-bit)

- SQL Server 2005 (64-bit) x64

- SQL Server 2008 (32-bit)

- SQL Server 2008 (64-bit) x64

- SQL Server 2008 R2 (32-bit)

- SQL Server 2008 R2 (64-bit) x64

- Microsoft SQL Server 2012 Release Candidate (RC) 0 (32-bit)

- Microsoft SQL Server 2012 RC 0 (64-bit) x64

Service accounts

Each service in SQL Server is a mechanism that is used to manage Windows or SQL authentication for SQL Server operations. During installation, you will be able to select which components to install. As a result, the SQL Server setup will install specific services. Since this book is focused on Database Engine, it will discuss only a few of the possible services: the Database Engine, SQL Server Agent, and SQL Server Integration Services (SSIS).

As a best practice, you should use separate accounts for each SQL Server service. The accounts should be configured with the lowest possible user rights. During the installation, SQL Server will assign default accounts to these services based on the host operating system. If you are running Windows 7 or Windows Server 2008 R2, you can use two new types of service accounts: a virtual account or a managed services account (MSA).

The primary purpose of both account types is to simplify administration for the database administrator. An *MSA* is a domain account whose password is automanaged by the domain controller. It can be used to start a Windows service, but not to log on to a computer. *Virtual accounts* are managed local accounts that are also automanaged. Both accounts can access network resources, but virtual accounts cannot be used with SQL Server failover cluster instances. If other servers and clients need to communicate with these services, you must configure the services to use domain accounts.

 Note When changing service accounts, always use SQL Server Configuration Manager.

Unlike with Windows Services Control Manager, the SQL Server tools will perform additional configurations, such as updating the Windows local security store.

Collation sequences

During some SQL Server engagements, you will likely encounter many people who just accept the default collation. In most cases, the default is sufficient; however, since it's responsible for case sensitivity, international characters, case sorting, accenting sensitivity, and rule sorting, you should definitely consider it prior to install. SQL Server allows collation specification at the server, database, and column level. As a best practice, you should use a single collation within your company.

Authentication modes

The final consideration is specific to authentication. During installation, you are given two choices of authentication: Windows and SQL Server. If you choose Windows, the SA login, which will be discussed in Chapter 25, "SQL Server security," will be disabled. Selecting Windows limits access to SQL Server to Windows accounts. If you select mixed mode authentication, you will have the ability to create accounts that are specific to SQL Server.

Installing SQL Server

This section will show you how to install SQL Server. Note that SQL Server can be installed using several methods, which include unattended, command prompt, configuration file, sysprep, and server core. This section will describe the simplest installation method, which is using the SQL Server 2012 Setup wizard. If you don't have a licensed copy of SQL Server, you can download an evaluation copy from the Microsoft website.

Installing SQL Server from the Setup Wizard

This exercise will quickly run through the installation process.

1. Either insert the SQL Server 2012 media into a DVD or CD drive or access it from a local or networked drive. Look in the root folder of the media and double-click *setup.exe*. If you are using an *.iso* file, you will need to use a tool to mount it or software such as WINRAR to extract the contents.

2. The SQL Server Installation 2012 Setup wizard will open. Select Installation from the left navigation area. On the right, click New SQL Server Stand-Alone Installation or Add Features to an Existing Installation, depending on your needs.

3. The installer will then execute a list of setup support rules. To view a complete list, click the Show Details button. Click OK.

4. If you have a product key, select the radio button labeled Enter the Product Key, and then enter the product key. If you don't have a product key, click the Specify a Free Edition radio button and select Evaluation from the list of available choices. Then click Next.

5. On the next page, check the box labeled "I accept the license terms." You also have the option of sending additional information to Microsoft about your installation. Make your choice and click Next. Note that the button labeled Next will not be enabled unless you accept the license terms. The installer will then install the necessary setup files.

6. After the setup files are installed, another set of setup support rules will run. Click Next.

7. Now you must select the server role. Select the SQL Server Feature Installation radio button, and click Next.

8. On the Feature Selection page, select the following: Database Engine Services, SQL Server Replication, SQL Server Data Tools, Client Tools Connectivity, Integration Services, Documentation Components, Management Tools - Basic, and Management Tools - Complete. The page should resemble Figure 2-1. This book will focus on these foundation features, but you can install others if you want, as well. Also, if you are installing a second instance of SQL Server 2012, the shared features will already be installed, so the Shared Features options will be grayed out.

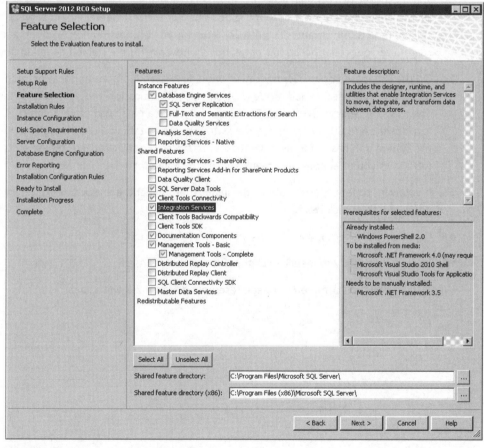

FIGURE 2-1 SQL Server 2012 Feature Selection page.

9. Toward the bottom of the page are options for specifying the directory where you want to install the features. Accept the defaults and click Next.

10. A few more installation rules will execute. If you have installed all the proper prerequisites, everything should run successfully. Click Next.

11. On the Instance Configuration page, select whether to install a default installation or a named instance. If a default instance is already installed, your only choice will be to install a named instance. The Named Instance text box will display the name you use to connect to the SQL Server—for example, ServerName\InstanceName\. The instance ID is used to identify installation directories and registry keys for an instance of SQL Server. Click Next.

12. The Disk Space Requirements page summarizes how much available space there is and how much is required. Click Next.

13. On the Server Configuration page, you specify the login accounts and startup types for the SQL Server services. If you want other services to communicate with SQL Server and vice versa, you must specify a domain account, an MSA, or a virtual account as the login account for Database Engine. For now, accept the defaults. For the SQL Server Agent service, change the startup type to Automatic. Click the Collation tab next to the Service Accounts tab. You can customize your collation on this page, but for now accept the default collation and click Next.

14. On the Database Engine Configuration page, first select your authentication mode. Select the radio button labeled Mixed Mode (SQL Server Authentication and Windows Authentication). Then specify a password for the SA account. Provide a password of your choice. Click the button labeled Add Current User. On the Data Directories tab, you can change the location where the system databases and user databases are stored. For now, accept the defaults. The final tab allows you to enable FileStream. Leave it disabled for now. Click Next.

15. If you want to report errors about the installation, select the check box on the Error Reporting page, and then click Next.

16. One last rules check is run. If everything passes, click Next.

17. You are now ready to install. Click the button labeled Install.

When the installation completes, a page resembling Figure 2-2 will appear.

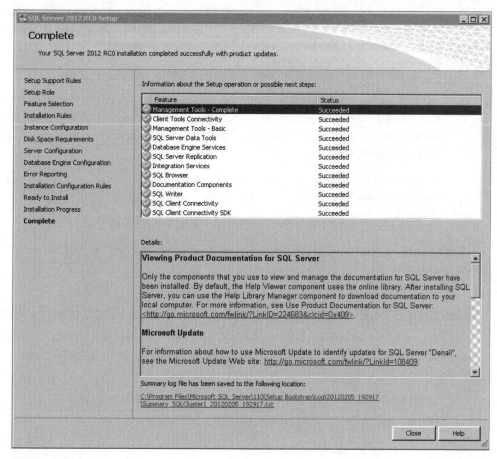

FIGURE 2-2 SQL Server 2012 setup summary page.

After installation

After your SQL Server installation is complete, there are certain things you should do. The following subsections describe a couple of them.

Assigning a TCP/IP port number to the SQL Server Database Engine

First, you may want to change the SQL Servers default TCP port from 1433 to a different port. This exercise describes how.

1. Open SQL Server Configuration Manager by clicking Start | All Programs | Microsoft SQL Server 2012 | Configuration Tools | SQL Server Configuration Manager.

2. In the left-hand navigation pane, expand SQL Server Network Configuration and click Protocols for MSSQLSERVER. If you are changing the port for a nondefault instance, then you will click Protocols for *<Instance Name>*.

3. Right-click TCP/IP in the left section.

4. You can configure each specific IP address, or you can configure the port for all IP addresses. To do so, click the IP Addresses tab, scroll to the bottom to locate IPALL, and change the port number to your desired port. Don't change the port, as this will require you to include the port number when connecting to this server.

5. Restart the instance of SQL Server that has been changed. Click SQL Server Service in the left navigation pane.

6. Select SQL Server (MSSQLSERVER), right-click, and select Restart.

Once this change is made, you are required to specify this port number when you connect to the SQL Server instance.

Opening a SQL Server instance port using Windows Firewall

If you attempt to connect to SQL Server from another machine now, the connection attempt will time out. To connect to this instance, you must open the port. You can do so using Windows Firewall, as follows:

1. Open Windows Firewall and click Start | Control Panel | Windows Firewall.

2. Toward the top of the page, click Advanced Settings.

3. Select Inbound Rules from the left navigation pane.

4. Click New Rule from the right navigation pane.

5. On the Rule Type page, select the radio button labeled Port, and click Next.

6. Ensure that the radio button labeled TCP is selected and enter **1433** in the text box labeled Specific Local Ports. Click Next.

7. Select the Allow the Connection radio button and click Next.

8. In the text box labeled Name, type a descriptive name for your inbound rule. Click Finish.

Now you should be able to connect to this instance of SQL Server using various client tools, which will be discussed later in this book.

How to upgrade to SQL Server 2012

Whether you are upgrading an existing server from one version to the next or installing a new version on a new server, you should carefully think through and plan this task. You have two upgrade choices: in-place or side-by-side. Each has advantages and disadvantages. Often your choice will depend on how much downtime your environment can support, the age or state of the existing systems, and funding. During an in-place upgrade, your system will be down for some time. If you are a member of a 24/7 organization, taking the system down may not be an option, and you will be required to do a side-by-side upgrade. Also, if you are looking to replace older or out-of-date machines, then side-by-side is your only option. With that said, purchasing new hardware has a cost, and if you don't have funding, then your only option is an in-place upgrade.

In-place upgrade

Just the thought of upgrading any software may send chills down your spine. Fortunately, the process of upgrading to SQL Server 2012 has been greatly improved over the years. SQL Server 2012 has several supported upgrade paths. Therefore, if you are currently running SQL Server on previous versions, you can quickly upgrade to SQL Server 2012 without upgrading to other versions. SQL Server 2005 with SP4 is the oldest version of SQL Server that has a direct upgrade path. If you are running a version older than this, you will need to upgrade to that version before you can perform an in-place upgrade to SQL Server 2012. For example, if you are currently running SQL Server 2000, you must upgrade to SQL Server 2005 with SP4 prior to running an in-place upgrade to SQL Server 2012.

Since this is an introductory book, how to actually perform the upgrade will not be covered; however, the following preupgrade checklist should assist you prior to an in-place upgrade:

- Ensure that your version of SQL Server has a supported upgrade path.

- Back up all your databases, including system databases.

- Run SQL Server Upgrade Advisor to prepare for the upgrade to SQL Server 2012.

- Verify that your hardware and software meet the minimum requirements for SQL Server 2012.

- Stop replication and make sure that the replication log is empty.

- Ensure that all the database server logons are stored in the master database.

- Estimate the disk space required for the components being upgraded and ensure that sufficient disk space is available.

When you are ready to upgrade, you will repeat most of the steps from the "Installing SQL Server" section of this chapter. The main differences will involve the configuration. The setup detects older version of SQL Server with support upgrade paths and then guides you through the process.

Side-by-side upgrade

This type of upgrade may not stress you as much as an in-place upgrade, simply because the old server remains in place and can be made available quickly in the event of an installation failure. You will follow the same steps as outlined in the "Installing SQL Server from the Setup Wizard" section of this chapter. Once you've completed the steps, you will need to migrate your security, databases, replication configuration, maintenance plans, and any other custom configurations that have been added to your SQL Server installation. This process gives you the advantage of having a stable rollback plan. In the event of an installation failure or some other type of catastrophe, you can always turn the other server back on and continue operations as normal. Figure 2-3 illustrates a side-by-side migration.

While this strategy offers several advantages, it could require that your organization purchase new hardware. In addition, this method may require that you have disk space that accommodates two identical databases. For organizations with very large databases, this could pose a problem.

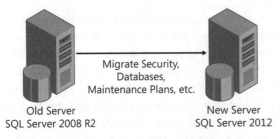

Old Server
SQL Server 2008 R2

Migrate Security,
Databases,
Maintenance Plans, etc.

New Server
SQL Server 2012

FIGURE 2-3 SQL Server 2012 side-by-side migration.

Summary

As outlined in this chapter, you can use several techniques and methods to upgrade SQL Server. Regardless of the method you choose, the end goal is typically the same. With any install or upgrade, you should allocate sufficient time to develop an effective strategy and outline the steps necessary for performing the tasks. The success of your plan depends heavily on these two factors.

CHAPTER 3

Using SQL Server 2012 administration and development tools

After completing this chapter, you will be able to

- Use SQL Server 2012 Books Online.

- Create solutions and projects with SQL Server Management Studio.

- Use Object Explorer.

- Use SQL Server Data Tools.

- Use SQL Server Configuration Manager.

Using SQL Server Books Online

Over the years, Microsoft SQL Server Books Online (BOL) has been criticized for its lack of content and its inability to effectively explain how to use various SQL Server tools and options. However, as the versions of SQL Server have progressed, so has the documentation. Unfortunately, the perception of BOL remains marred by the many years of criticism and, in some cases, its limited content. While BOL does not and probably will never provide a walk-through for every possible task, it does offer a good foundation and starting point for anyone interested in gaining general knowledge about all of the capabilities of SQL Server.

In previous versions of SQL Server BOL, content was installed locally by default. In Microsoft SQL Server 2012, this has changed slightly. When you open BOL for the first time, the Online Help Consent dialog box opens, as shown in Figure 3-1.

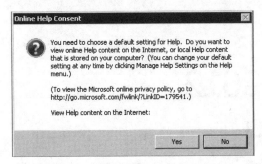

FIGURE 3-1 The SQL Server 2012 Online Help Consent dialog box displays the first time you open SQL Server Books Online.

You have the option of storing the help content locally or viewing it online. If you decide to view it online, you can always change the setting later. In the next exercise, you'll install BOL locally.

Install Books Online locally

1. Click the Yes button in the Online Help Consent dialog box Microsoft Help Viewer 1.1 displays.

2. Click the Help Library Manager icon.

3. In the Help Library Manager dialog box, click Install Content from Online. A fetch process begins that provides you with a list of available content.

4. From the list, click the Add button next to Books Online, located under the SQL Server 2012 category.

5. Click the Update button. The install process begins.

6. When the update is complete, click the Finish button.

7. Click Exit.

8. Close Microsoft Help Viewer.

9. Now open SQL Server Books Online by clicking Start | All Programs | Microsoft SQL Server 2012 | Documentation & Community | SQL Server Documentation.

10. In the left navigation section, you should see several SQL Server choices.

Take some time to explore the contents of BOL. If you are just getting started with SQL Server, or even if you are seasoned SQL Server veteran, you are bound to find all sorts of information that will provide insight into the full feature set available within SQL Server 2012.

Using SQL Server Management Studio

Your ability to efficiently manage and maintain your SQL Server environment has been greatly improved with the introduction of Microsoft SQL Server Management Studio (SSMS) in SQL Server 2005. Administrators can configure other SQL Server components, such as replication, availability groups, Microsoft SQL Server Agent, change data capture (CDC), and many other features that will be discussed later in this book. In addition, you can create databases and database objects, such as tables, views, and stored procedures. Finally, after building a database, you can also manage the data inside the database using SSMS.

Get started with SQL Server Management Studio

1. To open SSMS, click Start | All Programs | Microsoft SQL Server 2012 | SQL Server Management Studio.

2. When SSMS opens, the Connect to Server dialog box appears. Accept the defaults for every option except the Server Name drop-down list. Type your server name and click the Connect button.

Before you start using SSMS, let's take a quick tour of the environment. First, you may notice that the SSMS environment is very similar to that of most Microsoft products. At the very top is the main menu, which has several options available. Directly below the main menu is the Standard toolbar, which is loaded by default. If you right-click anywhere on either toolbar, a context menu appears. From this menu, you can select other choices that will add new items to the existing toolbars or add new toolbars to the menu. Below all the menus and to the left of the window is Object Explorer.

Object Explorer is a multifunctional window available in SSMS. As previously mentioned, it provides an intuitive interface for navigating and accessing server features and databases. Moreover, you can use Object Explorer to connect to multiple instances of SQL Server, Integration Services, Analysis Services, and Reporting Services instances. Once connected, you have the ability to create databases and database objects, configure other features and components, run performance reports, and perform a number of other functions. When you are connected to an instance of SQL Server, simply right-click to access additional functionality that further demonstrates the true power and flexibility of SSMS. For example, if you right-click the Databases folder, you can create, attach, or restore a database. You may have also noticed that Object Explorer has its own menu. This menu allows you to connect to or disconnect from an instance of SQL Server, refresh the items displayed in the window, and perform many other functions. You'll get started with Object Explorer in the next exercise.

Use Object Explorer

1. Open SSMS if you have not already done so. When prompted by the Connect to Server dialog box, ensure that Database Engine is selected from the Server Type drop-down list, type your server name in the Server Name drop-down list, and ensure that Windows Authentication is selected in the Authentication drop-down list.

2. If Object Explorer does not open, select Object Explorer from the View menu or press F8.

   Object Explorer will appear to the left of the SSMS window.

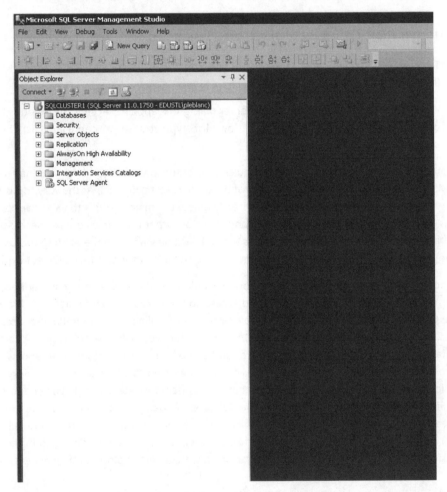

3. Near the top of Object Explorer, you should see the word *Connect* with a drop-down arrow located directly to the left. Click the drop-down arrow and use the menu that opens to connect to other SQL Server components. Since you have installed only a Database Engine, that is the only component that can be connected.

4. You can explore various server objects by expanding any of the folders displayed in Object Explorer. For example, expand the Management folder. You can now view and configure features such as Data Collection, Database Mail, and Extended Events.

5. Right-click the server name, which is the topmost item in the Object Explorer tree. From the context menu, select Reports | Standard Reports | Server Dashboards. This report provides you with a high-level overview of the server.

6. To view more detailed information, instead of selecting Server Dashboards from the report list, select Activity-All Active Sessions. This report reveals all active open sessions on that server.

7. In the toolbar located above Object Explorer, click the button labeled New Query. A new query window opens in which you can write queries to create objects, configure components, and query database objects.

 Note The preceding steps provide a quick overview of some of the SSMS functionality. Throughout this book, you'll learn more details and additional steps to help you take full advantage of the capabilities of SSMS.

While out of the box SSMS is configured to provide a full set of functionality to administrators and developers, it also provides you with the ability to make it your own. If you don't like Object Explorer on the left, you can move it, or if you don't like the font of the query editor, you can change it to one of your choice. You have several options available for configuration.

Personalize SQL Server Management Studio

1. Open SSMS if it is not already open.

2. Select Tools | Options.

3. In the Options dialog box, select Fonts and Colors.

4. Select Courier New from the Font drop-down list.

5. Select 16 from the Size drop-down list.

6. Click OK.

7. Open a query window and type **SELECT @@SERVERNAME**. Click the red exclamation point icon in the menu bar to execute the query.

8. Open Object Explorer if it is not already open.

9. Click the drop-down arrow located to the right of the words *Object Explorer*. Select Float from the menu.

10. Click and drag Object Explorer onto the left docking option that appears. This docks Object Explorer back in its original position. Explore a little and move it to other docking locations. Find the one that best fits your preference.

Using SQL Server Management Studio to create solutions and projects

While most of this chapter's content has been specific to administrators, SSMS does provide functionality for developers as well. In other words, you can create project-based solutions that help you organize your development and configuration scripts. Using SSMS, you can create a solution, which is a container of projects. Within SSMS, you can create two types of projects:

- SQL Server Scripts

- Analysis Services Scripts

In the next exercise, you will create a SQL Server Scripts project.

Create solutions and projects

1. Open SSMS if it is not already open.

2. From the menu select File | New | Project.

3. The New Project dialog box opens.

4. There are two Installed Templates to select from. Ensure that you select the SQL Server Management Studio Projects template. This choice provides two project types. Select SQL Server Scripts.

5. At the bottom of the screen, in the Name text box, type **SBS2012Chp3**.

6. Accept the defaults for the Location and Solution drop-down lists.

7. Type **SBS2012** in the Solution Name text box.

8. Click OK.

    To the right, you will notice a new docked window labeled Solution Explorer.

9. Right-click the Connections folder.

10. Select New Connection.

11. Type your server name in the Server Name drop-down list.

12. Click OK.

13. Right-click the Queries folder.

14. Select New Query.

15. Right-click the newly created query and select Rename.

16. Change the name of the query to **Select Server Name**. Ensure that you don't remove .sql.

17. In the query editor, type **SELECT @@SERVERNAME**.

18. Select File | Save All.

Using SQL Server Data Tools

SQL Server 2012 introduces a new development environment for SQL Server database developers called SQL Server Data Tools (SSDT). Although the primary purpose of this tool is development, it can be used for database deployment and database-level configurations. Using SSDT, you can create databases and database objects such as tables, views, stored procedures, and triggers. You can also edit data within the tables. In addition, you can execute queries and perform database schema compares.

SSDT replaces Business Intelligence Development Studio (BIDS). As a result, not only can you create and deploy databases, but you can also create Analysis Services, Integration Services, and Reporting Services projects. In addition, these projects can be checked into source control solutions such as Team Foundation Server.

Use SQL Server Data Tools

1. Click Start | Microsoft SQL Server 2012 | SQL Server Data Tools.

2. If this is your first time opening SSDT, you will be prompted with the following screen. The options available will vary depending on the software installed on your machine.

Choose Default Environment Settings

Microsoft®
SQL Server Data Tools

Before you begin using the application for the first time, you need to specify the type of development activity you engage in the most, such as Visual Basic or Visual C#. This information is used to apply a predefined collection of settings to the development environment that is designed for your development activity.

You can choose to use a different collection of settings at any time. From the Tools menu, choose Import and Export Settings and then choose Reset all settings.

Choose your default environment settings:

My Previous Settings
Business Intelligence Settings
General Development Settings
SQL Server Development Settings
Visual Basic Development Settings
Visual C# Development Settings

Description:
Optimizes the environment so you can focus on building SQL Server databases

[Start Visual Studio]   [Exit Visual Studio]

3. Select SQL Server Development Settings from the Choose Your Default Environment Settings list box.

4. Click Start Visual Studio.

5. Choose File | New | Project.

6. In the Recent Templates pane located in the left of the New Project dialog box, select SQL Server.

7. Select SQL Server Database Project from the project list.

8. In the Name text box, type **AdventureWorks**.

9. Accept the default for the Location drop-down list.

10. In the Solution Name text box, type **SBSChp3**.

11. Click OK.

12. In Solution Explorer, right-click the AdventureWorks project. Select Import | Database. The Import Database dialog box appears.

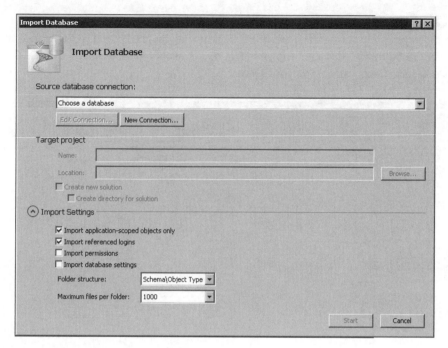

13. Click the New Connection button.

14. Type your server name in the Server Name drop-down list.

15. Select AdventureWorks2008R2 from the Select or Enter Database Name drop-down list.

16. Change the selection in the Folder Structure drop-down list to Object Type.

17. Click OK.

18. Accept all the defaults for the remaining items and click the Start button. The database import process begins.

19. Once all the objects have been imported, click the Finish button.

20. In Solution Explorer, expand the Tables folder.

21. Double-click the Address.sql item.

22. In the table designer view, locate AddressLine1 under the Name column. For that column, change the Data Type from nvarchar(60) to nvarchar(65).

23. Right-click the AdventureWorks project in Solution Explorer and select Publish from the context menu. Now the changes are deployed to the database on the server.

 Note The changes made in the design view are replicated to the script view. If the changes are made in the script view, they are replicated to the design view.

Using SQL Server Configuration Manager

SQL Server Configuration Manager, shown in Figure 3-2, allows you to manage the SQL Server services that have been installed on your server.

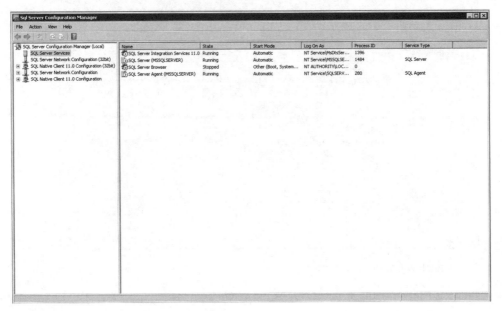

FIGURE 3-2 SQL Server Configuration Manager.

Using SQL Server Configuration Manager, you can perform the following actions:

- Start, stop, and pause a service
- Change service accounts
- Configure network protocols
- Configure advanced properties such as AlwaysOn and Filestream

Because these services are centralized, administrators are able to configure and manage services from one location.

Changing accounts and account passwords are actions often required or requested. For example, during installation you may have accepted the defaults for the service account that runs SQL Server, and now you need to change them. As a best practice, you should always use SQL Server Configuration Manager to make the changes because it not only changes the account, but also sets necessary changes to registry permissions so that the account has the proper permissions.

1. Open SQL Server Configuration Manager by clicking Start | All Programs | Microsoft SQL Server 2012 | Configuration Tools | SQL Server Configuration Manager.

2. In the left pane, right-click the SQL Server (MSSQLSERVER).

3. Click Properties in the context menu.

4. In the Properties dialog box, you will notice several tabs. Click each to view the available options.

5. With the Log On tab activated, click the Stop button.

6. Click the Start button.

7. Click OK.

8. Expand the SQL Server Network Configuration item.

9. Select Protocols from MSSQLSERVER.

10. If you want to enable the Named Pipes protocol, right-click and select Enable from the context menu.

Summary

In this chapter, you learned about several administrative and development tools included in Microsoft SQL Server 2012. Individually, each includes further tools that provide administrators and developers with the ability to create and manage SQL Server instances and objects at different levels. Together, they offer a comprehensive set of tools providing a one-stop shop for the functionality needed to maintain one to many instances of SQL Server.

Designing databases

CHAPTER 4

Designing SQL Server databases

After completing this chapter, you will be able to

- Understand the requirements and functions of each system database.

- Understand the SQL Server database structure.

- Create a database.

- Add and alter filegroups.

- Add files to filegroups.

- Detach and attach databases.

- Understand database recovery models.

The database is the container for all objects within Microsoft SQL Server for the relational engine. In this chapter, you will learn about the system databases that store vital information about the SQL Server instance. You will also learn fundamental techniques needed to create user-defined databases, along with methods you can use to control how and where data is stored. The methods include creating databases that consist of multiple filegroups and multiple data files. Finally, you will learn how to move databases from one instance of SQL Server to another, and you will explore database recovery models.

Understanding SQL Server system databases

Before you start creating Microsoft SQL Server 2012 databases, you should have a good understanding of the system databases that are created by default when you install an instance of SQL Server. Each of the following databases serves a specific purpose and is required to run SQL Server:

- master

- tempdb

- model

- msdb

- resource

- distribution

master database

The master database, as its name suggests, is the primary system database. Without it, SQL Server cannot start. The master database contains the most important information about objects within the SQL Server instance, such as the following:

- Databases
- AlwaysON
- Database mirroring
- Configurations
- Logins
- Resource Governor
- Endpoints

For example, if you want to quickly obtain a list of all the databases on an instance of SQL Server, you can execute the following query:

```
//The following code returns a list of all databases on an instance of SQL Server
Select * from sys.master_files
```

This query returns a list of databases and also additional configuration options that have been specified for each database. This approach is faster than using Microsoft SQL Server Management Studio (SSMS), where you view this information one database at a time.

tempdb database

The tempdb database is a global playground for temporary objects created by the internal processes that run SQL Server and temporary objects that are created by users or applications. These temporary objects included temporary tables and stored procedures, table variables, global temporary tables, and cursors. In addition to temporary objects, tempdb stores row versions for read-committed or snapshot isolation transactions, online index operations, and AFTER triggers. One important thing to note about tempdb is that it is re-created every time SQL Server is restarted. Although you can create objects in tempdb, you should never use it as a database where persisted information is stored.

model database

The model database is exactly what its name implies: a model for all databases that are created on an instance of SQL Server. In other words, it's used as a template each time you create a database. For example, if you want a particular table to exist in every database created on an instance of SQL Server, you will create that table in the model database. As a result, each time a database is created, it will include that table.

Note If the model database does not exist or is offline, tempdb cannot be created. This is because, as mentioned previously, it is re-created each time SQL Server is restarted. Since each database uses model as a template, and tempdb is no exception, it must exist to re-create tempdb at startup.

msdb database

The msdb serves primarily as the back end database for Microsoft SQL Server Agent. Whenever you create and/or schedule a SQL Server Agent job, the metadata for that job is stored in this database. In addition to SQL Server Agent data, msdb stores information for the following components:

- Service brokers
- Alerts
- Log shipping
- SSIS packages
- Utility control point (UCP)
- Database mail
- Maintenance plans

resource database

The resource database is a hidden, read-only database that is usually not discussed very often. The resource database's primary purpose is to improve the upgrade process from one version of SQL Server to the next. All system objects for an instance of SQL Server are stored within the resource database. This database cannot be backed up or restored. You should not attempt to change or move this database unless Microsoft Customer Support directs you to do so.

distribution database

The final system database is the distribution database. This database exists only when you have configured this instance as a distributor for replication. Prior to configuring replication, you must perform this configuration. All metadata and history for the various types of replication are stored within this database.

See Also For more information on replication, see Chapter 19, "Replication."

1. Open SQL Server Management Studio (SSMS) and connect to a server.

2. Object Explorer should be open. If it is not, press F8 to open it.

3. In Object Explorer, expand Databases.

4. You will see a folder labeled System Databases. Expand it.

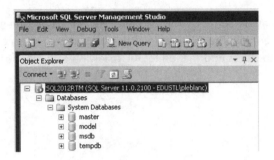

Understanding the SQL Server database structure

As mentioned previously, databases are the primary data storage objects within SQL Server. The database creation process, while very simple, always requires careful thought relating to the structure. Databases can be created using many different technologies and techniques. In this chapter, you will focus on using T-SQL and SSMS. By default, every SQL Server database consists of two files (see Figure 4-1):

■ The *data file* contains data and database objects such as tables, views, and stored procedures.

■ The *log file* contains information that assists in the recoverability of transactions in the database.

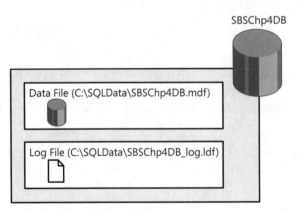

FIGURE 4-1 The SQL Server database structure consists of at least a single data file and a single log file.

Creating a database

There are two types of data files: primary and secondary. When a database is initially created, the primary data file is created. By default, it contains all the startup information for the database. As user-defined objects are created, they may also be stored in the primary data file. However, you may implement certain architectural strategies to improve the performance, scalability, and maintainability of your database. These strategies are discussed in the upcoming "Adding files and filegroups" section.

Prior to running the script, create two folders on the root of your C drive: SQLData and SQLLog.

Create your first database with SSMS

1. Open SSMS.

2. Open Object Explorer, if it is not already opened.

3. Click the arrow next to your server.

4. Right-click the Databases folder.

5. In the context menu, select New Database.

6. The New Database dialog box opens. Ensure that General is selected in the Select a Page section on the left.

7. In the Database Name text box, type **SBSChp4SSMS**.

8. In the Database Files section, locate the Path column. On the first row under the Path column, click the ellipsis button. Browse to C:\SQLData.

9. On the same row, under the File Name column, type **SBSChp4SSMS**.

10. On the second row, under the Path column, click the ellipsis button. Browse to C:\SQLLog.

11. On the same row, under the File Name column, type **SBSChp4SSMS_log**.

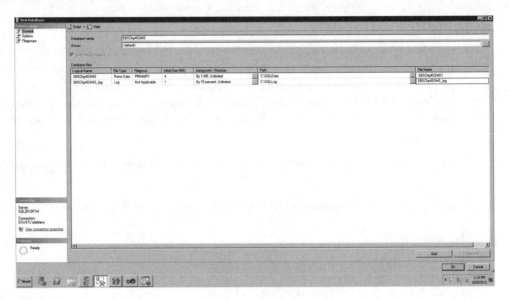

12. Click OK.

Create your first database with T-SQL

1. Click the button labeled New Query to open the query editor in SSMS.

2. Enter and execute the following T-SQL code:

```
--Use this script to create a database using T-SQL
USE master;
CREATE DATABASE SBSChp4TSQL
ON PRIMARY
(NAME='SBSChp4TSQL1', FILENAME = 'C:\SQLDATA\SBSTSQL1.mdf', SIZE=10MB, MAXSIZE=20,
FILEGROWTH=10%)
LOG ON
(NAME='SBSChp4TSQL_log', FILENAME = 'C:\SQLLog\SBSTSQL_log.ldf',
SIZE=10MB, MAXSIZE=200, FILEGROWTH=20%);
```

Understanding arguments

In the previous script, several arguments are used so that the database is placed in a specific directory and it grows at a certain rate. SQL Server provides a long list of arguments that can further extend how a database is created and where it resides. The previous script uses the following commonly used arguments:

- *database_name* is the name of the database, which must be unique to any of the databases that exist at the time of creation.

- *ON* specifies the filegroup and begins the section where the data file is defined.

- *LOG ON* begins the section where the log is defined.

- *Name* is the logical file name used by SQL Server when referencing the file. As with *database_name*, it must be unique.

- *FileName* is the operating system path and file name, including the file extension.

- *Size* specifies the initial size of the file in megabytes (MB) by default. Kilobytes (KB), gigabytes (GB), and terabytes (TB) can also be specified.

- *Maxsize* specifies the maximum size to which the file can grow (shown in megabytes by default).

- *Filegrowth* specifies the growth increment of the file. It is also shown in megabytes by default, but it can be specified as a percentage.

 Note This is not an exhaustive list of available database creation options. As you work more and more with SQL Server, you may discover a need for the other available options, which you can find in SQL Server Books Online.

Adding files and filegroups

Instead of placing user-defined objects in the primary data file, you have the option of adding a secondary data file to your database. These files types are usually distinguished by the file extension: primary files are usually suffixed with .mdf, while secondary files are suffixed with .ndf. Neither is a requirement; however, it is a best practice to use these extensions. The secondary data files are often used to spread data across disk subsystems or to add more disk space to a database in the event that the other data files have reached maximum capacity.

In addition to adding multiple files to a database, another best practice is to group the files using filegroups. When a database is created, the primary filegroup containing the primary data file is created by default. Additional filegroups are then created to ease database administration and typically to group data files together (see Figure 4-2).

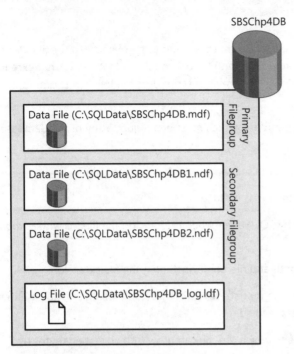

FIGURE 4-2 Database files and filegroups.

In the image are two filegroups:

- The primary filegroup contains the primary data file.

- The secondary filegroup contains two secondary data files.

Add files and filegroups using SSMS

1. Open SSMS and connect to a SQL server instance.

2. Expand the Databases folder.

3. Right-click the SBSChp4SSMS database and select Properties.

4. Select Filegroups from the Select a Page section of the Database Properties dialog box.

5. Click the Add button under the Rows section.

6. In the newly created row, under the Name column, type **SBSSSMSGroup1**.

7. In the second row, under the Default column, check the box.

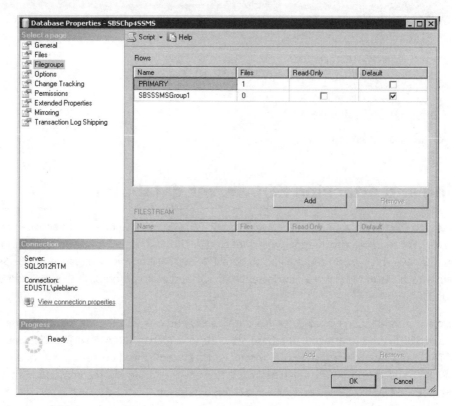

8. In the Select a Page section, select Files, and then maximize the window.

9. Click Add.

10. In the newly created row, under the Logical Name column, enter **SBSChp4SSMS1**.

11. In the Filegroup column, select SBSSSMSGroup1.

12. In the Path column, click the ellipsis button. Browse to C:\SQLData.

13. In the File Name column, enter **SBSChp4SSMS1.ndf**.

14. Click OK.

Add files and filegroups using T-SQL

1. Open the query editor in SSMS.

2. In the query editor, enter the following T-SQL code:

```
--Use this code to add a file and filegroup to a database
USE master;
ALTER DATABASE SBSChp4TSQL
    ADD FILEGROUP SBSTSQLGroup1;
```

```
ALTER DATABASE SBSChp4TSQL
    ADD File
    (
        NAME='SBSChp4TSQL2',
        FILENAME = 'C:\SQLDATA\SBSTSQL2.ndf',
        SIZE=10MB,
        MAXSIZE=20,
        FILEGROWTH=10%
    )
TO FILEGROUP SBSTSQLGroup1;
```

Detaching and attaching SQL Server databases

Now that you've created your database, what happens if you need to move it to another instance of SQL Server? For example, assume that you want to redistribute the free space on a server or decommission a server, which would require you to detach a database from one instance of SQL Server and then attach the database to a new instance of SQL Server. To accomplish this, you can use either T-SQL or SSMS.

There are currently two ways to attach a database to and one way to detach a database from an instance of SQL Server. To attach a database, you use *sp_attach* or CREATE DATABASE specifying the FOR ATTACH argument. Please note that the *sp_attach* system stored procedure has been deprecated and will be removed from future versions of SQL Server. As a result, it is recommended that you use only the CREATE DATABASE option when attaching databases.

Detach a SQL Server database using SSMS

1. Open SSMS.

2. Open Object Explorer, if it is not already open.

3. Expand the server node.

4. Expand the Databases folder.

5. Right-click the SBSChp4SSMS database.

6. Select Tasks | Detach.

7. In the Detach Database dialog box, check the boxes in the Drop Connections and Update Statistics columns.

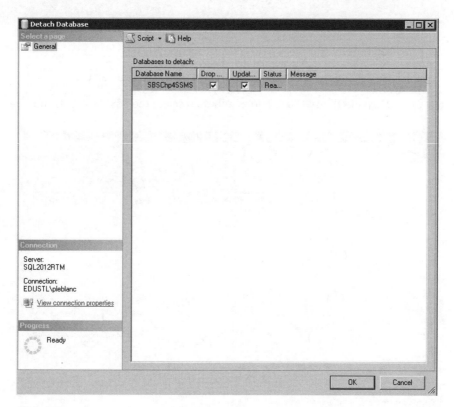

8. Click OK.

Now that the database is detached, you can copy the files to the new storage location and attach the database to a new instance of SQL Server.

Detach a SQL Server database using T-SQL

1. Open SSMS, and then open a new query window.

2. Enter and execute the following script:

```
USE Master;
EXEC sp_detach_db @dbname = 'SBSChp4TSQL';
```

Attach a SQL Server database using SSMS

1. Open SSMS.

2. Open Object Explorer, if it is not already open.

3. Expand the server node.

4. Right-click the Databases folder.

5. Click Attach.

6. Click the Add button.

7. In the Locate Database Files dialog box, expand the folder labeled C.

8. Locate and expand the SQLData folder, and then select the SBSChp4SSMS.mdf file.

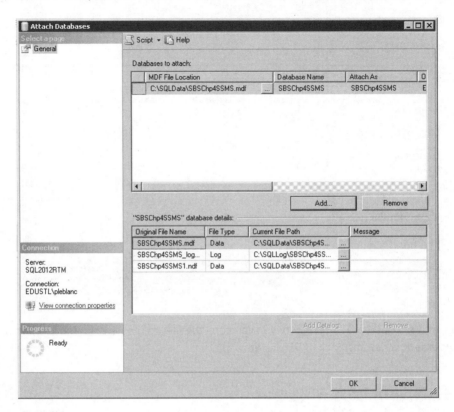

9. Click OK.

Attach a SQL Server database using T-SQL

1. Open SSMS, and then open a new query window.

2. Enter and execute the following script:

```
USE master;
CREATE DATABASE SBSChp4TSQL ON
(FILENAME = 'C:\SQLData\SBSTSQL1.mdf'),
(FILENAME = 'C:\SQLData\SBSTSQL2.ndf'),
(FILENAME = 'C:\SQLLog\SBSTSQL_Log.ldf')
FOR ATTACH;
```

Understanding database recovery models

A SQL Server database can be set to one of three recovery models:

- Simple
- Full
- Bulk-logged

The model determines how precisely a database may be restored.

Simple model

The simple model does not allow for transaction log backups. As a result, you cannot restore a database to a point in time. Your database is vulnerable to data loss when using this model. That said, using this model does ease the task of administration because SQL Server will reclaim space automatically from the transaction log.

Full model

With the full model, data loss is minimal when the transaction log is backed up on a regular basis. Every transaction is fully logged to the transaction log, and the transaction log will continue to grow until it is backed up. While this model does add administrative overhead, your data is protected from data loss.

Bulk-logged model

When you use the bulk-logged model, bulk operations are minimally logged, which reduces the size of the transaction log. Note that this does not eliminate the need to back up the transaction log. Unlike in the full recovery model, in the bulk-logged model you can restore only to the end of any backup; you cannot restore to some point in time.

Summary

You can create SQL Server databases using several different tools. In this chapter, you learned about two methods to create databases, but you are also able to use other tools such as SQL Server Data Tools, Windows PowerShell, and the C# and VB .NET programming languages. Each tool offers certain advantages and disadvantages, therefore you should take some time to explore all options available to ensure you use the tool that best fits your development needs.

CHAPTER 5

Creating your first table

After completing this chapter, you will be able to

- Develop a naming standard.

- Understand schemas.

- Understand the different SQL Server data types.

- Understand column properties.

- Create and alter tables.

- Understand computed columns.

- Add constraints to a table.

- Understand the FileTable feature.

- Create a database diagram.

Just as the database is the primary container of all objects on an instance of Microsoft SQL Server, the table is the primary container of all data on a SQL Server instance. Tables are the foundation of all objects, and without them a database is useless. The power in any application is the data that it accepts and stores. Without a relational database management system (RDBMS) to store and maintain that data, the application would likely not exist.

While this book's primary focus is SQL Server, it should be noted that databases come in many shapes and forms. For example, the most widely used database is a Microsoft Excel spreadsheet. Many people extract data or request data from an RDBMS and import that data into Excel. Once the data is in Excel, the end user may create a series of spreadsheets and workbooks that together provide a very robust reporting tool containing answers to many organizational questions.

The downside of this approach is that those Excel spreadsheets and workbooks become data silos that are typically stored on users' machines. If the spreadsheets and workbooks are not secured and backed up regularly, the information stored in them is vulnerable to a failure or catastrophe. In addition, the process to populate those spreadsheets and workbooks is often manual, and only one person understands how it works. Finally, by storing data in Excel, users are not able to realize the RDBMS benefits of multiuser concurrency and data integrity, which are the foundation of most database management systems.

The previously described downsides alone provide sufficient justification for using an RDBMS. Whether you are working with SQL Server or a similar system, most RDBMSs offer a way to centrally maintain and monitor access and availability to the data. Moreover, they provide governance on how the data is structured, organized, and delivered. These three key components are not typically available in something like an Excel spreadsheet. Using a robust RDBMS such as SQL Server provides administrators and developers with the ability to ensure that data is stored in a central location, and they can enforce naming standards and additional control that almost guarantee consistent and credible data across the organization.

In this chapter, you will first learn the importance of implementing and enforcing a naming standard. From there, you will be introduced to the various data types that are supported by SQL Server. Then you will create your first table using Microsoft SQL Server Management Studio (SSMS) and Transact-SQL (T-SQL). Finally, you will use the same methods to add constraints and keys to your tables.

Developing a naming standard

The first step in any database design project is to develop a naming standard that will be used during the design process. While naming standard development is definitely not a requirement, continuing without some standard could yield an unorganized database that may present challenges to developers when accessing the data. Inconsistent naming conventions often inhibit the development process indirectly. For a developer who is writing T-SQL to modify or retrieve data, naming standards provide clear paths to constructing T-SQL statements. For example, assume that you are designing a database that will store human resources data. You are asked to create a structure that houses information about individual employees, such as their name, address, phone number, and department. Assume that you have designed the database shown in Figure 5-1.

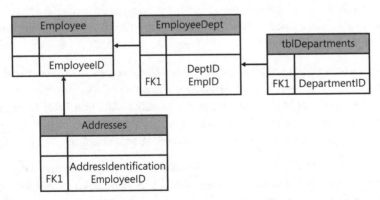

FIGURE 5-1 This simple database schema does not have naming conventions.

The database schema in Figure 5-1 shows four tables. Notice that each table uses a different naming convention. The name of the table that will store address information is plural, and the name of the table that will store department information is prefixed with *tbl*. There are other inconsistencies, but you should get the picture. If you were a developer new to this database, writing T-SQL against this database could pose a challenge. Since the table names vary, a developer would have to spend a significant amount of time becoming familiar with the database prior to writing queries. You may have also noticed the inconsistencies in the column names, which further complicate working with this database.

Enforcing governance with regard to naming objects within a database makes the database easier to work with. The following are some best practices:

- General standards

  - Do not use spaces within any object or column name.

  - Underscore characters are acceptable, but be aware that they can present some challenges with visualization tools.

  - Use PascalCase, which means capitalizing the first letter of each word that is used to name an object or column.

  - Do not use reserved keywords. Plural table and column names are acceptable, but singular is preferred in this book. This is completely a matter of preference.

- Table naming standards

  - Names should reflect the contents of the table.

  - Names must be unique to the database and the schema.

- Column naming standards

  - Names should be unique to each table.

  - Names should reflect the business use.

  - Select the appropriate data type, as discussed later in this chapter.

 Note Naming conventions for other objects are discussed when appropriate in context throughout this book.

Once this governance is put into place, the updated schema for the earlier sample database resembles Figure 5-2.

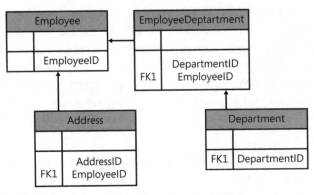

FIGURE 5-2 This database schema has naming conventions.

All the tables now have a common naming standard. Every new word begins with an uppercase letter, and the names are spelled completely. The main thing to notice is that each table name reflects the contents of the table.

Understanding schemas

While a database is the primary container of all objects, schemas offer another level of containment and organization within a database. Using a schema, a user can group objects of similar scope or ownership together. By default, the database owner (dbo) schema is automatically created within a database. Any object that is created is added to this schema. You can change this behavior in a couple of ways, as you will learn later in this book.

Consider the schema shown in Figure 5-2. You could create a schema containing information specific to the human resources department. However, if you extend the database to include sales information for each employee, you can place the new objects in a Sales schema.

Create a database schema using SSMS

1. Open SSMS and connect to a SQL Server instance.

2. Expand the Databases folder.

3. Expand the SBSChp4SSMS database.

4. Expand the Security folder.

5. Right-click the Schema folder and select New Schema from the context menu.

6. In the Schema – New dialog box, type **Sales** in the Schema Name text box and **dbo** in the Schema Owner text box.

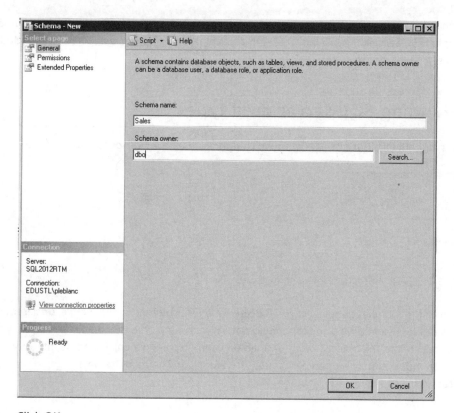

7. Click OK.

Create a database schema using T-SQL

1. Open the query editor in SSMS.

2. In the query editor, enter and execute the following T-SQL code:

```
--Use this code to create a SQL Server database with a single data and log file
USE SBSChp4TSQL;
GO
CREATE SCHEMA Sales;
GO
CREATE SCHEMA HumanResources;
GO
```

 Note As a best practice, try to create all schemas prior to creating tables. However, if that is not possible, you can always move a table or any other object from one to another using the ALTER SCHEMA ...TRANSFER statement.

A final thing to mention about schemas is that you can grant users permissions to schemas. In Chapter 25, "Security," you'll look in depth at several security aspects of SQL Server, including schemas.

Understanding SQL Server data types

SQL Server contains four distinct data type categories, as shown in Figure 5-3.

Numeric	Date and Time
Strings	Other

FIGURE 5-3 SQL Server contains four data type categories.

Each of the four categories contains subcategories. All columns within a table, declared variables, and parameters must have a corresponding data type. A data type simply specifies what type of data can be placed into the object (column, variable, parameter, and so on). Database integrity depends heavily on appropriately scoped data types; therefore, you should not always depend or rely on an application to enforce data type usage.

Numeric data types

The numeric data type has two subcategories: exact and approximate. Exact data types fit within a finite range of numbers. Table 5-1 lists and defines each exact numeric data type.

TABLE 5-1 Exact numeric data types

Data Type	Range	Storage
bigint	–9,223,372,036,854,775,808 to 9,223,372,036,854,775,807	8 bytes
int	–2,147,483,648 to 2,147,483,647	4 bytes
smallint	–32,768 to 32,767	2 bytes
tinyint	0 to 255	1 byte
money	–922,337,203,685,477.5808 to 922,337,203,685,477.5807	8 bytes
smallmoney	–214,748.3648 to 214,748.3647	4 bytes

If you need a column in a table that stores only values between 1 and 10, you should use a *tinyint*.

In addition to the data types in Table 5-1, the exact numeric category includes two more data types: *decimal* and *numeric*. They are slightly different from the others in that they allow decimal places, which are restricted by two values: precision and scale. Essentially, they are very similar in what and how they store data. Precision is the total number of digits that can be stored on both sides of the decimal place. This value can only be between 1 and 38. Scale is the number of digits that can be stored to the right of the decimal place and is specified only when precision is provided. This value will be between 0 and the specified precision. Therefore, if you wanted to store a four-digit number with only two digits to the right of the decimal place, you would use *decimal(4,2)*. Table 5-2 lists precision ranges and their corresponding storage requirements.

TABLE 5-2 Precision ranges and storage requirements

Precision	Storage
1–9	5 bytes
10–19	9 bytes
20–28	13 bytes
29–38	17 bytes

The approximate subcategory is similar to the *decimal* and *numeric* data types in that one accepts a precision value, which is *float*. The other does not accept a precision value; instead, it can store up to seven digits, which includes digits on both sides of the decimal. For example, if you attempt to store the number 1234.5678 in a *real* data type, the value rounds up to 1234.568. However, if you want to maintain the precision of that value, you can store it in a *float(25)*.

The main difference between the *decimal* and *float* data types is that you have a more precise level of storage with *decimal* than *float*. Table 5-3 lists precision ranges and their storage requirements for approximate *numeric* data types.

TABLE 5-3 Approximate precision ranges and storage requirements

nvalue	Precision	Storage
1–24	7 digits	4 bytes
25–53	15 digits	8 bytes

String data types

The string data type contains three subcategories: character, Unicode, and binary. Each contains three specific data types. The data types are similar in that each subcategory contains a fixed-length data type, a variable-length data type, and a data type that has been deprecated.

Note *n* defines the string length that can be stored. For variable-length data types, *max* can be specified for *n*, which indicates that the maximum storage size is 2 GB.

The character string subcategory will store non-Unicode data. The three types are as follows:

- **char(n)** Fixed-length string data type with a string length between 1 and 8,000.

- **varchar(n)** Variable-length string data type that can store up to 2 GB of data.

- **text** Deprecated data type. Replace it with a *varchar(max)*.

The Unicode string subcategory will store both Unicode and non-Unicode data. The three types are as follows:

- **nchar(n)** Fixed-length string data type with a string length between 1 and 4,000.

- **nvarchar(n)** Variable-length string data type that can store up to 2 GB of data.

- **ntext** Deprecated data type. Replace it with *nvarchar(max)*.

The binary string subcategory will store binary data. The three types are as follows:

- **binary(n)** Fixed-length binary data type with a string length between 1 and 8,000.

- **varbinary(n)** Variable-length binary data type with a string length up to 2 GB.

- **image** Deprecated data type. Replace with *varbinary(max)*.

As a best practice, you should use the fixed-length (*char, nchar, binary*) data types across all sub-categories when the values being stored are a consistent size. When the values are not consistent, you should use the variable-length data types (*varchar, nvarchar, varbinary*).

Date and time data types

Date and time data types are used widely in SQL Server databases. They offer the convenience of storing the date and time in various ways. There are six date and time data types.

- **time(n)** This data type stores the time of day without time-zone awareness based on a 24-hour clock. *time* accepts one argument, which is fractional seconds precision. You can pro-vide only values between 0 and 7. As the number increases, so does the fractional precision. If you specify a data type of *time(2)*, you can store a value similar to 11:51:04:24. Changing *2* to *3* increases the precision to three numbers, similar to 11:51:04:245.

- **date** This data type stores a date value between 01-01-01 and 12-31-9999.

- **smalldatetime** This data type stores a date and time value. The value of the date is between 1/1/1900 and 6/6/2079. The time precision is down to seconds. A value of 4/1/2012 11:15:04 can be stored using this data type.

- **datetime** This data type is similar to *smalldatetime*, but it offers a larger date range and a higher level of precision with regard to time. It offers the same date range as the *date* param-eter, 01-01-01 to 12-31-9999, and it has a more precise value of time. A value of 4/1/2012 11:15:04:888 can be stored using this data type.

- **datetime2(n)**   This data type is similar to *datetime*, but it offers extended flexibility of time. Unlike with *datetime*, you can control the fractional second precision with a value. You can provide only values between 0 and 7. If you specify a data type of *datetime2(2)*, you can store a value similar to 4/1/2012 11:51:04:24. Changing *2* to *3* increases the precision to three numbers, similar to 4/1/2012 11:51:04:24.

- **datetimeoffset**   This data type includes all the capabilities of *datetime2*, and it also has time-zone awareness. This makes it unique among the date and time data types. Using this data type, you can store the time-zone offset along with the date and time. A value of 4/1/2012 03:10:24 -06:00 can be stored using this data type.

Other data types

In addition to the data types covered in the preceding sections, SQL Server includes several other data types. Table 5-4 lists each additional data type with a brief description.

TABLE 5-4   Other SQL Server 2012 data types

Data Type	Description
cursor	A temporary copy of data that will be used for recursive or iterative processes. Of all the data types, this is the only one that cannot be included as part of a table.
rowversion(timestamp)	This data type automatically generates an 8-byte value similar to 0x0000000000000001. *rowversion* replaces the *timestamp* data type, which has been deprecated. This data type is typically used to detect changes in data.
hierarchyid	This is a positional data type. It represents a position in a hierarchy. *hierarchyid* is used to organize data such as a bill of materials and organizational charts.
sql_variant	This is the chameleon of data types. *sql_variant* can assume the identity of just about any data type in the list of SQL Server data types. Prior to performing any types of operations on it, you must convert it to the respective data type. For example, if you want perform addition, you must cast this data type to an int or some other numeric data type that supports that operation.
xml	You can store actual XML data using this data type.
geospatial	SQL Server supports two geospatial data types: GEOGRAPHY and GEOMETRY. GEOGRAPHY represents data in a round-earth coordinate system. GEOMETRY is a flat or planar data type in which you can store points, lines, and other geometric figures.
filestream	This data type allows you to store common unstructured data such as documents and images. SQL Server has been coupled with the NTFS file system, allowing the storage of *varbinary(max)* on the file system.

Since the data types in Table 5-4 are typically used for advanced operations, details regarding how to use them are beyond the scope of this book. If you feel the need to delve deeper into these data types, you can search SQL Server Books Online for some great examples.

Understanding column properties

You're almost ready to create your first table. Before doing so, however, you must understand that a table contains one or more columns, which make up the rows of a table. Each column stores very specific information. You can configure certain properties for a given column based on the selected data type, which is a property itself.

The most common property is Allow Nulls. This simply means that you can insert a row into the table without supplying a value. For example, say you have a table that contains FirstName, MiddleName, and LastName. Every person does not have a middle name; therefore, that value should be optional. When designing your table, consider the business logic behind the value when deciding nullability.

 Note NULL is a special value in the database world. It does not mean empty; rather, it represents the absence of a value and is different from an empty string.

The second most common property is Is Identity. It is second because it is only available for most numeric data types. When you set this value for a column, SQL Server automatically generates a number as each row is inserted. You can customize or configure the starting point and how the number will increment using the properties that are available. You will learn how to configure the identity value later in this chapter.

SQL Server 2012 introduces a new autonumber-generating mechanism called Sequence, which is a schema-bound object that generates a sequence of numeric values based on certain options specified during its creation. Chapter 12, "Modifying data," discusses this topic at length.

Creating tables

Admittedly, creating tables with SSMS is much easier than with T-SQL. The biggest disadvantage to using SSMS, though, is not having very portable code. Once T-SQL is written, it can be saved and executed against the same instance or another instance of SQL Server without your having to re-create the script, but this is not the case with SSMS. If you use the table designer to create a table, you are required to perform the same steps on another instance of SQL Server if you want to re-create the table. Nevertheless, it is worth knowing and understanding the steps. You should learn how to create the table using T-SQL not only because most things on SQL Server are accomplished using T-SQL, but also because it allows for easy portability.

Now it is time to create a table of your own. Create a table named Addresses using the information provided in Table 5-5.

TABLE 5-5 Address table requirements

Name	Data Type	Length	Allow Nulls	Identity
AddressID	int	NA	No	Yes (start at 1 increment by 1)
StreetAddress	varchar	125	No	NA
StreetAddress2	varchar	75	Yes	NA
City	varchar	100	No	NA
State	char	2	No	NA
EmployeeID	int	NA	No	NA

Create a table using SSMS

1. With SSMS open, expand the Databases folder.

2. Expand the SBSChp4SSMS database.

3. Expand the Security folder.

4. Right-click the Schemas folder.

5. Select New Schema from the menu.

6. In the Schema – New dialog box, type **HumanResources** in the Schema Name text box.

7. Type **dbo** in the Schema Owner text box.

8. Click OK.

9. Right-click the Tables folder. The table designer opens.

10. Select New Table from the menu.

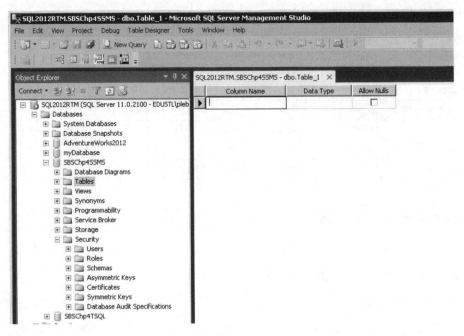

11. In the Column Name column, type **AddressID**.

12. Click in the Data Type column and select int from the drop-down list.

13. In the Column Properties tab that is located at the bottom of the table designer window, scroll down and expand Identity Specification.

14. Set the Is Identity property to Yes.

15. In the next row of the column list, type **StreetAddress** in the Column Name column.

16. Click in the Data Type column and select varchar from the drop-down list, changing the character string length to 125.

17. Uncheck the box under the Allow Nulls column.

18. Repeat steps 16–18 for each additional column, setting the property according to the specifications.

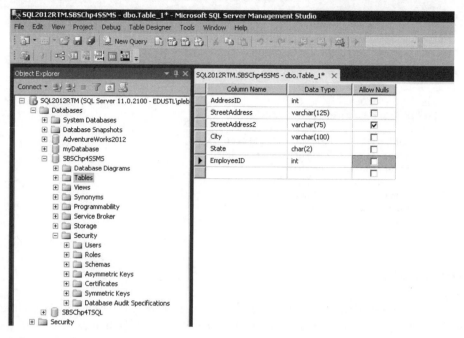

19. Select View | Properties. The Properties window opens.

20. Locate and click in the Schema property. Select HumanResources from the drop-down list.

21. Locate and expand the Regular Data Space Specification property. In the Filegroup or Partition Scheme Name property, ensure that SBSSSMSGroup1 is selected.

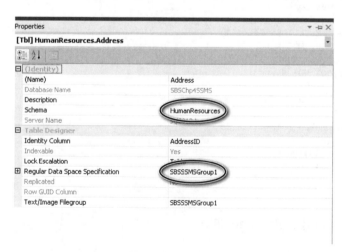

22. Click the Save button.

23. Type **Address** in the text box in the Choose Name window.

24. Click OK.

1. Open the query editor in SSMS.

2. In the query editor, enter and execute the following T-SQL code:

```
USE SBSChp4TSQL;
CREATE TABLE HumanResources.Address
(
      AddressID int NOT NULL IDENTITY(1,1),
      StreetAddress varchar(125) NOT NULL,
      StreetAddress2 varchar(75) NULL,
      City varchar(100) NOT NULL,
      State char(2) NOT NULL,
      EmployeeID int NOT NULL
) ON [SBSTSQLGroup1];
```

Altering tables

Now you are equipped with the skills you need to create tables with T-SQL and SSMS, but what if someone asks you to change one of your tables? How will you make that change? Not to worry— just as you created the tables with T-SQL and SSMS, you can also modify the tables. You can add columns, change columns, and drop columns using either tool.

Prior to walking through the next set of steps, execute the following script:

```
USE SBSChp4TSQL;
  CREATE TABLE HumanResources.Employee
  (
        EmployeeID int NOT NULL IDENTITY(1,1),
        FirstName varchar(50) NOT NULL,
        MiddleName varchar(50) NULL,
        LastName varchar(50) NOT NULL
  ) ON [SBSTSQLGroup1];
USE SBSChp4SSMS;CREATE TABLE HumanResources.Employee
  (
        EmployeeID int NOT NULL IDENTITY(1,1),
        FirstName varchar(50) NOT NULL,
        MiddleName varchar(50) NULL,
        LastName varchar(50) NOT NULL
  ) ON [SBSSSMSGroup1];
```

Add a column to an existing table using SSMS

1. Ensure that SSMS is open and you are connected to your server.

2. Expand the Databases folder.

3. Expand the SBSChp4SSMS database.

4. Expand the Tables folder.

5. Right-click the HumanResources.Employee table and select Design.

6. Type **Gender** in the first empty row in the Column Name column.

7. In the Data Type column, type **char(1)**.

8. In the Allow Nulls column, uncheck the box.

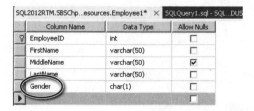

9. Click Save.

Add a column to an existing table using T-SQL

1. Open the query editor in SSMS.

2. In the query editor, enter and execute the following T-SQL code:

```
--Use this code to add the Gender column to the Employee table
USE SBSChp4TSQL;
ALTER TABLE HumanResources.Employee
    ADD Gender char(1) NOT NULL;
```

Understanding computed columns

Not only can you insert data directly into columns, but you can also derive columns from other columns. These columns are known as *computed* columns. Typically, computed columns will extend or enhance the data that is stored in traditional columns.

Add a computed column using SSMS

1. Ensure that SSMS is open and you are connected to your server.

2. Expand the Databases folder.

3. Expand the SBSChp4SSMS database.

4. Expand the Tables folder.

5. Right-click the HumanResources.Employee table and select Design.

6. Under Gender, in the next row, type **FullName** and press the Tab key.

7. In the Column Properties section at the bottom of the table designer screen, locate and expand the Computed Column Specification property.

8. In the Formula property, type **LastName+', '+FirstName**.

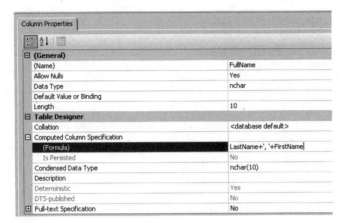

9. Click Save.

Add a computed column using T-SQL

1. Open the query editor in SSMS.

2. Use this code to add the FullName column to the Employee table:

```
--Use this code to add the Gender column to the Employee table
USE SBSChp4TSQL;
ALTER TABLE HumanResources.Employee
    ADD FullName          AS LastName+', '+FirstName;
```

Adding constraints to a table

SQL Server 2012 allows you to add several constraints to a table. The primary goal of most constraints is data integrity. In other words, their purpose is to improve the validity and consistency of your data. This section covers five constraints: primary key, default, unique, check, and foreign key.

Primary key constraints

As previously stated, a primary key is a column that contains a unique list of values. Often an integer column is added to a table with the identity property and is used as the primary key. However, you can create a primary key from almost any column or combination of columns. The main limitations are that the column cannot allow nulls, the values must be unique, and you can have only one primary key per table. Since you've already created two tables, you'll create primary keys on those tables. Both the Employee and Address tables have ID values that are unique and can be used as primary keys.

Default constraints

Default constraints are perfect when you have a column that typically contains a specific value. A really good candidate for this is a column that has a data type of *bit*. The *bit* data type only accepts 1 or 0 (true or false). If you add an Active column to the Employee table that specifies whether an employee is currently working for the company, the default value will probably be true or 1. Therefore, you should set the default value for that column accordingly.

Unique constraints

Unique constraints are sometimes confused with primary keys. These constraints simply ensure that duplicate values cannot be inserted into the corresponding column. For example, assume that you must add a column for Social Security numbers to the Employee table. Since Social Security numbers are truly unique values, you should add a unique constraint to ensure that a given Social Security number is entered only once.

Check constraints

The final constraint, check, allows you to check the value that is being inserted against logical expressions. This constraint is similar to the foreign key column in that it controls what values are inserted. The foreign key column gets its values from another table, while check constraints use expressions.

Add constraints using SSMS

Execute the following query prior to following the steps in this exercise:

```
USE SBSChp4TSQL;
ALTER TABLE HumanResources.Employee
    ADD Active bit NOT NULL;

ALTER TABLE HumanResources.Employee
    ADD SocialSecurityNumber varchar(10) NOT NULL;


USE SBSChp4SSMS;
ALTER TABLE HumanResources.Employee
    ADD Active bit NOT NULL;

ALTER TABLE HumanResources.Employee
    ADD SocialSecurityNumber varchar(10) NOT NULL;
```

1. Ensure that SSMS is open and you are connected to your server.

2. Expand the Databases folder.

3. Expand the SBSChp4SSMS database.

4. Expand the Tables folder.

5. Right-click the HumanResources.Employee table, and then select Design.

6. Right-click the EmployeeID column, and then select Set Primary Key from the context menu.

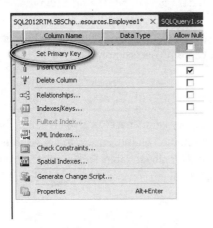

7. Select the Active column.

8. In the Properties window, locate Default Value or Binding property.

9. Type **1** as the property value.

10. In the menu bar, click the Manage Indexes and Keys icon.

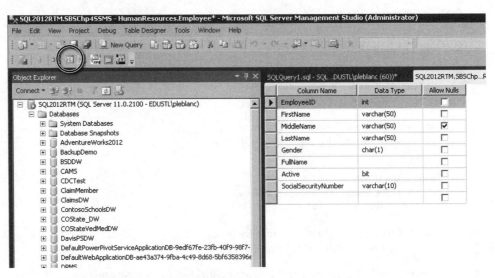

11. Click the Add button in the Indexes/Keys window.

12. Locate the Name property and type **UQ_Employee_SSN** as the property value.

13. Locate the Is Unique property and set the value to Yes.

14. Locate the Type property and set the value to Unique Key.

15. Locate and click on the Columns property and then click on the ellipsis next to EmployeeID (ASC). On the next window, select SocialSecurityNumber under the Column Name drop-down list. Click OK.

16. Click Close.

17. In Object Explorer, expand the HumanResources.Employee table if it is not already expanded.

18. Right-click the Constraints column, and then select New Constraint from the context menu.

19. In the Check Constraint dialog box, change the value for the Name property to **CK_Employee_Gender_MF**.

20. Click the Value box for the Expression property, and click the ellipsis that appears.

21. In the Expression box, enter **([Gender = 'F' OR [Gender] = 'M')**.

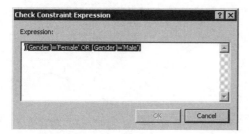

22. Click Close.

23. Click Save.

Add a constraints using T-SQL

1. Open the query editor in SSMS.

2. In the query editor, enter and execute the following T-SQL code:

```
USE SBSChp4TSQL;
ALTER TABLE HumanResources.Employee
    ADD CONSTRAINT PK_HumanResourcesEmployee_EmployeeID
        PRIMARY KEY (EmployeeID);

ALTER TABLE HumanResources.[Address]
    ADD CONSTRAINT PK_HumanResourcesAddress_AddressID
        PRIMARY KEY (AddressID);ALTER TABLE HumanResources.Employee
    ADD CONSTRAINT DF_HumanResourcesEmployee_Active_True DEFAULT(1) FOR Active;

ALTER TABLE HumanResources.Employee
    ADD CONSTRAINT UQ_HumanResourcesEmployee_SocialSecurityNumber
    UNIQUE (SocialSecurityNumber);
```

Foreign key constraints

The integrity of data is the most important concern in a database. If you allow the insertion of bad data, then that is what is going to come out. Foreign keys play a vital role in enforcing the referential integrity of the database. You may have noticed the EmployeeID column in the Address table. To ensure that only employee IDs that exist in the Employee table are inserted into the Address table, you need to create a foreign key constraint.

Create foreign key constraints using SSMS

Prior to following the steps of this exercise, execute this script:

```
USE SBSChp4SSMS
ALTER TABLE HumanResources.Address
    ADD CONSTRAINT PK_HumanResourcesAddress_AddressID
        PRIMARY KEY (AddressID);
```

1. Ensure that SSMS is open and you are connected to your server.

2. Expand the Databases folder.

3. Expand the SBSChp4SSMS database.

4. Expand the Tables folder.

5. Expand the HumanResources.Address table.

6. Right-click the Keys folder and select New Foreign Key.

7. In the Foreign Key Relationships dialog box, locate the Name property and type **FK_Employee_To_Address_On_EmployeeID** as the value.

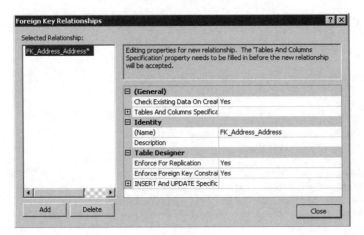

8. Click in the text box next to the Table and Columns Specification property.

9. Click the ellipsis button that appears.

10. In the Tables and Columns dialog box, select Employee(HumanResources) from the Primary Key Table drop-down list.

11. Select EmployeeID from the drop-down list directly below the Primary Key Table drop-down list.

12. In the drop-down list to the right, select EmployeeID.

13. Click OK.

14. Click Close.

15. Click Save.

16. If a warning window appears, click Yes.

Create foreign key constraints using T-SQL

1. Open the query editor in SSMS.

2. In the query editor, enter and execute the following T-SQL code:

```
USE SBSChp4TSQL;
ALTER TABLE HumanResources.Address
    ADD CONSTRAINT FK_Employee_To_Address_On_EmployeeID
        FOREIGN KEY (EmployeeID)
            REFERENCES HumanResources.Employee(EmployeeID);
```

Note The foreign key constraint must be created on the table where the key column is not the primary key.

Understanding the FileTable

SQL Server 2012 introduces a new type of table, the FileTable. This table builds on the existing FileStream technology. Therefore, you must enable the FileStream capabilities prior to creating a FileTable. The FileTable feature allows you to store various types of documents, and you can also directly query the attributes exposed by the Windows file system using T-SQL.

FileStream is an advanced feature of SQL Server, and a detailed description of it is beyond the scope of this book. However, an introduction to the FileTable is necessary because it offers some unique capabilities to the RDBMS. It brings together SQL Server and the Windows file namespace. As a result, integrated SQL Server services such as full-text and semantic search can query the unstructured data stored in the FileTable.

Creating database diagrams

One of the most unused features of SSMS is the diagramming tool. Sure, it may not be as robust as some third-party diagramming tools, but on the other hand, it is a very intuitive product. It has all the features needed to provide a visual representation of a database.

Create a database diagram using SSMS

1. To create a database diagram, expand the AdventureWorks2012 database.

2. Expand the Database Diagram folder.

3. You are prompted to create support objects for diagramming if this is the first time you have created a diagram in this database. Click Yes.

4. Right-click the Database Diagrams folder and select New Database Diagram. Select the tables that are shown in the following image by holding down the Shift key as you click the tables.

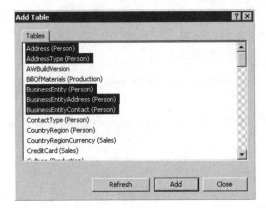

5. Click Add.

   You will see a database diagram that includes a complete list of columns for each table and, most important, the foreign key relations between the tables.

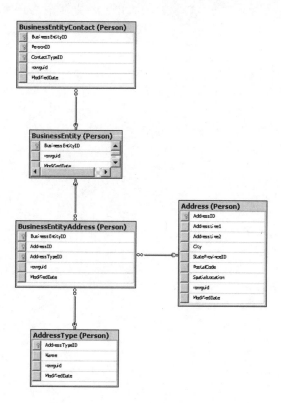

Summary

This chapter has taken you on a journey through several new concepts, technologies, and tools. You created tables that contain columns of varying data types. In addition, you learned how to add constraints to the tables and columns that assist in ensuring the consistency and validity of the inserted or modified data. As you progress through this book, all the knowledge you gained in the chapter will continue to be helpful as you build on what you have learned here—the ride has just begun.

CHAPTER 6

Building and maintaining indexes

After completing this chapter, you will be able to

- Understand the structure of an index.

- Understand the different types of indexes.

- Create different types of indexes.

- Add included columns and filters to an index.

- Place an index in a filegroup.

- Disable and drop an index.

An *index* is an on-disk data structure that is based on tables and views. Indexes make the retrieval of data faster and efficient, in most cases. However, overloading a table or view with indexes could adversely affect the performance of other operations such as inserts or updates.

In this chapter, you will be introduced to the basic structure of clustered, nonclustered, and columnstore indexes, and you will learn the differences between each of the aforementioned index types. You will also learn how to create, alter, and drop clustered and nonclustered indexes.

Index structure overview

Indexes can be categorized into two primary types: clustered and nonclustered. There are several other types of indexes, and detailing these is beyond the scope of this book, but you can find more information in SQL Server Books Online. The indexes are created on a column or columns on tables and views. The purpose of clustered and nonclustered indexes is to improve how the Microsoft SQL Server Database Engine accesses the data.

While both index types may improve read operations, there is also a possibility that they could negatively affect the performance of some operations like inserts and updates. Therefore, you need to be selective when creating indexes. In most cases, highly transactional databases are indexed differently than those that support mostly read operations. In the next set of exercises, you will create a clustered index.

1. Open SQL Server Management Studio (SSMS) and connect to a server.

2. Expand the Databases folder.

3. Expand the AdventureWorks2012 database.

4. Expand the Tables folder.

5. Expand the dbo.DatabaseLog table.

6. Right-click the Indexes folder.

7. Select New Index | Clustered Index.

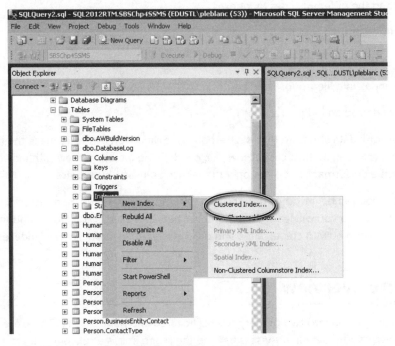

8. In the New Index dialog box, click the Add button.

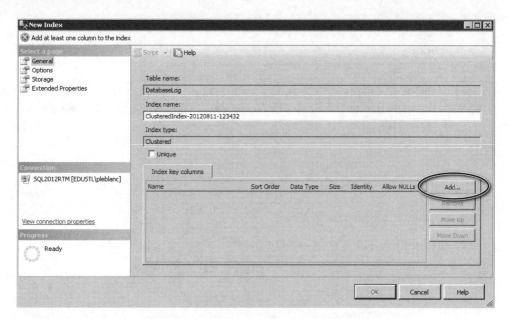

9. In the Select Columns dialog box, check the box next to the PostTime column.

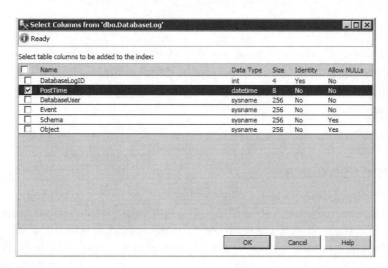

10. Click OK.

11. Click Ascending in the New Index dialog box.

12. In the newly available drop-down list, select Descending.

13. In the Name text box, type **CIX_DatabaseLog_PostTime**.

14. Click OK.

> **Note** In Chapter 5, "Creating your first table," you learned how to create primary keys. By default, a primary key will create a clustered index; however, this is not a requirement.

Create a clustered index using T-SQL

1. Open the query editor in SSMS.

2. In the query editor, enter and execute the following T-SQL code:

```
--Use this script to create a clustered index
USE AdventureWorks2012;
CREATE CLUSTERED INDEX CIX_DatabaseLog_PostTime
ON dbo.DatabaseLog
(
     PostTime DESC
)
WITH(DROP_EXISTING = ON);
```

> **Note** In the preceding script an index option, DROP_EXISTING, is used, which drops the index if it exists and re-creates it. Additional index options are discussed later in this chapter.

Clustered index structure

Before continuing with the index, let's take a brief detour to discuss the structure of a clustered index. Each table or view can have only one clustered index. This is because a clustered index changes the way the data is stored and sorted. Both clustered and nonclustered indexes store information in a *balanced tree*, or *B-tree*. A B-tree identifies similar data and groups it together. The fast access of the data that an index provides can be attributed to the fact that searches on a B-tree are based on key values. Since a B-tree groups records with similar keys together, the Database Engine will need to navigate only a few pages to find the records.

See Also *You can find more information about creating indexed views in Chapter 15, "Views."*

Let's start at the top. Both indexes have a single root page where navigation begins. This root page contains index pages that hold index rows. Figure 6-1 shows the root level.

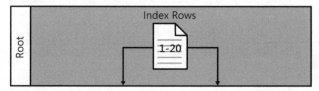

FIGURE 6-1 The root level of a clustered index.

Within these index rows are keys and pointers. The keys are the columns you included when you created the index. The pointers bring you to the next levels of the tree. They could point to the intermediate level or the leaf level. Where they point depends on the size of the index rows and the number of rows in the table. Figure 6-2 displays the root and intermediate levels of a clustered index.

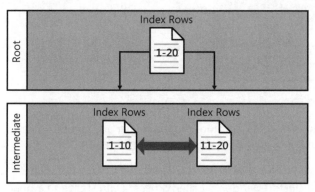

FIGURE 6-2 The root and intermediate levels of a clustered index.

Notice how the data is evenly distributed across the two pages at the intermediate level.

Note If you create a very large key clustered index that has multiple key columns, fewer keys will fit on a page. As a result, you could have more pages and maybe even more levels. As a best practice, consider choosing a narrow key, which should minimize the number of pages in the intermediate level. For this reason, integers make an excellent choice for clustered indexes, especially when using identity columns.

The bottom level, or leaf level, contains all the data. In other words, the data is stored in the clustered index, but only at the leaf level. Thus, the clustered index keeps the data in the table ordered by the key. To get to this leaf level, you will have pointers from either the root or the intermediate level (see Figure 6-3).

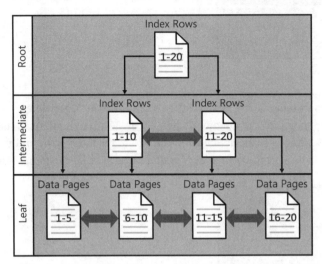

FIGURE 6-3 A complete clustered index B-tree.

As you navigate the B-tree, notice how the data becomes more granular and spread out, but it remains well balanced. This is what makes the B-tree so powerful.

Note A table that does not have a clustered index is called a *heap*. Data stored in a heap does not have any organization and could return data very slowly. As a best practice, consider adding a clustered index to all tables in your database.

Nonclustered index structure

The B-tree structure of the nonclustered index is similar to that of a clustered index. The B-tree has a root and leaf level, as depicted in Figure 6-4.

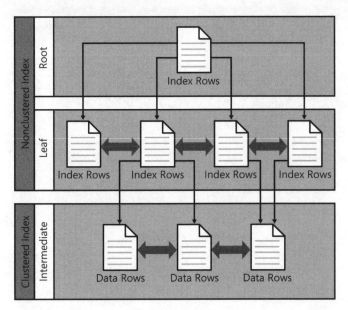

FIGURE 6-4 A nonclustered index structure.

Notice that the leaf level of the nonclustered index contains index rows instead of data rows. The leaf level contains bookmarks that direct it to data rows (leaf level) in the clustered index that contains the data. Since the nonclustered index does not contain any data, it does not affect the way data is stored or sorted. As a result, you can have multiple nonclustered indexes on a single table. In Microsoft SQL Server, you can create an index that includes a column or columns that are already part of an existing index. As a result, you should always consider changing or replacing an existing index prior to adding new indexes.

Note You can create a nonclustered index on tables that are heaps. In that case, the leaf level of the nonclustered index will contain row identifier lookups. While you can create nonclustered indexes on heaps, the results may not be the same because a clustered index does not exist.

1. Open SSMS and connect to a server.

2. Expand the Databases folder.

3. Expand the AdventureWorks2012 database.

4. Expand the Tables folder.

5. Expand the Sales.SalesOrderHeader table.

6. Right-click the Indexes folder.

7. Select New Index | Non-Clustered Index.

8. In the Index Name text box, type **IX_SalesOrderHeader_OrderDate**.

9. Click Add.

10. Check the box next to the OrderDate column.

11. Click OK.

12. Click OK.

Create a nonclustered index using T-SQL

1. Open the query editor in SSMS.

2. In the query editor, enter and execute the following T-SQL code:

```
--Use this script to create a nonclustered index
USE AdventureWorks2012;
CREATE NONCLUSTERED INDEX IX_SalesOrderHeader_DueDate
ON Sales.SalesOrderHeader
(
    DueDate
);
```

Columnstore index structure

SQL Server 2012 introduces a new type of nonclustered index called the *columnstore index*, which is available only if you're using the Enterprise version of SQL Server. Instead of storing the data rows contiguously across pages, all the data contained within a column is stored contiguously down a set of pages. Figure 6-5 illustrates how the data is stored.

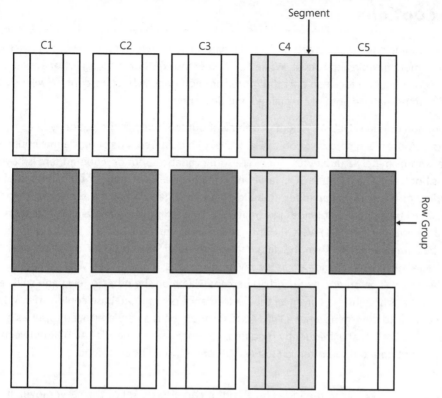

FIGURE 6-5 The columnstore index structure.

So instead of storing all the data in one structure, it is horizontally partitioned into row groups. Within a columnstore index is a *segment*. A segment contains all the values from one column of a row. The segments are broken down into row groups. Segments for the same sets of rows are stored within a *row group*.

This is a very different type of index than the traditional clustered and nonclustered indexes. Therefore, you should carefully consider your needs prior to using the columnstore index in your database. Here are few scenarios in which you should use a columnstore index:

- The database is mostly read.

- Most updates are appending the new data.

- The database is a data warehouse.

These characteristics are uncommon in traditional operational databases. As a result, it is recommended that columnstore indexes be used only on data warehouses. Another contributing factor to why columnstore indexes should currently be used only on data warehouses is that you cannot update a table that has a columnstore index. This may or may not change in future releases of SQL Server. The index has to be removed for any updates to occur. As a result, you should avoid creating this type of index on tables that are frequently updated or that require small lookup queries.

Adding index options

Now that you have some basic index creation skills, it's time to add a few options to your indexes to make them a little more flexible and robust. While SQL Server indexes boast a long list of available options, in this section you will focus on only the more common ones. A brief description will be provided for those options that are not fully explained and described.

The most common option is FILLFACTOR. If you think about the name of the option, you can almost derive its purpose. Each data page on the leaf level of a clustered index holds a maximum amount of data, approximately 8,060 bytes. There are some variances, but describing them is beyond the scope of this book. FILLFACTOR tells SQL Server how full the leaf-level pages of the index should be when rebuilding or reorganizing an index. Rebuilding and reorganizing an index are part of index maintenance and will be discussed at length in Chapter 21, "Managing and maintaining indexes and statistics." If you do not specify a FILLFACTOR during index creation, it will be 100. This means the data pages will be completely full. When the data changes through insert, update, or delete operations, then the page will have to change or, as we say in the database world, *split*. When a page splits, 50 percent of the data will be on one page and 50 percent will be on the other. A few page splits are not too bad, but if this is a regular occurrence, the performance of your database could suffer. While the explanation of how to determine what a FILLFACTOR should be is a very advanced topic, as a baseline, if you have a table that is frequently modified, consider setting the FILLFACTOR between 70 and 80. If a table is not updated too often, a FILLFACTOR of 90 should be sufficient.

> **Note** FILLFACTOR can be set at the index level, but it can also be set at the server level. If you open the Properties dialog box on the server and go to Database Settings, you can set the Default Index fill factor.

The next option, which is tightly coupled with FILLFACTOR, is PAD_INDEX. This option has the same effect on pages in the index structures as FILLFACTOR, but instead of data pages, it controls how full the intermediate-level pages will be. Unlike with FILLFACTOR, you cannot set a value for PAD_INDEX; it inherits the value from FILLFACTOR.

When an index is created, the data has to be sorted, and this requires the containing database to have sufficient space for this operation, which could cause performance problems. However, using the SORT_IN_TEMPDB option relocates the sort operations to tempdb. As a best practice, tempdb should be stored on a separate set of disks from other databases. Not only can doing this improve performance, but it also allows you to transfer disk space requirements to tempdb.

Table 6-1 provides a list of the additional index options and a brief description of each.

TABLE 6-1   Additional index options

Option	Description
IGNORE_DUP_KEY	During a multirow insert that contains duplicate key values, setting this option to ON will ensure that only one unique row is inserted and the integrity of the index is not violated.
STATISTICS_NORECOMPUTE	Statistics are vital to SQL Server with regard to determining how a query will be executed. As such, statistics need to be updated regularly. You can stop statistics from automatically recomputing by setting this option to ON.
ONLINE	Index maintenance is pivotal. You must rebuild and reorganize your indexes on a regular basis. However, when these operations are performing, users cannot access the data. Setting this option to ON allows data access. Please note that you must own the Enterprise version of SQL Server to use this option; Chapter 21 discusses this option further.
ALLOW_ROW_LOCKS	When accessing data, if this option is set to ON, SQL Server will lock the accessed rows.
ALLOW_PAGE_LOCKS	When accessing data, if this option is set to ON, SQL Server will lock the accessed pages.
MAX_DOP	Using this option, you can control how many processors are used during index creation.
DATA_COMPRESSION	This option is available only in the Enterprise version of SQL Server. There are two types of compression: ROW and PAGE. Both are discussed in detail in Chapter 7, "Table compression."

Take some time and explore the index options. Create indexes with some of these options for practice and to further extend your knowledge.

Change index options using SSMS

1. Open SSMS and connect to a server.

2. Expand the Databases folder.

3. Expand the AdventureWorks2012 database.

4. Expand the Tables folder.

5. Expand the dbo.DatabaseLog table.

6. Expand the Indexes folder.

7. Right-click the CIX_DatabaseLog_PostTime index and select Properties.

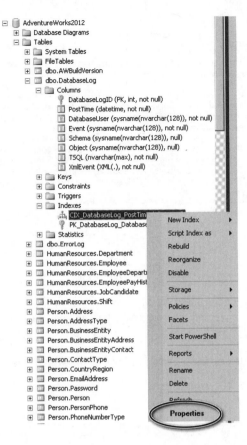

8. In the Index Properties dialog box, select Options from the Select a Page section.

9. Locate the Sort in tempdb property and change the value to True.

10. Locate the Fill Factor property and change the value to 80.

11. Locate the Pad Index property and change it to True.

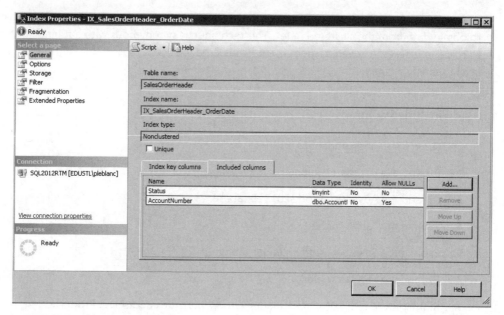

12. Click OK twice.

Change index options using T-SQL

1. Open the query editor in SSMS.

2. In the query editor, enter and execute the following T-SQL code:

```
--Use this script to add index options to an index
USE AdventureWorks2012;
CREATE CLUSTERED INDEX CIX_DatabaseLog_PostTime
ON dbo.DatabaseLog
(
     PostTime DESC
)
WITH(DROP_EXISTING = ON, SORT_IN_TEMPDB = ON, FILLFACTOR = 80, PAD_INDEX = ON);
```

Adding included columns

Recall from the discussion of nonclustered indexes that the leaf level contains bookmark lookups to the leaf level of the clustered index. This operation can sometimes slow down the processing of a query. To circumvent this issue, SQL Server allows you to add additional information in the leaf level of a nonclustered index. You do so by adding the INCLUDED argument to your index creation script.

In short, the included column improves the performance of a query by eliminating the need for it to obtain data from the clustered index. This technique is synonymous with a tuning strategy known as *covering indexes*. A covering index is a nonclustered index that has all the information at the leaf level to satisfy a query.

Add included columns to an index using SSMS

1. Open SSMS and connect to a server.

2. Expand the Databases folder.

3. Expand the AdventureWorks2012 database.

4. Expand the Tables folder.

5. Expand the Sales.SalesOrderHeader table.

6. Expand the Indexes folder.

7. Right-click the IX_SalesOrderHeader_OrderDate index and select Properties.

8. In the Index Properties dialog box, select the Included Columns tab.

9. Click the Add button.

10. Check the boxes next to the Status and AccountNumber columns.

11. Click OK.

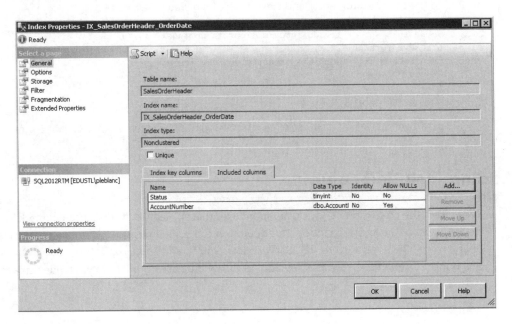

12. Click OK twice.

Add included columns to an index using T-SQL

1. Open the query editor in SSMS.

2. In the query editor, enter and execute the following T-SQL code:

```
--Use this script to add included columns to an index
USE AdventureWorks2012;
CREATE NONCLUSTERED INDEX IX_SalesOrderHeader_OrderDate
ON Sales.SalesOrderHeader
(
     OrderDate
)
INCLUDE(Status, AccountNumber)
WITH(DROP_EXISTING = ON);
```

Adding filters to indexes

Just as included columns enhance the capabilities of a nonclustered index, so do filters. Filtered indexes optimize nonclustered index performance by using a filtered predicate to refine data down to a small subset. As a result, you have a smaller index that requires less storage and maintenance, and offers improved performance. Filtered indexes are ideal for columns that contain a smaller set of pertinent values for queries.

Add a filter to an index using SSMS

1. Open SSMS and connect to a server.

2. Expand the Databases folder.

3. Expand the AdventureWorks2012 database.

4. Expand the Tables folder.

5. Expand the Sales.SalesOrderHeader table.

6. Expand the Indexes folder.

7. Right-click the IX_SalesOrderHeader_OrderDate index and select Properties.

8. Click Filter in the Select a Page section of the Index Properties dialog box.

9. Type **OnlineOrderFlag = 0** in the Filter Expression text box.

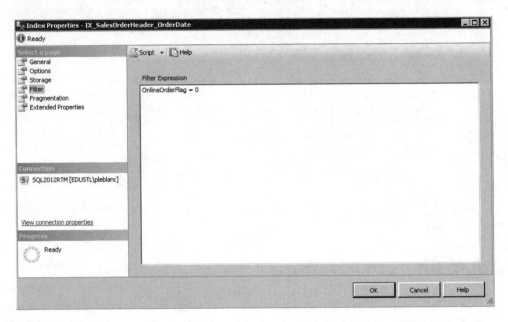

10. Click OK twice.

Add a filter to an index using T-SQL

1. Open the query editor in SSMS.

2. In the query editor, enter and execute the following T-SQL code:

```
--Use this script to add a filter to an index
USE AdventureWorks2012;
CREATE NONCLUSTERED INDEX IX_SalesOrderHeader_OrderDate
ON Sales.SalesOrderHeader
(
    OrderDate
)
INCLUDE(Status, AccountNumber)
WHERE(OnlineOrderFlag = 0)
WITH(DROP_EXISTING = ON);
```

Placing indexes

The last argument determines where the index will reside on disk. If you do not provide a location, the index will be placed in the same filegroup as the base table. We discussed filegroups earlier. However, if you prefer, you can place an index in a different filegroup or partition.

See Also *Chapter 4, "Designing SQL Server databases," discusses filegroups, and Chapter 8, "Table partitioning," covers partitions in depth.*

If you want to place an index in a filegroup other than the PRIMARY filegroup, you must first have a filegroup that includes a data file. The following code adds a second filegroup and one data file to the AdventureWorks2012 database:

```
USE master;
ALTER DATABASE AdventureWorks2012
     ADD FILEGROUP AW2012FileGroup2;

ALTER DATABASE AdventureWorks2012
ADD FILE
(
     NAME = IndexFile,
 FILENAME = 'C:\SQLData\IndexFile.ndf',
 SIZE = 5MB,
 MAXSIZE = 100MB,
 FILEGROWTH = 5MB
)
TO FILEGROUP AW2012FileGroup2;
```

Now with the pieces in place, in the next exercise you'll modify an existing index to move it to the new filegroup.

Place an index in a filegroup using SSMS

1. Open SSMS and connect to a server.

2. Expand the Databases folder.

3. Expand the AdventureWorks2012 database.

4. Expand the Tables folder.

5. Expand the Sales.SalesOrderHeader table.

6. Expand the Indexes folder.

7. Right-click the IX_SalesOrderHeader_OrderDate index and select Properties.

8. Select Storage in the Select a Page section.

9. Select AW2012FileGroup2 from the Filegroup drop-down list.

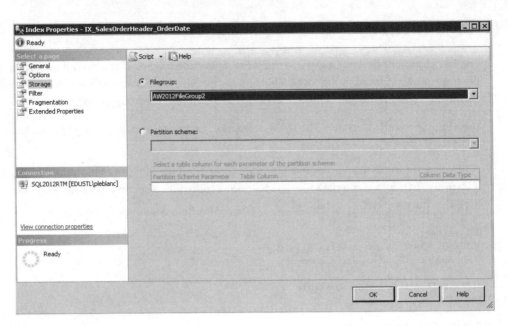

10. Click OK twice.

Place an index in a filegroup using T-SQL

1. Open the query editor in SSMS.

2. In the query editor, enter and execute the following T-SQL code:

```
--Use this script to place an index in a filegroup
USE AdventureWorks2012;
CREATE NONCLUSTERED INDEX IX_SalesOrderHeader_OrderDate
ON Sales.SalesOrderHeader
(
    OrderDate
)
INCLUDE(Status, AccountNumber)
WHERE(OnlineOrderFlag = 0)
WITH(DROP_EXISTING = ON)
ON AW2012FileGroup2;
```

Disabling and dropping indexes

Often an index is created and after some time a database administrator or developer may realize that it is really not needed. As a result, the administrator or developer typically will want to remove the index. In some cases, instead of removing the index, it may be a good idea to disable it. This will allow you to verify how performance is affected without actually dropping the index.

Disable an index using SSMS

1. Open SSMS and connect to a server.

2. Expand the Databases folder.

3. Expand the AdventureWorks2012 database.

4. Expand the Tables folder.

5. Expand the Sales.SalesOrderHeader table.

6. Expand the Indexes folder.

7. Right-click the IX_SalesOrderHeader_OrderDate index and select Disable.

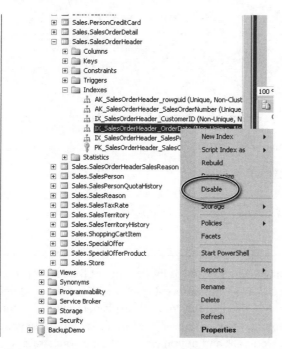

8. Click OK.

Disable an index using T-SQL

1. Open the query editor in SSMS.

2. In the query editor, enter and execute the following T-SQL code:

```
--Use this script to disable an index
USE AdventureWorks2012;
ALTER INDEX IX_SalesOrderHeader_OrderDate
    ON Sales.SalesOrderHeader DISABLE;
```

Drop an index using SSMS

1. Open SSMS and connect to a server.

2. Expand the Databases folder.

3. Expand the AdventureWorks2012 database.

4. Expand the Tables folder.

5. Expand the Sales.SalesOrderHeader table.

6. Expand the Indexes folder.

7. Right-click the IX_SalesOrderHeader_OrderDate index and select Delete.

8. Click OK.

Drop an index using T-SQL

1. Open the query editor in SSMS.

2. In the query editor, enter and execute the following T-SQL code:

```
--Use this script to drop an index
USE AdventureWorks2012;
DROP INDEX CIX_DatabaseLog_PostTime
    ON dbo.DatabaseLog;
```

Summary

Developing indexing strategies for any RDBMS system is more of an art than a science. Each database—and more specifically, each table—has different characteristics that may force you to adopt techniques that encompass one or more of the concepts explained in this chapter. In some cases, you may give birth to a new method that has never been used. Regardless of your approach, you should carefully consider every argument and option when deciding your strategy.

PART III

Advanced database design topics

CHAPTER 7

Table compression

After completing this chapter, you will be able to

- Understand the different types of compression.

- Understand how to compress a table or index.

- Determine when to compress a table or index.

We often hear that disk space is cheap and that we should not be too concerned if databases are growing at an excessive rate. Just buy more disks. Well, what most managers do not realize is that we are not talking about disks that you buy at some large electronic store. Microsoft SQL Server and other RDBMSs require fast redundant sets of disks. That coupling takes disk price from cheap to often very expensive. In addition, if you must include high availability and disaster recovery as part of your topology, then your costs are doubled.

To offset some of the cost, SQL Server includes a feature that allows you to compress your data at different levels—specifically, tables and indexes. You can actually compress any of the following:

- A table that is stored as a heap (it does not have a clustered index)

- A table that has a clustered index

- A nonclustered index

- An indexed view

- A partition (see Chapter 8, "Table partitioning")

Not only can you reduce the disk requirements of SQL Server with compression, but in most cases you can also improve the overall performance of your disk subsystems and query request times. The actual compression rate is dependent upon two primary factors: data characteristics and the corresponding data type. While not all data types are affected by compression, most are. Table 7-1 lists the affected data types.

TABLE 7-1 Data types affected by compression

smallint	int	bigint	decimal	numeric
real	float	money	smallmoney	bit
datetime	datetime2	datetimeoffset	char	nchar
binary	rowversion			

SQL Server has two types of compression: data and backup. Throughout this chapter, you will focus on data compression.

 Note Data compression is supported only in the Enterprise version of SQL Server 2012.

Understanding row compression

The great thing about SQL Server compression is that it is completely transparent to applications that need to access the underlying data. While compression does change how the data is physically stored, developers do not have to change anything syntactically in their code.

Row compression, by nature, is not a very complicated process. Basically, it identifies the data type of each column, converts it to variable length, and finally reduces the amount of required storage to only what is needed. As a result, compression increases the amount of data that can be stored on a page. In addition, it may reduce the amount of metadata associated with a record.

For example, if you have a column that has a data type of *smallint*, by default it will allocate 2 bytes of storage. However, the value inserted into the column may require only 1 byte of storage. If that is the case, enabling compression on that table will reduce the amount of allocated storage to only what is needed: 1 byte. This process is repeated for every column in the table or index.

As stated, you can compress a table or index. During creation, you have the option of specifying a table option that will compress the data within a table. Continuing the trend, you can compress data with T-SQL and Microsoft SQL Server Management Studio (SSMS).

Compress a table or index using SSMS

1. Open SSMS and connect to a server.

2. Expand the server node in Object Explorer.

3. Expand the AdventureWorks2012 database.

4. Expand the Tables folder and right-click the Sales.SalesOrderDetail table.

5. From the context menu that appears, select Storage | Manage Compression.

6. When the Data Compression Wizard appears, check the box labeled Do Not Show This Starting Page Again, and click Next.

   The next page, Select Compression Type, is where all the magic happens.

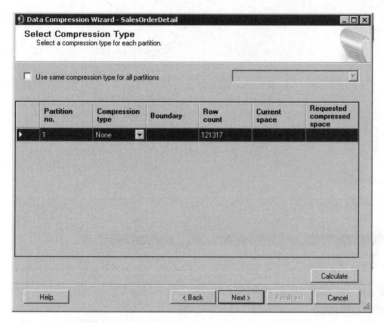

7. Check the box labeled Use Same Compression Type for All Partitions.

8. Select Row from the drop-down list, and click Calculated in the bottom-right corner.

   As you can see, you will save approximately 3 MB of disk space by implementing row compression on the table.

9. Click Next.

   The Select an Output Option page is where you specify how and when to compress the data.

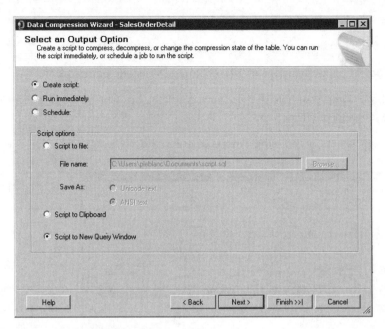

10. Click Run Immediately.

11. Click Next and the Summary page appears.

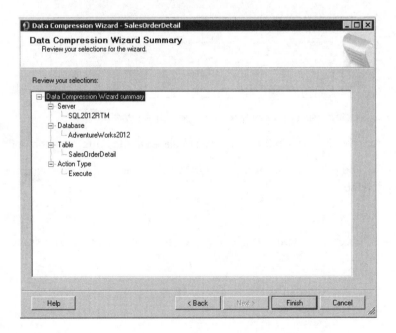

12. Review the summary information and click Finish.

13. The Compression Wizard Progress page appears.

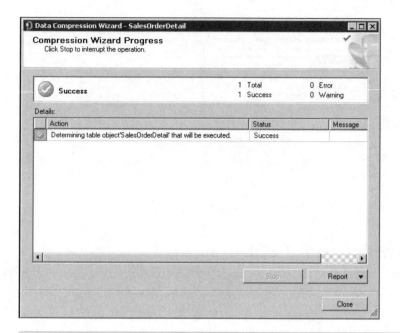

 Note Compressing the heap or the clustered index does not compress the nonclustered indexes. If you want to compress the nonclustered indexes, you must do so individually.

Compress a nonclustered index using SSMS

1. In Object Explorer, expand Sales.SalesOrderHeader.

2. Expand the Indexes folder.

3. Right-click the IX_SalesOrderHeader_SalesPersonID nonclustered index and select Storage | Manage Compression.

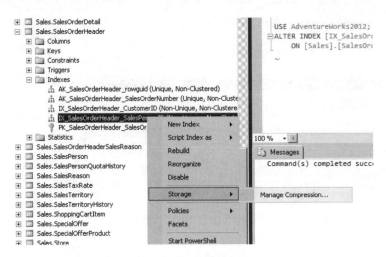

4. Repeat steps 9–13 from the previous exercise.

Row compression with T-SQL

If you prefer using T-SQL over SSMS, you can execute the following code to compress the clustered index on the Sales.SalesOrderHeader table and the IX_SalesOrderHeader_SalesPersonID nonclustered index:

```
--Use this code to row compress the Sales.SalesOrderHeader table
USE AdventureWorks2012;
ALTER TABLE [Sales].[SalesOrderHeader]
    REBUILD WITH(DATA_COMPRESSION = ROW);

--Use this code to row compress a nonclustered index on the Sales.SalesOrderHeader table
ALTER INDEX IX_SalesOrderHeader_SalesPersonID
    ON Sales.SalesOrderHeader
    REBUILD WITH(DATA_COMPRESSION = ROW);
```

You can also compress a table during initial creation with T-SQL. The following code creates a table that has a primary key that will be row compressed:

```
--Use this code to row compress a table during creation
USE AdventureWorks2012;
CREATE TABLE dbo.Ch7RowCompression
(
    ID int PRIMARY KEY,
    FirstName varchar(50),
    LastName varchar(50),
    BirthDate datetime
)
WITH (DATA_COMPRESSION = ROW);
```

Note that nothing about creating a table changes—however, you must add the option at the end, which appears in bold in the previous script. Now whenever data is inserted into the table, it will be row compressed. Using this method will compress the clustered index on the table or, if the clustered index does not exist, it will compress the heap.

Understanding page compression

Page compression further extends row compression by performing a few additional steps. Page compression performs three operations:

- Row compression
- Prefix compression
- Dictionary compression

As you can see, page compression includes row compression as part of its process. Nothing changes with the row compression process—it's just the first step in page compression. After the row compression is complete, the next step is prefix compression.

During this step, each column is scanned for a value that will reduce the storage space for each column. Once the value is identified, a row for each column is stored in the page header. All the information is called the compression information (CI), which is stored below the page header. The identified values (prefixed values) are located in each column and replaced with a pointer to the value in the CI section. Figure 7-1 illustrates the process.

Prior to Prefix Compression		
Page Header		
iiijj	iiiij	ijkl
iiijkk	jjjj	ijkl
iiikkk	iiiikk	jjjj

After Prefix Compression		
Page Header		
iiijkk	iiiikk	ijkl
4j	4j	[empty]
[empty]	0jjjj	[empty]
3kkk	[empty]	0jjjj

FIGURE 7-1 Prefix compression is the first step of page compression.

The prefixes that will reduce the size of the data are moved to the page header, and the actual column values are modified to include pointers to the CI, as shown in Figure 7-1. The value 3kkk represents the first three characters in the prefix and kkk.

The next step is dictionary compression, which scans the entire page instead of a single column. The values that are repeated—for example, 4j—are moved to the CI section of the page header and replaced with references to the values, as shown in Figure 7-2.

After Prefix Compression		
Page Header		
iiijkk	iiiikk	ijkl
4j	4j	
0	0	[empty]
[empty]	1	[empty]
3kkk	[empty]	1

FIGURE 7-2 Dictionary compression is the final step of page compression.

The process of page compression with SSMS or T-SQL is exactly the same as with row compression. The difference is that you specify PAGE instead of ROW.

Compress a page using SSMS

1. Repeat steps 1–7 from the "Compress a table or row using SSMS" exercise.

2. On the Select Compression Type page, select Page from the drop-down list.

3. Click Calculate. It may take a few seconds to yield results.

4. Click Next.

5. Click Run Immediately.

6. Click Next.

7. Click Finish.

Page compression with T-SQL

Just as with row compression, you have the ability to page compress data with T-SQL. The following script will page compress the clustered index on the Sales.SalesOrderDetail table and one of the nonclustered indexes:

```
--Use this code to page compress the Sales.SalesOrderDetail table
USE AdventureWorks2012;
ALTER TABLE Sales.SalesOrderDetail
    REBUILD WITH(DATA_COMPRESSION = PAGE);

--Use this code to page compress a nonclustered index on the Sales.SalesOrderDetail table
ALTER INDEX IX_SalesOrderDetail_ProductID
    ON Sales.SalesOrderDetail
    REBUILD WITH(DATA_COMPRESSION = PAGE);
```

The biggest advantages of using T-SQL are the portability and reusability of the code. While SSMS offers a very intuitive and flexible user interface, if you want to reproduce the steps in a different environment, you have to replicate the steps for each table or index. However, when you use T-SQL, it is as simple as executing a query.

Estimating effects of compression

Refer back to Figure 7-1, which shows a button labeled Calculated that returns an estimate of how much space will be used from row or page compressing a table or index. Performing the steps to estimate space savings on each individual table or index in a database can be an arduous task. Fortunately, SQL Server provides a stored procedure (discussed in detail in Chapter 17, "Stored procedures") that you can use to perform the same action.

Moreover, with a little time and skill, you can build a process that loops over every table or index in a database and yields the results of the stored procedure call. The following script estimates the space savings for a single index on the Production.TransactionHistory table:

```
exec sp_estimate_data_compression_savings
    @schema_name = 'Production',
    @object_name = 'TransactionHistory',
    @index_id = 1,
    @partition_number = NULL,
    @data_compression = 'row'
```

This script could take several minutes to execute depending on how much data there is and the type of compression that you select. The size_with_requested_compession_setting(KB) column estimates the size of the table or index if compressed. You should consider these results along with other factors mentioned in the next section when determining whether to compress a table or index.

Compression considerations

You will want to carefully consider whether to implement row or page compression prior to doing so. As with most things, compression does not come without a cost. While the data remains compressed in memory, when it is selected, it is decompressed. In addition, when new rows are inserted, the data is row and/or page compressed. When rows are updated or deleted, row-compressed objects should persist their current level of compression. However, page compression may be recalculated depending upon the number of changes that occur to the data.

As a result, determining which objects to compress is highly dependent upon what activities are performed on the corresponding objects. As a general starting point, those objects that are updated frequently should be row compressed. Those objects that are mostly read should be page compressed. There are certainly other issues to think about, but these are good starting points. Also, tables that are only appended to (in other words, data is added to the end) should be page compressed.

Summary

Deciding what to compress and when takes some definite testing and analysis of your current database. Compression in most cases should save space, and it may even provide some performance improvements to your overall database environment. The process of compression can be applied to certain objects in your database using SSMS or T-SQL. This chapter examined the two types of compression, row and page, and you walked through the steps to implement both types of compression. In addition, you learned how to estimate the amount of space savings that you can expect to gain by either implementation.

CHAPTER 8

Table partitioning

After completing this chapter, you will be able to

- Understand table partitioning.
- Create a partition function.
- Create a partition scheme.
- Partition a table.

The concept of partitioning is not very difficult to explain or comprehend. For example, assume you have a table that contains sales data, and you would like to divide the data into segments based on the year of sale. Logically, the table would resemble Figure 8-1.

	OrderID	OrderNumber	OrderDate
2010	1	SUS1	1/1/2010
	2	SUS2	1/2/2010
2011	3	SUS3	3/2/2011
	4	SUS4	4/5/2011
2012	5	SUS5	2/2/2012
	6	SUS6	10/2/2012

FIGURE 8-1 Logical table partitioning.

As shown in Figure 8-1, dividing the data by year is simple to illustrate. When data is added to the table, it will be placed in the appropriate location based on the year of the sale. Partitioning tables offers several benefits, primarily in the form of simplified maintenance, potential performance improvements, and the ability to physically store data in a single database across several disks.

So how can partitioning be handled physically as data is inserted into a Microsoft SQL Server table? The process consists of the following three steps:

1. Create a partition function.
2. Create a partition scheme.
3. Apply the partition scheme to a table.

You will examine each step in the sections that follow.

Creating a partition function

While the logical—or you could even say *manual*—partitioning process is straightforward, the process of partitioning a table in SQL Server is not that much more difficult. The first step is to create a partition function. This function is what will be used to align or map the data to the corresponding partition based on a column in the table.

 Note In SQL Server, you can partition tables that have indexes and those that do not have indexes.

Using partition function arguments

When creating a partition function, you must specify or provide a few pieces of information. The first and most obvious is a name. The next is the input parameter type, which is the data type of the column that will be used for partitioning. The only data types that cannot be used are *text*, *ntext*, *image*, *xml*, *timestamp*, *varchar(max)*, *nvarchar(max)*, and *varbinary(max)*; alias data types; and common language runtime (CLR) user-defined data types. Typically, a date or integer column is used for the partitioning function. The final two, the boundary and the side of the boundary (RIGHT or LEFT), work together as a team to determine specifically how the data will be partitioned. The first is the boundary value, which acts as a constraint on each partition. This value is equal to *n* + 1 the number of values supplied. For example, refer back to Figure 8-1 and note that the values would be 2010, 2011, and 2012, and a fourth partition that contains all the data greater than 2012. The last argument defines on which side of the boundary, LEFT or RIGHT, the boundary will reside.

 Note In Microsoft SQL Server 2012, the number of partitions that can be created on a table or index has been increased to 15,000.

 Note For ease of maintenance and, often, improved performance, it is recommended that you place each partition in a separate filegroup. When creating your filegroups, you must always include one more than the number of boundaries specified in your partition function. The filegroups should be placed on different disks to physically separate I/O. The following script adds several filegroups to the AdventureWorks2012 database:

```
ALTER DATABASE AdventureWorks2012;
    ADD FILEGROUP Sales2005;
--Use this code to add multiple filegroups to the AdventureWorks2012 database
USE master;
ALTER DATABASE AdventureWorks2012
ADD FILE
```

```
(
     NAME = 'Sales2005',
  FILENAME = 'C:\SQLData\Sales2005File.ndf',
  SIZE = 5MB,
  MAXSIZE = 200MB,
  FILEGROWTH = 5MB
)
TO FILEGROUP Sales2005;

ALTER DATABASE AdventureWorks2012
     ADD FILEGROUP Sales2006;

ALTER DATABASE AdventureWorks2012
ADD FILE
(
     NAME = 'Sales2006',
  FILENAME = 'C:\SQLData\Sales2006File.ndf',
  SIZE = 5MB,
  MAXSIZE = 200MB,
  FILEGROWTH = 5MB
)
TO FILEGROUP Sales2006;

ALTER DATABASE AdventureWorks2012
     ADD FILEGROUP Sales2007;

ALTER DATABASE AdventureWorks2012
ADD FILE
(
     NAME = 'Sales2007',
  FILENAME = 'C:\SQLData\Sales2007File.ndf',
  SIZE = 5MB,
  MAXSIZE = 200MB,
  FILEGROWTH = 5MB
)
TO FILEGROUP Sales2007;

ALTER DATABASE AdventureWorks2012
     ADD FILEGROUP Sales2008;

ALTER DATABASE AdventureWorks2012
ADD FILE
(
     NAME = 'Sales2008',
  FILENAME = 'C:\SQLData\Sales2008File.ndf',
  SIZE = 5MB,
  MAXSIZE = 200MB,
  FILEGROWTH = 5MB
)
```

```
TO FILEGROUP Sales2008;
ALTER DATABASE AdventureWorks2012
     ADD FILEGROUP Sales2009;

ALTER DATABASE AdventureWorks2012
ADD FILE
(
     NAME = 'Sales2009',
  FILENAME = 'C:\SQLData\Sales2009File.ndf',
  SIZE = 5MB,
  MAXSIZE = 200MB,
  FILEGROWTH = 5MB
)
TO FILEGROUP Sales2009;
```

While SQL Server 2012 offers a very robust user interface that encompasses all the steps required to partition a table or index, you will use T-SQL initially to work through the partitioning process.

Create a partitioning function using T-SQL

1. Open the query editor in Microsoft SQL Server Management Studio (SSMS).

2. In the query editor, enter and execute the following T-SQL code:

```
--Use this code to create a partition function
USE AdventureWorks2012;
CREATE PARTITION FUNCTION fnPOOrderDate (datetime)
AS RANGE LEFT
FOR VALUES('20051231','20061231','20071231','20081231')
```

The preceding script results in the division or partitioning illustrated in Figure 8-2.

Partition	1	2	3	4	5
Values or Ranges	OrderDate <= 12/31/2005	OrderDate between 1/1/2006 and 12/31/2006	OrderDate between 1/1/2007 and 12/31/2007	OrderDate between 1/1/2008 and 12/31/2008	OrderDate > 12/31/2008
	Anything Less Than 2006	Only 2006	Only 2007	Only 2008	Anything Greater Than 2008

FIGURE 8-2 Partition function data distribution.

Creating a partition scheme

As mentioned previously, using filegroups as part of your partitioning strategy offers several advantages. To ensure that you place the correct data in the correct filegroup, you will use a *partition scheme*. The partition scheme assigns or maps the partitions created by the function to filegroups.

Specifying partition scheme arguments

You can specify four arguments when creating a partition scheme:

- The name, whose definition and purpose are obvious.

- The name of the partition function, which must be created prior to creating the scheme. The partitions created by the specified function will be mapped to the filegroups provided when creating the scheme.

- ALL, which when used, limits the number of filegroups to one.

- The last argument, which accepts a comma-delimited list of filegroups.

The partitions are assigned to the filegroups in the order in which they are listed, starting with the first partition specified in the function.

Create a partitioning scheme using T-SQL

1. Open the query editor in SSMS.

2. In the query editor, enter and execute the following T-SQL code:

```
--Use this code to create a partition function
USE AdventureWorks2012;
CREATE PARTITION SCHEME schPOOrderDate
AS PARTITION fnPOOrderDate
TO(Sales2005, Sales2006, Sales2007, Sales2008, Sales2009);
```

Partitioning tables and indexes

As previously stated, both tables and indexes can be partitioned. More specifically, you can partition the following:

- A table without a clustered index (heap)

- A clustered index

- A unique index

- A nonclustered index

When partitioning a clustered index, the column that has been specified as the partitioning column must be included in the clustering key. If you are partitioning a clustered or nonclustered index that is not unique, the partitioning column is not required as part of the key. However, if you do not include it, SQL Server will add it to the index by default. With regard to unique indexes, clustered or nonclustered, you must include the partitioning column as part of the unique index key.

Partition a table using SSMS

1. Open SSMS and connect to a server.

2. In the query editor, enter and execute the following T-SQL code:

```
USE [AdventureWorks2012];
IF(OBJECT_ID('dbo.PurchaseOrderHeader')) IS NOT NULL
    DROP TABLE dbo.PurchaseOrderHeader
GO
CREATE TABLE dbo.[PurchaseOrderHeader](
    [PurchaseOrderID] [int] NOT NULL,
    [RevisionNumber] [tinyint] NOT NULL,
    [Status] [tinyint] NOT NULL,
    [EmployeeID] [int] NOT NULL,
    [VendorID] [int] NOT NULL,
    [ShipMethodID] [int] NOT NULL,
    [OrderDate] [datetime] NOT NULL,
    [ShipDate] [datetime] NULL,
    [SubTotal] [money] NOT NULL,
    [TaxAmt] [money] NOT NULL,
    [Freight] [money] NOT NULL,
    [TotalDue] money,
    [ModifiedDate] [datetime] NOT NULL
);
```

3. In Object Explorer, expand the Databases folder.

4. Expand the AdventureWorks2012 database.

5. Expand the Tables folder.

6. Right-click the dbo.PurchaseOrderHeader table.

7. Select Storage | Create Partition from the context menu.

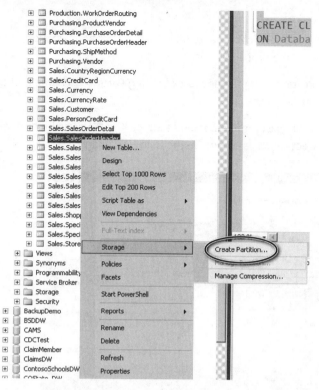

8. On the Create Partition Wizard page, click Next.

9. On the Select a Partitioning Column page, click the radio button next to the OrderDate column.

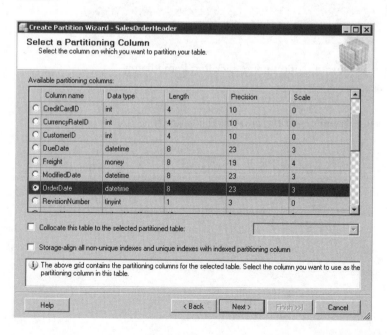

10. Click Next.

11. On the Select a Partition Function page, click Existing Partition Function and select fnPOOrderDate from the drop-down list.

12. On the Select a Partition Scheme page, click Existing Partition Scheme and select schPOOrderDate from the drop-down list.

13. Because you chose an existing function and scheme, the Map Partitions page should be pre-filled with the correct values, as shown in the following image.

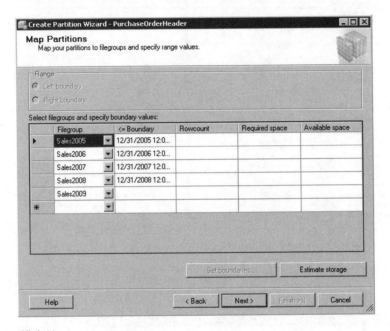

14. Click Next.

15. On the Select an Output Option page, click Run Immediately.

16. Click Next.

17. Review the summary information, and then click Finish.

18. Click Close.

Partition a table using T-SQL

1. Open the query editor in SSMS.

2. In the query editor, enter and execute the following T-SQL code:

```
USE [AdventureWorks2012];
IF(OBJECT_ID('dbo.PurchaseOrderHeader')) IS NOT NULL
    DROP TABLE dbo.PurchaseOrderHeader
GO
CREATE TABLE dbo.[PurchaseOrderHeader](
    [PurchaseOrderID] [int] NOT NULL,
    [RevisionNumber] [tinyint] NOT NULL,
    [Status] [tinyint] NOT NULL,
    [EmployeeID] [int] NOT NULL,
    [VendorID] [int] NOT NULL,
    [ShipMethodID] [int] NOT NULL,
    [OrderDate] [datetime] NOT NULL,
    [ShipDate] [datetime] NULL,
    [SubTotal] [money] NOT NULL,
    [TaxAmt] [money] NOT NULL,
    [Freight] [money] NOT NULL,
    [TotalDue] money,
    [ModifiedDate] [datetime] NOT NULL
) ON schPOOrderDate(OrderDate);
```

 Note The preceding script creates a standard table. However, note that the last line in bold tells SQL Server to create the table using the specified partition scheme and OrderDate as the partition column.

Partition a table using SSMS

1. Open SSMS and connect to a server.

2. In the query editor, enter and execute the following T-SQL code:

```
USE [AdventureWorks2012];
CREATE CLUSTERED INDEX CIX_PurchaseOrderHeader_OrderDate
ON dbo.PurchaseOrderHeader(OrderDate)
```

3. In Object Explorer, expand the Databases folder.

4. Expand the AdventureWorks2012 database.

5. Expand the Tables folder.

6. Expand Indexes.

7. Right-click the CIX_PurchaseOrderHeader_OrderDate index and select Properties from the context menu.

8. Click Storage in the Select a Page section.

9. Click Partition Scheme and select schPOOrderDate from the drop-down list.

10. Click under the Table Column column (toward the bottom of the screen).

11. Select OrderDate from the drop-down list.

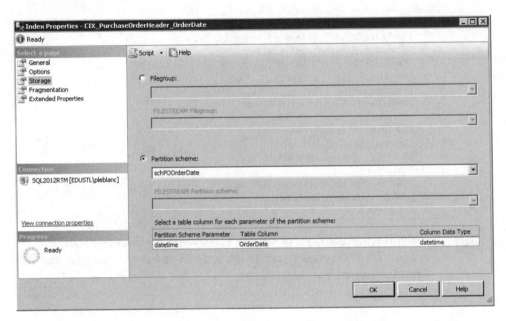

12. Click OK.

Partition an index using T-SQL

1. Open the query editor in SSMS.

2. In the query editor, enter and execute the following T-SQL code:

```
USE [AdventureWorks2012];
CREATE CLUSTERED INDEX CIX_PurchaseOrderHeader_OrderDate
ON dbo.PurchaseOrderHeader(OrderDate)
WITH(DROP_EXISTING = ON)
ON schPOOrderDate(OrderDate);
```

Summary

This chapter presented a brief overview of SQL Server partitioning, including an introduction to the key concepts and terms needed to gain a general understanding of the partitioning process. You followed a step-by-step demonstration on how to create a partition function and scheme that you can use to partition a table or index. You will need to investigate several advanced topics once you have acquired a basic understanding of partitioning. As your database architectures become more complex and your data space requirements grow, consider looking into further partition topics, including modifying, splitting, and aligning partitions.

CHAPTER 9

Database snapshots

After completing this chapter, you will be able to

- Understand database snapshots.

- Identify database snapshot prerequisites.

- Create and view a database snapshot.

- Drop a database snapshot.

- Revert to a database snapshot.

A *database snapshot* is a static, read-only copy of an existing Microsoft SQL Server database. The existing database is referred to as the *source* database when discussing database snapshots. When a snapshot is created, it is an exact read-only replica of the source database at that point in time. As the source database changes, the snapshot will be updated to ensure that it is synchronized.

This chapter covers the information you need to determine when, how, and why to implement snapshots. Specifically, the chapter outlines the limitations and prerequisites of using snapshots, and you will learn how to create snapshots and view snapshots. Finally, you will learn how to use a snapshot as a backup in the event that a backup does not exist, and also how to drop a snapshot when it is no longer needed.

Understanding database snapshot prerequisites and limitations

When creating a database snapshot, you must ensure that your source database constantly and consistently remains available. The following is a list of the most common prerequisites and limitations of the source database:

- Database snapshots are supported only in the Enterprise version of SQL Server 2012.

- The source and the snapshot database must reside on the same SQL Server instance.

- The source database cannot be dropped, detached, or restored.

- Source database files cannot be dropped.

- Performance could be negatively affected due to increased I/O on the source.

While the snapshot itself provides a read-only copy of the source database, you should consider several limiting factors prior to implementing snapshots in your environment. The following is a list of the common snapshot limitations:

- The snapshots must reside on the same server as the source database.

- Snapshots cannot be backed up, restored, or detached.

- Changes in the source database will cause the snapshot database to grow. Therefore, you should ensure that you have disk space available equal to the size of your source database.

- If a snapshot runs out of space, it must be deleted and re-created.

Again, this is not an exhaustive list of the limitations, but these are the ones that typically impact if and when database snapshots will work in your environment.

Creating and viewing database snapshots

T-SQL is the primary mechanism used to create database snapshots. The syntax is similar to a traditional database creation script, with a few small modifications. The following pseudocode depicts a sample syntax script:

```
CREATE DATABASE <database snapshot name>
ON
(
    NAME = <Logical Name of source database file>,
    FILENAME = <File Path where file will be stored and the name of the file>
)
AS SNAPSHOT OF <source database name>
```

If the source database has multiple data files, you must specify each in the script. This is demonstrated in the following exercise.

Create a database snapshot using T-SQL

1. Open the query editor in Microsoft SQL Server Management Studio (SSMS).

2. In the query editor, enter and execute the following T-SQL code:

```
--Use this script to create a snapshot of a database
USE master;
CREATE DATABASE SBSChp4TSQL_snapshot_42012200
ON
(
    NAME = SBSChp4TSQL1,
    FILENAME = 'C:\SQLDATA\SBSChp4TSQL1_snapshot_data.ss'
),
```

```
(
    NAME = SBSChp4TSQL2,
    FILENAME = 'C:\SQLDATA\SBSChp4TSQL2_snapshot_data.ss'
)
AS SNAPSHOT OF SBSChp4TSQL;
```

View a database snapshot with SSMS

1. Open SSMS and connect to a server.

2. In Object Explorer, expand the Databases folder.

3. Expand the Database Snapshots folder.

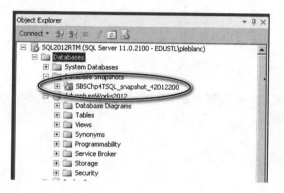

Dropping database snapshots

At some point, you may decide that a database snapshot is no longer useful, or you may decide that it is consuming too much space and you would like to start with a fresh snapshot. You can drop a snapshot using SSMS or T-SQL.

Drop a database snapshot using SSMS

1. Open SSMS and connect to a server.

2. In Object Explorer, expand the Databases folder.

3. Expand the Database Snapshots folder.

4. Right-click the database snapshot that you want to drop, and select Delete from the context menu.

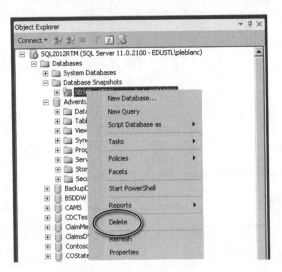

5. Check the box labeled Close Existing Connections.

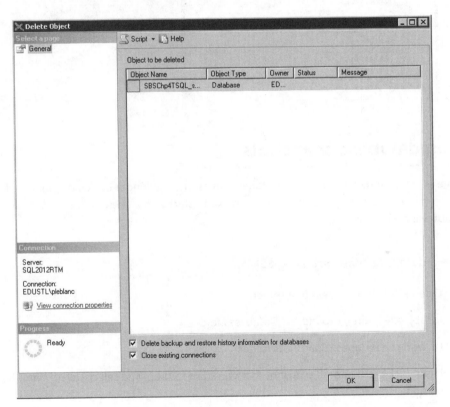

6. Click OK.

Drop a database snapshot using T-SQL

1. Open the query editor in SSMS.

2. In the query editor, enter and execute the following T-SQL code:

```
--Use this script to create a snapshot of a database
USE master;
CREATE DATABASE SBSChp4TSQL_snapshot_42012400
ON
(
    NAME = SBSChp4TSQL1,
    FILENAME = 'C:\SQLDATA\SBSChp4TSQL14_snapshot_data.ss'
),
(
    NAME = SBSChp4TSQL2,
    FILENAME = 'C:\SQLDATA\SBSChp4TSQL24_snapshot_data.ss'
)
AS SNAPSHOT OF SBSChp4TSQL;
```

3. Open a new query window.

4. In the new query editor window, enter and execute the following T-SQL code:

```
--Use this script to drop a database snapshot
USE master;
DROP DATABASE SBSChp4TSQL_snapshot_42012400;
```

Reverting to a database snapshot

One of the biggest advantages you can leverage by creating database snapshots is that you may be able to use them as a backup to a database backup. For example, assume that someone has accidently deleted data from a table in your database, or a table has been dropped. How would you restore that object? You could use a database backup; however, if you created a database snapshot, you could use that snapshot instead. The snapshot may offer an even more recent version of the database schema and data than your last backup.

Revert to a database snapshot using T-SQL

1. Open the query editor in SSMS.

2. In the query editor, enter and execute the following T-SQL code:

```
--Use this script to create a snapshot of a database
USE master;
RESTORE DATABASE SBSChp4TSQL FROM DATABASE_SNAPSHOT = 'SBSChp4TSQL_snapshot_42012400';
```

Restoring from a database snapshot is a viable option in some cases, but it is not a complete copy of the database. Therefore, if the source database becomes corrupt, you cannot revert to the snapshot. Here are a few more limitations that you may encounter:

- The source database must have only one snapshot.

- If any of the files are read-only or offline, you cannot revert to a snapshot.

- Any changes that occurred after the reverted snapshot was taken will be lost.

Summary

As discussed in this chapter, database snapshots offer organizations several ways to leverage a copy of the data and schema that may have not been available before. They are commonly used as sources for reports and ad-hoc querying. In addition, you can use them as a source of backup in the case of data loss. Regardless of your reason for leveraging snapshots, you must take into account the additional disk space requirements and the potential for performance degradation when you consider using this feature.

CHAPTER 10

The SELECT statement

After completing this chapter, you will be able to

- Write a SELECT statement.

- Sort your results.

- Filter a SELECT statement with the WHERE clause.

- Use comparison operators.

- Use the BETWEEN operator.

- Use the WHERE clause with multiple conditions.

- Search for a list of values.

- Use a wildcard search.

- Create aliases.

- Use the JOIN operator.

- Limit the data returned in your result set.

- Use the UNION keyword to combine result sets.

So far in this book, you have learned how to create databases and tables, but what happens after an application has added data to the database? How do you get the data out? Microsoft SQL Server data retrieval is a very straightforward and simple process. To retrieve or access data inside a SQL Server database, you use a SELECT statement, which is the topic of this chapter.

Writing a SELECT statement

While the SELECT statement offers a plethora of arguments that can make it very complex, in its simplest form it consists of two keywords: a list of columns and a table name.

Write a SELECT statement

1. Open Microsoft SQL Server Management Studio (SSMS) and connect to a server.

2. In Object Explorer, expand the Databases folder.

3. Expand the AdventureWorks2012 database.

4. Expand the Tables folder.

5. Expand the HumanResources.Department table.

6. Open the query editor in SSMS.

7. In the query editor, enter the following T-SQL code:

   ```
   USE AdventureWorks2012;
   SELECT
   FROM
   ```

8. Drag the Columns folder underneath the table in Object Explorer to the right of the keyword SELECT. Ensure that there is a space after the SELECT keyword.

9. Drag the HumanResources.Department table from Object Explorer to the right of the keyword FROM. Ensure that there is a space after the FROM keyword.

   ```
   --Use this query to select data from the HumanResources.Department table
   in the AdventureWorks2012 database
   USE AdventureWorks2012;
   SELECT DepartmentID, Name, GroupName, ModifiedDate
   FROM [HumanResources].[Department]
   ```

10. Execute the query and review the results.

	DepartmentID	Name	GroupName	ModifiedDate
1	1	Engineering	Research and Development	2002-06-01 00:00:00.000
2	2	Tool Design	Research and Development	2002-06-01 00:00:00.000
3	3	Sales	Sales and Marketing	2002-06-01 00:00:00.000
4	4	Marketing	Sales and Marketing	2002-06-01 00:00:00.000
5	5	Purchasing	Inventory Management	2002-06-01 00:00:00.000
6	6	Research and Development	Research and Development	2002-06-01 00:00:00.000
7	7	Production	Manufacturing	2002-06-01 00:00:00.000
8	8	Production Control	Manufacturing	2002-06-01 00:00:00.000
9	9	Human Resources	Executive General and Administration	2002-06-01 00:00:00.000
10	10	Finance	Executive General and Administration	2002-06-01 00:00:00.000
11	11	Information Services	Executive General and Administration	2002-06-01 00:00:00.000
12	12	Document Control	Quality Assurance	2002-06-01 00:00:00.000
13	13	Quality Assurance	Quality Assurance	2002-06-01 00:00:00.000
14	14	Facilities and Maintenance	Executive General and Administration	2002-06-01 00:00:00.000
15	15	Shipping and Receiving	Inventory Management	2002-06-01 00:00:00.000
16	16	Executive	Executive General and Administration	2002-06-01 00:00:00.000

Note If you want to return every column in a table, you can replace the column list with an asterisk (*) because every column was included in the SELECT statement:

```
USE AdventureWorks2012;
SELECT *
FROM [HumanResources].[Department]
```

Sorting results

Now that you can retrieve data, you may want to do certain things with the results of the query. For example, often you'll want to sort data. To sort data in SQL Server 2012, you use the ORDER BY clause. This clause sorts the data in the order specified, either ascending (ASC) or descending (DESC).

Order the result set

1. Open the query editor in SSMS.

2. In the query editor, enter and execute the following T-SQL code:

```
--Use this query to sort the results of a query
USE AdventureWorks2012;
SELECT *
FROM [HumanResources].[Department]
ORDER BY DepartmentID DESC
```

Instead of returning the results starting with DepartmentID 1, as shown in the previous image, the results start with DepartmentID 16. The following image shows the new results.

	DepartmentID	Name	GroupName	ModifiedDate
1	16	Executive	Executive General and Administration	2002-06-01 00:00:00.000
2	15	Shipping and Receiving	Inventory Management	2002-06-01 00:00:00.000
3	14	Facilities and Maintenance	Executive General and Administration	2002-06-01 00:00:00.000
4	13	Quality Assurance	Quality Assurance	2002-06-01 00:00:00.000
5	12	Document Control	Quality Assurance	2002-06-01 00:00:00.000
6	11	Information Services	Executive General and Administration	2002-06-01 00:00:00.000
7	10	Finance	Executive General and Administration	2002-06-01 00:00:00.000
8	9	Human Resources	Executive General and Administration	2002-06-01 00:00:00.000
9	8	Production Control	Manufacturing	2002-06-01 00:00:00.000
10	7	Production	Manufacturing	2002-06-01 00:00:00.000
11	6	Research and Development	Research and Development	2002-06-01 00:00:00.000
12	5	Purchasing	Inventory Management	2002-06-01 00:00:00.000
13	4	Marketing	Sales and Marketing	2002-06-01 00:00:00.000
14	3	Sales	Sales and Marketing	2002-06-01 00:00:00.000
15	2	Tool Design	Research and Development	2002-06-01 00:00:00.000
16	1	Engineering	Research and Development	2002-06-01 00:00:00.000

Note If a clustered index exists on the table, and ORDER BY is not specified, the results are usually returned in the order specified when the clustered index was created. However, when logic is relying on data ordered in a specific way, you should always specify ORDER BY.

Filtering data with the WHERE clause

So far, you have simply returned all the rows in a table. In the real world, this is probably not what you will do—most times, you will need to return only subsets of data. For example, assume you want to write a query that searches for a specific department or all departments that start with the letter *P*. To accomplish this, you will include the WHERE clause as part of your SELECT statement. The WHERE clause always follows the FROM statement and precedes the ORDER BY clause. There are several different implementations of the query clause, among them the following, which are discussed in the sections that follow:

- Comparison operators

- The BETWEEN operator

- A WHERE clause with multiple conditions

- A search for a list of values

- A wildcard search

Using comparison operators

SQL Server offers several comparison operators, such as = (equals), < (less than), > (greater than), and >= (greater than or equal to), among others. Coupling these operators with the WHERE clause can assist you in limiting data in several ways.

Use the equality operator

1. Open the query editor in SSMS.

2. In the query editor, enter and execute the following T-SQL code:

```
--Use this query to filter data using the equality operator
USE AdventureWorks2012;
SELECT *
FROM [HumanResources].[Department]
WHERE DepartmentID = 4
```

	DepartmentID	Name	GroupName	ModifiedDate
1	4	Marketing	Sales and Marketing	2002-06-01 00:00:00.000

Use the greater than operator

1. Open the query editor in SSMS.

2. In the query editor, enter and execute the following T-SQL code:

```
--Use this query to filter the results of query using the greater than operator
USE AdventureWorks2012;
SELECT *
FROM [HumanResources].[Department]
WHERE DepartmentID > 4
```

Using the BETWEEN operator

In some cases, you may want to search your data for a sequential range of data. For example, you may want to return all the sales from May 1, 2007, through December 12, 2007. You could use a couple of the comparison operations, but SQL Server offers you a more elegant solution: the BETWEEN operator.

Use the BETWEEN operator

1. Open the query editor in SSMS.

2. In the query editor, enter and execute the following T-SQL code:

```
--Use this query to filter the results of a query using the BETWEEN operator
USE AdventureWorks2012;
SELECT
     AccountNumber,
     SalesOrderID,
     OrderDate
FROM Sales.SalesOrderHeader
WHERE
     OrderDate BETWEEN '5/1/2007' AND '12/31/2007'
```

 Note When using the BETWEEN operator, note that it is an inclusive range for numbers, which means that the two values specified in the clause will be included in the filter.

In the previous example, the result set would include all order data that occurred between 5/1/2001 12 AM and 12/31/2007 12 AM. As such, it would not return anything that happened during the day of 12/31/2007 after midnight. If you were required to include the values for that data, you could write the query as follows:

```
SELECT
    AccountNumber,
    SalesOrderID,
    OrderDate
FROM Sales.SalesOrderHeader
WHERE
    OrderDate >= '5/1/2007 00:00:00' AND OrderDate<= '12/31/2007'
```

Using the WHERE clause with multiple conditions

Sometimes you may need to specify multiple filters in one statement. For example, perhaps you want to find sales in a certain date range but also only for a specific product. In that case, you can use the AND or OR operator to combine both filters.

Write a WHERE clause with multiple conditions

1. Open the query editor in SSMS.

2. In the query editor, enter and execute the following T-SQL code:

    ```
    --Use this query to filter the results with multiple conditions
    USE AdventureWorks2012;
    SELECT
        SalesOrderDetailID,
        OrderQty,
        ProductID,
        ModifiedDate
    FROM Sales.SalesOrderDetail s
    WHERE
        ModifiedDate BETWEEN '5/1/2007' AND '12/31/2007' AND
        ProductID = 809
    ```

Searching for a list of values

Another typical scenario involves retrieving a result set based on a list of values. For example, you may need to return all sales for a particular list of products. Using the IN operator, SQL Server determines whether items in a specified list match the specified value.

Use the IN operator

1. Open the query editor in SSMS.

2. In the query editor, enter and execute the following T-SQL code:

```
--Use this query to filter the results with the IN operator
USE AdventureWorks2012;
SELECT
    SalesOrderDetailID,
    OrderQty,
    ProductID,
    ModifiedDate
FROM Sales.SalesOrderDetail s
WHERE
    ProductID IN (776, 778, 747, 809)
```

Using a wildcard search

The final variation of the WHERE clause covered here is the wildcard search. For example, suppose you want to return all the departments at your organization that start with the letters *PR*. To do this, you use a LIKE comparison. When you use LIKE, SQL Server can determine if a specified character or string of characters matches a value in your database.

Use the LIKE comparison

1. Open the query editor in SSMS.

2. In the query editor, enter and execute the following T-SQL code:

```
--Use this query to filter the results using LIKE
USE AdventureWorks2012;
SELECT
    *
FROM HumanResources.Department
WHERE
    Name LIKE 'Pr%'
```

The *Pr%* used in the preceding query tells SQL Server to return all departments whose name starts with *Pr* and any following characters.

The LIKE syntax does not use a typical regular expression wildcard set. As demonstrated in the previous script, the % represents any string of zero or more characters. In addition, other wildcard characters are as follows:

- _ (a single character)

- *[abc]* (a single character in a set)

- *[^abc]* (a single character not in the set)

Creating aliases

You can create *aliases*, which can be a shorter or more understandable name, for table and column names, making it easier to work with aggregations, expressions, and queries that involve multiple tables. In addition, your database may contain very cryptic column names, and you may want to provide names that are more meaningful to applications and end users. Using aliases allows you to rename or shorten the names of tables and columns.

Alias a table and column

1. Open the query editor in SSMS.

2. In the query editor, enter and execute the following T-SQL code:

```
--Use this query to alias a table and column
USE AdventureWorks2012;
SELECT
      DepartmentID,
      Name AS DepartmentName,
      GroupName AS DepartmentGroupName
FROM HumanResources.Department AS d
```

In the preceding query, the Name column is renamed DepartmentName, the GroupName column is renamed DepartmentGroupName, and the table has been aliased as simply d. Now you can reference the table as d instead of the entire table name throughout the query. The use of table aliases is explained in the next section.

Note The AS keyword used in the previous query is optional when aliasing items within a SQL Server query. This means the original table name cannot be used any longer, so HumanResources.Department.DepartmentName will no longer resolve in the query.

Using the JOIN operator to return data from multiple tables

You have focused primarily on retrieving data from a single table thus far. In practice, it is highly unlikely that your queries will reference just one table—most of the time, you will be required to return data from multiple tables. To do this, you use the JOIN operator. While there are several types of JOINs, in this chapter, you will focus on the three most commonly used:

- INNER

- LEFT OUTER

- RIGHT OUTER

Using INNER JOIN

Of the three most commonly used JOIN operators, INNER JOIN is the one that you will likely use on a regular basis. INNER JOIN is an equality match between two or more tables. For example, assume you have a table that contains products and another that contains sales, and you want to find only the products that have been sold. Basically, you are looking for the intersection of the two tables on some value. Figure 10-1 illustrates the intersection.

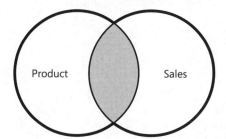

FIGURE 10-1 An INNER JOIN intersection.

The shaded section of Figure 10-1 depicts the rows that will be returned from a query that would join the Sales and Product tables.

The JOIN syntax

Regardless of whether you are writing an INNER join or an OUTER join, you start with a basic SELECT statement. You'll use the following query as your starting point:

```
USE AdventureWorks2012;
SELECT
      p.FirstName,
      p.LastName
FROM Person.Person p
```

The table in the FROM clause should include a column with values that exist in the table you plan on joining. In this case, you would like to include an email address in the result set. To accomplish this, you must reference a second table in the query, as illustrated in the following query:

```
USE AdventureWorks2012;
SELECT
      p.FirstName,
      p.LastName,
      ea.EmailAddress
FROM Person.Person AS p
INNER JOIN Person.EmailAddress AS ea
      ON p.BusinessEntityID = ea.BusinessEntityID
```

The INNER JOIN keywords have been included, which allows you to specify a second table in the query. The INNER JOIN or any JOIN must be coupled with the ON keyword. In the ON clause, you specify which column or columns will be used to connect (JOIN) the two tables. The key to successfully joining any two tables is to identify their intersecting data, which is commonly aligned across primary key and foreign key relationships (see Chapter 5, "Creating your first table"). If you want to perform a LEFT OUTER or RIGHT OUTER JOIN in the preceding query, you replace INNER with either LEFT OUTER or RIGHT OUTER.

 Note You can join multiple tables in one SELECT statement by including additional JOIN and ON couplings.

Write an INNER JOIN query

1. Open the query editor in SSMS.

2. In the query editor, enter and execute the following T-SQL code:

```
--Use the query to perform an INNER JOIN on two tables
USE AdventureWorks2012;
SELECT
      p.ProductID,
      p.Name AS ProductName,
      sd.OrderQty,
      sd.UnitPrice
FROM Production.Product AS p
INNER JOIN Sales.SalesOrderDetail sd
      ON p.ProductID = sd.ProductID
```

Using OUTER JOINs

There are two basic types of OUTER JOINs: LEFT and RIGHT. They both provide very similar functionality, but there is a slight difference that depends on the order of the tables in the query. Using the previous product sales example, if you begin reading the query from left to right, which table do you encounter first? The Production.Product table, which makes it the left table. The second table you encounter (continuing to read to the right) is Sales.SalesOrderDetail, the right table. This trend continues throughout the query.

Therefore, if you want to retrieve a list of products regardless of their existence in the Sales.SalesOrderDetail table, a LEFT OUTER JOIN should be your choice. Figure 10-2 illustrates a LEFT OUTER JOIN.

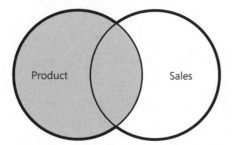

FIGURE 10-2 A LEFT OUTER JOIN intersection.

On the other hand, if you are trying to retrieve all sales, whether or not they are associated with a product, you should choose a RIGHT OUTER JOIN. Figure 10-3 illustrates a RIGHT OUTER JOIN.

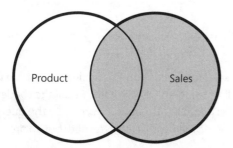

FIGURE 10-3 A RIGHT OUTER JOIN intersection.

Regardless of the type of OUTER JOIN, the syntax is similar to that of an INNER JOIN. You replace INNER with either LEFT OUTER or RIGHT OUTER.

1. Open the query editor in SSMS.

2. In the query editor, enter and execute the following T-SQL code:

```
--Use this query to perform a LEFT OUTER JOIN
USE AdventureWorks2012;
SELECT
      p.ProductID,
      sd.ProductID,
      p.Name AS ProductName,
      sd.OrderQty,
      sd.UnitPrice
FROM Production.Product AS p
LEFT OUTER JOIN Sales.SalesOrderDetail sd
      ON p.ProductID = sd.ProductID
```

The following image shows the results of the LEFT OUTER JOIN query.

	ProductID	ProductID	ProductName	OrderQty	UnitPrice
1...	879	879	All-Purpose Bike Stand	1	159.00
1...	712	712	AWC Logo Cap	1	8.99
1...	355	NULL	Guide Pulley	NULL	NULL
1...	378	NULL	Hex Nut 17	NULL	NULL
1...	401	NULL	HL Hub	NULL	NULL
1...	524	NULL	HL Spindle/Axle	NULL	NULL
1...	361	NULL	Thin-Jam Hex Nut 1	NULL	NULL
1...	418	NULL	Internal Lock Washer 10	NULL	NULL
1...	424	NULL	Thin-Jam Lock Nut 1	NULL	NULL
1...	464	NULL	Lock Washer 5	NULL	NULL
1...	438	NULL	Lock Nut 5	NULL	NULL
1...	507	NULL	LL Mountain Rim	NULL	NULL
1...	458	NULL	Lock Nut 4	NULL	NULL
1...	481	NULL	Metal Plate 3	NULL	NULL
1...	2	NULL	BB Ball Bearing	NULL	NULL

If you scroll down the result set, you should start to see NULL values in those columns that are part of the Sales.SalesOrderDetail table. This is a direct result of using an OUTER JOIN. Recall the shaded area of Figure 10-2 illustrating the result set of a LEFT OUTER JOIN. The rows returned by the query are what you should expect. Not only are the products associated with sales returned, but so are those without sales.

Limiting the data returned in your result set

Besides using a WHERE clause in your query, you have several other ways to limit the data returned in your result set. While there is a long list of methods and techniques you can use, SQL Server offers keywords that provide a very simplistic approach to limiting your result set.

Using TOP

The TOP keyword limits the number of rows that are returned in a result to either a specific number of rows or a specific percentage of rows. TOP should always be used with the ORDER BY clause. In most cases, you will be looking for the highest or lowest set of values for a given column, and sorting the data will provide you with that information. For example, if you want to return the top five sales in your Sales table, you add TOP (5) immediately following the keyword SELECT. In addition, you include an ORDER BY clause specifying the column that contained the actual sales value for each row as the ordering column.

Write a TOP query

1. Open the query editor in SSMS.

2. In the query editor, enter and execute the following T-SQL code:

```
--Use this query to return the top 5 sales
USE AdventureWorks2012;
SELECT TOP(5)
      SalesOrderID,
      OrderDate,
      SalesOrderNumber,
      TotalDue
FROM Sales.SalesOrderHeader
ORDER BY
      TotalDue DESC
```

Using DISTINCT and NULL

DISTINCT returns a unique or distinct list of values of each specified column in a SELECT statement. If there are any duplicate values in the list, all but one duplicate value will be removed. For example, if you execute the following query, the result returns a list of products with some of the product names repeated several times:

```
USE AdventureWorks2012;
SELECT
     p.Name AS ProductName
FROM Production.Product AS p
INNER JOIN Sales.SalesOrderDetail sd
    ON p.ProductID = sd.ProductID
```

By placing DISTINCT immediately following the SELECT keyword, you remove any duplicates from the list.

Moreover, if you want to limit the result to only products that have not shipped, you add the WHERE clause. In this example, the WHERE clause needs to identify all the SalesOrderProduct rows that contain a NULL CarrierTrackingNumber.

The NULL value is a special value. It is actually not a value at all—it's the absence of a value. As a result, there are special comparison values that can be used when referencing it in a WHERE clause. If you are searching for NULLs, you would use the following:

```
WHERE <column name> IS NULL
```

If you are searching for columns that are NOT NULL, you would use this:

```
WHERE <column name> IS NOT NULL
```

In this example, you are searching for all products that have not shipped—in other words, all the rows in the result set that have a NULL value for the SalesOrderDetail CarrierTrackingNumber column.

The next step is to remove all columns, if any are listed, besides the Product Name column from the column list. If not, then the distinctness of each row will be based on all the columns in the SELECT statement instead of solely on the Product Name column. Finally, if it has not already been included, place the DISTINCT keyword between the SELECT keyword and the column name.

Write a query that includes DISTINCT

1. Open the query editor in SSMS.

2. In the query editor, enter and execute the following T-SQL code:

```
--Use this query to return a distinct list of products that have not been shipped
USE AdventureWorks2012;
SELECT DISTINCT
        p.Name AS ProductName
FROM Production.Product AS p
INNER JOIN Sales.SalesOrderDetail sd
        ON p.ProductID = sd.ProductID
WHERE
        sd.CarrierTrackingNumber IS NULL
        ORDER BY productname
```

Using UNION to combine result sets

Often you will have two SELECT statements that may need to be combined into one result for consumption by an application or end user. Using the UNION keyword, you can accomplish just that. UNION has two variations:

- Just UNION, which removes any duplicate rows in your result set.

- UNION ALL, which includes duplicates. If duplicates are possible, you should use UNION ALL; it is much faster because it does not have to include DISTINCT.

The following pseudocode illustrates the use of UNION:

```
SELECT column1, column2 FROM TABLE1
UNION
SELECT column1, column2 FROM TABLE2
```

When writing a query with UNION, both SELECT statements must contain the same number of columns, and the data types must match for each column. When using UNION, provide only one ORDER BY clause after the last SELECT statement.

Write a query that includes UNION

1. Open the query editor in SSMS.

2. In the query editor, enter and execute the following T-SQL code:

```
--Use this query to return a list of products that are black and silver
USE AdventureWorks2012;
SELECT
      Name AS ProductName
FROM Production.Product
WHERE
      Color = 'Black'
UNION
SELECT
      Name AS ProductName
FROM Production.Product
WHERE
      Color = 'Silver'
```

Summary

The potential of the SELECT statement is limited only by your knowledge of the table and data relationships and how you can manipulate them with the SELECT syntax. In this chapter, you learned about the commonly used SELECT methods, which should provide a solid foundation for your T-SQL experimentation. You explored several methods that will assist you in joining data from multiple tables and then limiting the result.

PART IV

Using Transact-SQL (T-SQL)

CHAPTER 11

Advanced data retrieval topics

After completing this chapter, you will be able to

- Write PIVOT and UNPIVOT queries.

- Write a paging query.

- Write a common table expression.

- Use a variable.

Chapter 10, "The SELECT statement," provided a solid introduction to data retrieval using the SELECT query. In this chapter, you will build on that introductory knowledge and examine a few advanced topics that will enhance how you return the data and what data is returned. As you interact with Microsoft SQL Server data more and more, you may encounter situations in which the basic concepts are not enough. This chapter will supply you with additional skills to help you solve more advanced problems.

Pivoting and unpivoting data

The concept of pivoting data in SQL Server refers to restructuring the data into another format. There are two forms available: PIVOT and UNPIVOT.

Using the PIVOT operator

Assume that the data is stored in a format similar to that shown in Table 11-1.

TABLE 11-1   Row-by-row data

SalesOrderID	CustomerID	SalesPersonID
43659	29825	279
43660	29672	279
43661	29734	282
43662	29994	276
43663	29565	280
43664	29898	283

Each row in the table represents an order placed by a customer and the salesperson who took the order. Instead of displaying this information on a row-by-row basis, you can use the PIVOT operator to return the number of orders placed for each customer, grouped by salesperson. Table 11-2 illustrates the pivoting of a small sample of the data.

TABLE 11-2 Pivoting data

SalesPersonID	29825	29672	29734	29994	29565	29898
279	5	1	0	2	1	0
282	6	2	1	3	2	1
275	7	3	2	4	3	2
280	2	5	5	2	1	1
283	3	6	6	3	2	2

The first column in the table represents the salespeople, and each subsequent column represents a customer and how many sales were made to that customer. The first row in each column, besides the column that contains SalesPersonID, contains a CustomerID.

In the next exercise, you will write your own pivot query.

Write a pivot query

1. Open the query editor in Microsoft SQL Server Management Studio (SSMS).

2. In the query editor, enter and execute the following T-SQL code:

```
SELECT SalesOrderID, CustomerID, SalesPersonID
FROM Sales.SalesOrderHeader
WHERE SalesPersonID IS NOT NULL
```

This query represents the foundation of the pivot. It returns the row-by-row data.

3. Directly above this query, enter the following T-SQL code:

```
USE AdventureWorks2012;
SELECT
    SalesPersonID, [29486] AS Cust1,
    [29487] AS Cust2, [29488] AS Cust3, [29491] AS Cust4,[29492] AS Cust5, [29512] AS
Cust6
FROM
(
```

This part of the query represents how the data will be returned.

4. Finally, directly below the query in step 2, enter the following query:

```
) AS p
PIVOT
(
COUNT(SalesOrderID)
FOR CustomerID IN
(
[29486],[29487],[29488],[29491],[29492],[29512])
) AS pvt
ORDER BY SalesPersonID
```

This part of the query specifies the PIVOT operator, what to aggregate, and which customers to include in the result set.

5. The final query should resemble the following:

```
USE AdventureWorks2012;
SELECT SalesPersonID, [29486] AS Cust1, [29487] AS Cust2, [29488] AS Cust3,
[29491] AS Cust4,[29492] AS Cust5, [29512] AS Cust6
FROM
(
SELECT SalesOrderID, CustomerID, SalesPersonID
FROM Sales.SalesOrderHeader
WHERE SalesPersonID IS NOT NULL
) AS p
PIVOT
(
COUNT(SalesORderID)
FOR CustomerID IN
(
[29486],[29487],[29488],[29491],[29492],[29512])
) AS pvt
ORDER BY SalesPersonID
```

6. Execute the query and it will return the following pivoted results.

	SalesPersonID	Cust1	Cust2	Cust3	Cust4	Cust5	Cust6
1	274	0	0	0	1	0	0
2	275	6	6	0	3	5	0
3	276	0	0	0	0	0	0
4	277	6	5	0	0	1	0
5	278	0	0	0	0	0	0
6	279	0	0	0	0	0	0
7	280	0	0	0	0	0	0
8	281	0	0	0	0	0	0
9	282	0	0	0	0	0	0
10	283	0	0	0	0	0	0
11	284	0	0	0	0	0	0
12	285	0	0	1	0	0	3
13	286	0	0	3	0	0	1
14	287	0	0	0	0	0	0

As you can see, each row aggregates to show a distinct list of salespeople and how many sales have been made to each customer in the pivot list.

Using the UNPIVOT operator

If your data resembles the data shown in the previous figure, and you want to have each row represent a customer sale, you use the UNPIVOT operator. The result set would look exactly as shown in Table 11-1. In the next exercise, you'll write an UNPIVOT query.

Write an UNPIVOT query

1. Open the query editor in SSMS.

2. In the query editor, enter and execute the following T-SQL code:

```
USE AdventureWorks2012
GO
IF(OBJECT_ID('dbo.unPvt')) IS NOT NULL
      DROP TABLE dbo.unPvt
GO
CREATE TABLE dbo.unPvt
(
      SalesPersonID int,
      Cust1 int,
      Cust2 int,
      Cust3 int,
      Cust4 int,
      Cust5 int,
      Cust6 int
)
GO
INSERT INTO dbo.unPvt
(
      SalesPersonID, Cust1, Cust2, Cust3, Cust4, Cust5, Cust6
)
VALUES
      (274, 5, 6, 4, 2, 6, 7),
      (275, 1, 7, 2, 3, 6, 8),
      (276, 0, 2, 8, 9, 6, 3),
      (277, 6, 3, 1, 7, 6, 1),
      (278, 5, 4, 9, 0, 2, 0),
      (279, 2, 1, 0, 1, 8, 9)
GO
```

This is not actually part of the UNPIVOT query, but it is data that needs to be provided in order to show a practical example.

3. Open a new query window in SSMS and enter the following:

```
SELECT SalesPersonID, Cust1, Cust2, Cust3, Cust4, Cust5, Cust6
FROM unPvt
```

This is the foundation of the UNPIVOT query that provides the base data.

4. Directly above this query, enter the following:

```
USE AdventureWorks2012
GO
SELECT SalesPersonID, Customer, Sales
FROM
(
```

This represents the data that will be returned when the final query is executed.

5. Directly below the statement in step 2, enter the following:

```
) up
UNPIVOT
(
        Sales FOR Customer IN
        (
            Cust1, Cust2, Cust3, Cust4, Cust5, Cust6
        )
)AS unpvt;
GO
```

This part of the query includes the UNPIVOT operator that, instead of aggregating data like PIVOT, includes a list of customers that will be included in the row-by-row result set.

6. The final query will resemble the following:

```
USE AdventureWorks2012
GO
SELECT SalesPersonID, Customer, Sales
FROM
(
     SELECT SalesPersonID, Cust1, Cust2, Cust3, Cust4, Cust5, Cust6
     FROM unPvt
) up
UNPIVOT
(
        Sales FOR Customer IN
        (
            Cust1, Cust2, Cust3, Cust4, Cust5, Cust6
        )
)AS unpvt;
GO
```

7. Execute the query.

As shown here, each row represents the number of sales made to a given customer.

	SalesPersonID	Customer	Sales
1	274	Cust1	5
2	274	Cust2	6
3	274	Cust3	4
4	274	Cust4	2
5	274	Cust5	6
6	274	Cust6	7
7	275	Cust1	1
8	275	Cust2	7
9	275	Cust3	2
10	275	Cust4	3
11	275	Cust5	6
12	275	Cust6	8
13	276	Cust1	0
14	276	Cust2	2
15	276	Cust3	8
16	276	Cust4	9

Paging data

A common request for application functionality is paging data. Instead of having the entire result returned, it is often preferable to have a short list broken down by a page and some number of rows. Prior to SQL Server 2012, developers or DBAs could use several techniques to simulate paging, but with SQL Server 2012, we now have true native database-side paging.

SQL Server 2012 introduces a keyword coupling that provides an elegant and efficient paging solution. Using OFFSET and FETCH, you can write a single query that returns data one page at a time to a client application or end user:

- **OFFSET**   Denotes how many rows to skip before the query starts returning rows

- **FETCH**   Specifies how many rows to return after OFFSET has been processed

OFFSET is synonymous with the page number and FETCH with the number of rows that will be displayed per page.

Both OFFSET and FETCH have a few additional arguments that must be included in the syntax. The following is sample syntax for writing a paging query:

```
SELECT <column list>
FROM <table name>
ORDER BY <column name>
OFFSET <rows to start on> ROWS
FETCH NEXT <number of rows to return> ROW ONLY
```

With OFFSET, you can provide an integer value or an expression (see Chapter 14, "Advanced T-SQL topics") that specifies the starting row. You must also include the ROWS keyword. FETCH requires the NEXT keyword, an integer or expression that specifies the number of rows to return, and the ROWS keyword.

1. Open the query editor in SSMS.

2. In the query editor, enter and execute the following T-SQL code:

```
--Use this script to write a paging query
USE AdventureWorks2012;
SELECT
      ProductID,
      ProductNumber,
      Name AS ProductName,
      ListPrice
FROM Production.Product
ORDER BY ProductID
OFFSET 0 ROWS
FETCH NEXT 10 ROWS ONLY
```

An additional, and probably the most important, requirement is that this pair must be preceded by an ORDER BY clause. The column specified in the ORDER BY clause determines the order and what rows will be returned. The following query is modified slightly, so that instead of starting at the first row, the offset is changed to 10:

```
USE AdventureWorks2012;
SELECT
      ProductID,
      ProductNumber,
      Name AS ProductName,
      ListPrice
FROM Production.Product
ORDER BY ProductID
OFFSET 10 ROWS
FETCH NEXT 10 ROWS ONLY
```

When OFFSET is changed, notice that a new set of products is returned.

Writing expressions

You will often need to combine the values of two columns together into a single value. A brief introduction to this concept appeared in the "Understanding computed columns" section of Chapter 5, "Creating your first table," where the FirstName and LastName columns of table were concatenated together to form one column. You can also do this inline during a SELECT statement, as shown in the following script:

```
USE AdventureWorks2012;
SELECT
      FirstName+' '+LastName AS FullName
FROM Person.Person
```

Note In SQL Server, the plus sign (+) is used for concatenating strings.

The results of this query will be a single column that contains the value of both columns with a space in between, as shown in Figure 11-1.

FIGURE 11-1 This abbreviated result of a query uses an inline expression.

While the preceding example is very basic, SQL Server does allow you to create expressions that are based on constants, other expressions, scalar functions, or variables. By using these arguments, you can perform logical, Boolean, and ranking calculations. To demonstrate, in the next exercise you'll write a query with a constant expression.

Write a query with a constant expression

1. Open the query editor in SSMS.

2. In the query editor, enter and execute the following T-SQL code:

```
--Use this script to write a query with an expression
USE AdventureWorks2012;
SELECT
    (SubTotal+TaxAmt)*1.05 AS TotalDue
FROM SaleS.SalesOrderHeader
```

Using variables

During data retrieval, you may encounter a situation where you need to temporarily store a value for later use in your query. It may be a value from a SELECT statement or a constant value that will be used later in a query. In order to use a variable, you must first declare it. Next, you prefix the variable with an at (@) symbol. Finally, you specify the data type that will be stored in the variable. The syntax for declaring a variable is as follows:

```
DECLARE @variable int
```

Once the variable is declared, you assign values to it. There are three methods to do so: you can use the SET keyword, which is the preferred method; you can assign a value using the SELECT statement; or you can assign a value during the declaration of the variable. The syntax for assigning values to a variable using these methods is as follows:

```
--Use this syntax to assign a value using the SET keyword
DECLARE @variable int
SET @variable = <value>

--Use this syntax to assign a value using a SELECT statement
SELECT @variable = <column or expression>
FROM <table name>

--Use this syntax to assign a value to a variable when it is declared
DECLARE @variable int = <value>
```

Write a query that uses a variable

1. Open the query editor in SSMS.

2. In the query editor, enter the following T-SQL code:

   ```
   USE AdventureWorks2012;
   DECLARE @ProductID int = 1;
   ```

   This part of the code declares and assigns a value to the ProductID variable.

3. In the query editor, directly below the statement entered in step 2, enter the following T-SQL code and execute the query:

   ```
   SELECT
       ProductID,
       ProductNumber,
       Name AS ProductName
   FROM Production.Product
   WHERE ProductID = @ProductID
   ```

   This part of the code selects product information with an equality WHERE clause using the variable as the filter value.

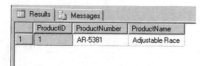

Summary

The topics introduced in this chapter provided a glimpse of how powerful the T-SQL programming language can be. You learned how to use the PIVOT and UNPIVOT operators to physically change the structure of a result set. In addition, you were introduced to the new paging constructs in Microsoft SQL Server 2012. Finally, you learned how to write expressions and return them as part of a result set. These concepts can assist you in solving more complex problems, and you will be introduced to several more throughout this book.

Modifying data

After completing this chapter, you will be able to

- Insert data into SQL Server tables.

- Update data in tables.

- Delete data from tables.

- Merge data.

- Return output data.

So far in this book, you have worked with tables that contain data. In most cases, a client-based application will be the primary mechanism for inserting and modifying data in Microsoft SQL Server tables. However, a situation may arise in which you need to add or modify data inside your database tables. SQL Server offers several different ways of modifying data. In this chapter, you will learn how to perform simple inserts, updates, and deletes. You will also see how to merge data from two sources into one and return output data.

Inserting data into SQL Server tables

Although you can use several techniques and methods to insert data into SQL Server tables, the best approach is to start with the two simplest ways:

- INSERT INTO statement

- SELECT INTO statement

Using the INSERT INTO statement

The first method to insert data into SQL Server tables involves using an INSERT INTO statement, which can add one row or multiple rows. Using this method, you can insert data into all columns, specific columns, identity columns, and several other variations.

Insert a single row into a table using the INSERT INTO statement

1. Open the query editor in Microsoft SQL Server Management Studio (SSMS).

2. In the query editor, enter and execute the following T-SQL code:

```
USE AdventureWorks2012;
INSERT INTO HumanResources.Department(Name, GroupName, ModifiedDate)
VALUES('Payroll', 'Executive General and Administration', '6/12/2012');
```

> **Note** The column list is optional in the INSERT INTO statement, but for purposes of clarity, it's always recommended. If it is not included, the values are inserted into the table based on the order of the columns. The identity columns are not included in the order.

Every column in the table does not have to appear in the INSERT statement. You must specify a value in the VALUES clause for all columns that have been listed. In the preceding query, DepartmentID was omitted from the column list. Executing the following query will show the new row:

```
USE AdventureWorks2012;
SELECT
     DepartmentID, Name, GroupName, ModifiedDate
FROM HumanResources.Department
ORDER BY DepartmentID DESC;
```

	DepartmentID	Name	GroupName	ModifiedDate
1	17	Payroll	Executive General and Administration	2012-06-12 00:00:00.000
2	16	Executive	Executive General and Administration	2002-06-01 00:00:00.000
3	15	Shipping and Receiving	Inventory Management	2002-06-01 00:00:00.000
4	14	Facilities and Maintenance	Executive General and Administration	2002-06-01 00:00:00.000
5	13	Quality Assurance	Quality Assurance	2002-06-01 00:00:00.000
6	12	Document Control	Quality Assurance	2002-06-01 00:00:00.000
7	11	Information Services	Executive General and Administration	2002-06-01 00:00:00.000
8	10	Finance	Executive General and Administration	2002-06-01 00:00:00.000
9	9	Human Resources	Executive General and Administration	2002-06-01 00:00:00.000
10	8	Production Control	Manufacturing	2002-06-01 00:00:00.000

Since DepartmentID is an identity column, a value was automatically inserted into the column. If you want to insert a value into an identity column, you can use the SET IDENTITY_INSERT statement. When inserting into an identity column, you must explicitly list each column in the column list.

Insert data into an identity column using the INSERT INTO statement

1. Open the query editor in SSMS.

2. In the query editor, enter and execute the following T-SQL code:

```
USE AdventureWorks2012;
SET IDENTITY_INSERT HumanResources.Department ON
INSERT INTO HumanResources.Department(DepartmentID, Name, GroupName, ModifiedDate)
VALUES(18, 'International Marketing', 'Sales and Marketing', '5/26/2012');
SET IDENTITY_INSERT HumanResources.Department OFF
```

Both of the aforementioned approaches insert only a single row. By leveraging the VALUES clause, you can insert multiple rows into a table with a single statement.

Using sequence numbers

Prior to Microsoft SQL Server 2012, the only mechanism for autonumber generation in SQL Server was an identity column. In the latest release, Microsoft introduced the sequence number. A sequence number is a user-defined object that behaves similarly to an identity column in that it automatically generates numeric values. However, unlike the identity column, it is not associated to a specific object within the database. As a result, the numbers generated by the sequence can be used by multiple tables.

Sequences do have a few limitations that may deter some database developers from using them. The first limitation is that the numbers generated by the sequence are not guaranteed to be unique. Second, these numbers can be changed, which is a big difference from identity columns. Finally, the likelihood of gaps within the numbers is greater, especially when the sequence is shared across multiple tables.

The basic syntax is as follows:

```
CREATE SEQUENCE <SCHEMA>.<SEQUENCE NAME>
AS int
START WITH <SOME NUMBER>
INCREMENT BY <SOME NUMBER>;
```

> **Note** You should know two things about the preceding script. First, the data type specified can be any integer database, and by default it is *bigint*. Second, the START WITH keywords are optional.

1. Open the query editor in SSMS.

2. In the query editor, enter and execute the following T-SQL code:

```
USE AdventureWorks2012
GO
IF(OBJECT_ID('dbo.States')) IS NOT NULL
     DROP TABLE dbo.States
GO
CREATE TABLE dbo.States
(
     StateID int PRIMARY KEY,
     StateName varchar(50),
     StateAbbrev char(2)
)
GO
```

The preceding script creates a table that will be used to demonstrate using the sequence. Note that IDENTITY was not specified for the DepartmentID column.

3. Open a new query window, and enter and execute the following T-SQL code:

```
USE AdventureWorks2012
GO
CREATE SEQUENCE dbo.StateSeq
AS int
START WITH 1
INCREMENT BY 1
GO
```

In this script, the *int* data type was specified, and using the START WITH and INCREMENT keywords, the sequence will start at 1 and increment by 1. In other words, the first INSERT statement that uses the sequence will begin with 1, the next with 2, the next with 3, and so on.

4. Open a new query window, and enter and execute the following T-SQL code:

```
USE AdventureWorks2012
GO
INSERT INTO dbo.States(StateID, StateAbbrev, StateName)
VALUES  (NEXT VALUE FOR dbo.StateSeq, 'LA', 'Louisiana')
INSERT INTO dbo.States(StateID, StateAbbrev, StateName)
VALUES  (NEXT VALUE FOR dbo.StateSeq, 'TX', 'Texas')
INSERT INTO dbo.States(StateID, StateAbbrev, StateName)
VALUES  (NEXT VALUE FOR dbo.StateSeq, 'FL', 'Florida')
GO
SELECT * FROM dbo.States
```

In the preceding query, the NEXT VALUE FOR keywords are specified in place of an actual value for the StateID. A new value is generated for each selected incremented by 1. You can see this in the result set that is displayed after the execution of the query.

Insert multiple rows into a table using the INSERT INTO statement

1. Open the query editor in SSMS.

2. In the query editor, enter and execute the following T-SQL code:

```
USE AdventureWorks2012;
INSERT INTO HumanResources.Department
VALUES
    ('International Sales', 'Sales and Marketing', '5/26/2012'),
    ('Media Control', 'Quality Assurance', '5/26/2012')
```

Instead of writing a single INSERT statement for each row, you can supply a comma-delimited list of values for each row in the VALUES clause. The following figure illustrates the result of the multirow insert.

	DepartmentID	Name	GroupName	ModifiedDate
1	19	Media Control	Quality Assurance	2012-05-26 00:00:00.000
2	18	International Sales	Sales and Marketing	2012-05-26 00:00:00.000
3	17	Payroll	Executive General and Administration	2012-06-12 00:00:00.000
4	16	Executive	Executive General and Administration	2002-06-01 00:00:00.000
5	15	Shipping and Receiving	Inventory Management	2002-06-01 00:00:00.000
6	14	Facilities and Maintenance	Executive General and Administration	2002-06-01 00:00:00.000
7	13	Quality Assurance	Quality Assurance	2002-06-01 00:00:00.000
8	12	Document Control	Quality Assurance	2002-06-01 00:00:00.000

In addition to using the VALUES clause to insert multiple rows, you can insert multiple rows from an existing table into another table using a SELECT statement.

Insert data using a SELECT statement

1. Open the query editor in SSMS.

2. In the query editor, enter and execute the following T-SQL code:

```
USE AdventureWorks2012;
INSERT INTO HumanResources.Department(Name, GroupName, ModifiedDate)
SELECT
    Name+' USA', GroupName, ModifiedDate
FROM HumanResources.Department
WHERE DepartmentID IN (20, 19)
```

Using the SELECT INTO statement

The second method you can use to insert data into SQL Server tables is the SELECT INTO statement. This method actually creates a new table and inserts all the rows from the SELECT statement into that newly created table.

1. Open the query editor in SSMS.

2. In the query editor, enter and execute the following T-SQL code:

```
USE AdventureWorks2012;
SELECT
      DepartmentID, Name, GroupName, ModifiedDate
INTO dbo.Department
FROM HumanResources.Department
```

The new table may have similar characteristics to the table schema that acts as the source. However, column lengths—both string and numerical—may change, and the keys, indexes, and constraints will not be created on the new table. Therefore, you should avoid using SELECT INTO as a permanent table.

Updating data in tables

Now that you have some data in the database, you will learn how to change that data just in case the incorrect values were inserted. SQL Server includes an UPDATE statement that you can use to modify one row or several rows. You should be cautious when issuing an UPDATE statement, as it is highly unlikely that every row in a table needs updating. Therefore, always consider including a WHERE clause with every UPDATE statement. If WHERE is not included, you could accidentally update every row, which could cost you your job.

Update a single row

1. Open the query editor in SSMS.

2. In the query editor, enter and execute the following T-SQL code:

```
USE AdventureWorks2012;
UPDATE HumanResources.Department
SET Name = Name +' Europe'
WHERE DepartmentID = 19
```

This UPDATE statement uses an expression to append Europe to the Name column for a single row in the Department table.

	DepartmentID	Name	GroupName	ModifiedDate
1	19	Media Control Europe	Quality Assurance	2012-05-26 00:00:00.000
2	18		Sales and Marketing	2012-05-26 00:00:00.000
3	17	Payroll	Executive General and Administration	2012-06-12 00:00:00.000
4	16	Executive	Executive General and Administration	2002-06-01 00:00:00.000
5	15	Shipping and Receiving	Inventory Management	2002-06-01 00:00:00.000
6	14	Facilities and Maintenance	Executive General and Administration	2002-06-01 00:00:00.000
7	13	Quality Assurance	Quality Assurance	2002-06-01 00:00:00.000
8	12	Document Control	Quality Assurance	2002-06-01 00:00:00.000
9	11	Information Services	Executive General and Administration	2002-06-01 00:00:00.000

As a precaution, you should add an additional filter to the WHERE clause to ensure that the UPDATE statement is not repeatable. In other words, if the query was accidently run twice, it would have no effect on the data. This is especially important when performing a concatenation or mathematical change. The following query shows how to accomplish this:

```
USE AdventureWorks2012;
UPDATE HumanResources.Department
SET Name = Name +' Europe'
WHERE DepartmentID = 19
AND NAME NOT LIKE '% Europe'
```

The new filter that uses LIKE ensures that if you rerun the query, it will have no effect on the data that would have previously updated.

Updating rows while referencing multiple tables

You may encounter a situation where you need to reference additional tables when updating a row. The additional tables could be used to limit the rows that will be updated, or they could provide a value that will be used in an expression as part of the update. Using the JOIN clause, you can reference additional tables just as you do with a SELECT statement.

Update rows while referencing multiple tables

1. Open the query editor in SSMS.

2. In the query editor, enter and execute the following T-SQL code:

```
USE AdventureWorks2012;
UPDATE Production.Product
SET ListPrice = p.ListPrice * 1.05
FROM Production.Product p
INNER JOIN Production.ProductSubcategory ps
    ON p.ProductSubcategoryID = ps.ProductSubcategoryID
WHERE
    ps.Name = 'Socks'
```

The preceding query uses the Production.ProductSubcategory table to limit the number of rows updated to only those that are included in the Socks subcategory. The ListPrice for each row that is in this subset is increased by 5 percent.

Deleting data from tables

Before moving on to a discussion on removing data from SQL Server tables, please heed the following statement and try never to forget it: as with the UPDATE statement, always consider including a WHERE clause when executing a DELETE statement. If you do not include WHERE as part of the DELETE statement, all the data will be removed after the query is executed. SQL Server does not explicitly have an undo button. There are ways to incorporate a mechanism that will offer an undo operation, but you should always practice including a WHERE clause.

There are two primary methods of removing data from SQL Server: the DELETE statement and the TRUNCATE statement. Both remove data, with the main difference being that you can limit the number of rows deleted when using the DELETE statement and you cannot do so with TRUNCATE.

Use DELETE to delete a single row

1. Open the query editor in SSMS.

2. In the query editor, enter and execute the following T-SQL code:

```
USE AdventureWorks2012;
DELETE FROM HumanResources.Department
WHERE DepartmentID = 22
```

Delete rows while referencing multiple tables

1. Open the query editor in SSMS.

2. In the query editor, enter and execute the following T-SQL code:

```
USE AdventureWorks2012;
DELETE FROM HumanResources.Department
FROM HumanResources.Department d
LEFT OUTER JOIN HumanResources.EmployeeDepartmentHistory ed
    ON d.DepartmentID = ed.DepartmentID
WHERE ed.DepartmentID IS NULL
```

In the preceding query, the HumanResources.EmployeeDepartmentHistory table is used to identify those departments in the HumanResources.Department table that are not associated with any rows in the referenced table. Coupling that LEFT OUTER JOIN reference with the WHERE clause ensures that only those rows are deleted.

Use TRUNCATE to delete all rows

1. Open the query editor in SSMS.

2. In the query editor, enter and execute the following T-SQL code:

```
USE AdventureWorks2012;
TRUNCATE TABLE dbo.Department
```

Remember that the TRUNCATE statement removes all rows from the referenced table. Prior to executing this statement, you should ensure that this is exactly what you intend to do. Once the statement is executed, all the data will be removed.

Merging data

The MERGE statement is a hybrid that can insert, update, and delete data in a single query. Depending on how you write the query, it can perform almost any combination of insert, update, and delete. A MERGE statement is typically used to perform an *upsert*, which is a logical combination of inserting and updating data. MERGE checks for the existence of a row, and if the row does not exist, a new row is added. If the row does exist, then it is updated.

In general, the MERGE statement joins between a source table and a destination table. The source table contains the data that will be either added to or updated in the destination table. The destination table will accept the inserts or updates.

Use MERGE to insert and update data

1. Open the query editor in SSMS.

2. In the query editor, enter and execute the following T-SQL code:

```
USE AdventureWorks2012;
MERGE dbo.Department destination
    USING HumanResources.Department source
        ON destination.Name = source.Name
    WHEN MATCHED THEN
        UPDATE
            SET destination.Name = source.Name,
                destination.GroupName = source.GroupName,
                destination.ModifiedDate = source.ModifiedDate
    WHEN NOT MATCHED BY TARGET THEN
        INSERT (Name, GroupName, ModifiedDate)
        VALUES (source.Name, source.GroupName, source.ModifiedDate);
```

In the preceding query, the dbo.Department table is the destination table and will be either updated or inserted into. The HumanResources.Department table is the source table and will provide the data to the destination table. Similar to JOIN, the ON keyword is used to perform the match between the two tables. In other words, if there is a match between the two values from each table (WHEN MATCHED), then update the rows. If there is not a match (WHEN NOT MATCHED), then insert those rows.

 Note You can use additional keywords to further extend the functionality of the MERGE statement. You can base inserts and updates on either the target or the source.

Returning output data

After performing INSERT, UPDATE, DELETE, or MERGE operations, you may have a need to archive or audit the affected rows. Using the OUTPUT clause, you can return that data to whatever interface is processing the request. The results of OUTPUT can be inserted into a table or simply returned to the calling client.

Output the results of an INSERT statement

1. Open the query editor in SSMS.

2. In the query editor, enter and execute the following T-SQL code:

```
USE AdventureWorks2012;
INSERT INTO HumanResources.Department
    OUTPUT inserted.DepartmentID, inserted.Name, inserted.GroupName, inserted.
ModifiedDate
VALUES('International Marketing', 'Sales and Marketing', '5/26/2012');
```

The OUTPUT statement simply returns those rows affected by the input to the client. To output the data from an insert, you reference a logical table name inserted. This table exists within the scope of the query, and the data can be accessed only then.

Output the results of an UPDATE statement

1. Open the query editor in SSMS.

2. In the query editor, enter and execute the following T-SQL code:

```
USE AdventureWorks2012;
UPDATE HumanResources.Department
SET Name = Name +' Europe'
OUTPUT
    deleted.Name AS OldName,
    inserted.Name AS UpdateValue
WHERE DepartmentID = 25
```

When outputting data from an update, you will have access not only to the logical inserted table, but also to a deleted table. The deleted table contains the values before the update, and the inserted table contains the values after the update.

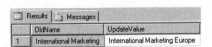

As previously mentioned, the typical use of the OUTPUT clause is to audit changes to data. More often than not, companies require that applications track deletions in their databases. By taking advantage of the OUTPUT clause, you can implement a mechanism that does just that.

Insert OUTPUT data into a table

1. Open the query editor in SSMS.

2. In the query editor, enter and execute the following T-SQL code:

```
USE AdventureWorks2012;
GO
CREATE TABLE dbo.Department_Audit
(
    DepartmentID int NOT NULL,
    Name nvarchar(50) NOT NULL,
    GroupName nvarchar(50) NOT NULL,
    DeletedDate datetime NOT NULL
        CONSTRAINT DF_Department_Audit_DeletedDate_Today DEFAULT(GETDATE())
)
```

> **Note** The default constraint in the preceding script uses the GETDATE scalar function, which will insert the current date and time when a row is added to the table. You could also track user names, host names, and other connection string properties by using other system scalar functions. Scalar functions are discussed in detail in Chapter 13, "Built-in scalar functions."

3. In the query editor, enter and execute the following T-SQL code:

```
USE AdventureWorks2012;
DELETE FROM dbo.Department
OUTPUT deleted.Departmentid, deleted.Name, deleted.GroupName
INTO dbo.Department_Audit(DepartmentID, Name, GroupName)
WHERE DepartmentID = 16
```

The preceding query deletes a single row from the Department table and also inserts the contents of the deleted row into an audit table.

4. To view the current contents of the audit table, execute the following query:

```
USE AdventureWorks2012;
SELECT *
FROM dbo.Department_Audit
```

You will see the exact data that the Department table contained prior to the deletion.

Summary

The ability to manipulate data is vital in any RDBMS. Typically, the sources of most data modifications are from a client application. However, there will always be times when you need to use T-SQL to make changes to your data. As you learned in this chapter, SQL Server provides a powerful set of methods that offer the flexibility and extensibility to handle most of your data changes.

Built-in scalar functions

After completing this chapter, you will be able to

- Return and manipulate date and time values using date and time functions.

- Convert data with the CAST and CONVERT functions.

- Manipulate string values.

- Add logic to T-SQL statements using built-in functions.

Microsoft SQL Server boasts a plethora of built-in scalar functions whose purposes and results vary depending on type and use. Within SQL Server, scalar functions are grouped into 12 categories. Of those, we will discuss four categories in this chapter: date and time, conversion, string, and logical. Several new scalar functions have been added to SQL Server 2012.

Note If you would like to explore all the available built-in scalar functions, refer to the "Built-in Functions (Transact-SQL)" page on MSDN: *http://msdn.microsoft.com/en-us/library/ms174318.*

Using date and time functions

As stated in Chapter 5, "Creating your first table," SQL Server allows date and time values to be stored in several formats. While you are able to store date and time values in almost any possible format, it's optimal to use SQL Server functions to return date and time values in a format that meets your needs. Using these functions, you can do the following:

- Return date and time values of varying precision

- Return parts of date and time values

- Derive date and time values from date and time parts (a new feature in SQL Server 2012)

- Get date and time differences

- Modify date and time values

- Validate date and time values

Return date and time values

1. Open the query editor in Microsoft SQL Server Management Studio (SSMS).

2. In the query editor, enter and execute the following T-SQL code:

```
SELECT GETDATE() AS GETDATE, SYSDATETIME() AS SYSDATETIME;
```

The result set will be a single date and time value equal to the date and time you executed the query.

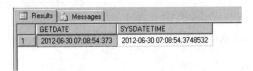

You should notice immediately that the precision of the values is different. The *GETDATE()* function returns a *DATETIME* data type, and the *SYSDATETIME* function returns a *datetime2(7)*. The latter of the two is a more precise value, which is the reason you see more numbers after the final decimal place.

Return parts of data and time values

1. Open the query editor in SSMS.

2. In the query editor, enter and execute the following T-SQL code:

```
SELECT
        DAY(GETDATE()) AS DAY,
        MONTH(GETDATE()) AS MONTH,
        YEAR(GETDATE()) AS YEAR,
        DATENAME(WEEKDAY, GETDATE()) AS DATENAMEWeekDay,
        DATEPART(M, GETDATE()) AS DATEPART,
        DATEPART(WEEKDAY, GETDATE()) AS DatePartWeekDay,
        DATENAME(MONTH, GETDATE()) AS DateNameMonth
```

The following image shows the result set from the query.

The return values for the first three functions—*DAY, MONTH,* and *YEAR*—are obvious. However, the last two functions, *DATENAME* and *DATEPART*, offer a little more functionality. Unlike the first three functions, both *DATENAME* and *DATEPART* accept an additional parameter known as *datepart*. The *datepart* parameter tells the function which part of the date to return. Table 13-1 lists all the available *datepart*s that can be used as parameters.

TABLE 13-1 Valid *datepart* arguments

datepart	Abbreviations
year	yy, yyyy
quarter	qq, q
month	mm, m
dayofyear	dy, y
week	wk, ww
weekday	dw
hour	hh
minute	mi, n
second	ss, s
millisecond	ms
microsecond	mcs
nanosecond	ns
TZoffset	tz
ISO_WEEK	Isowk, isoww

Each *datepart* argument typically returns an integer value. However, you may have noticed that string values are included in the previous figure when using *month* and *weekday* as the *datepart* argument for the *DATENAME* function. This is the main distinction between the two functions. The *DATEPART* function returns the data type as an integer value. Since the *DATENAME* function can return string values, its return data type is *nvarchar*.

Deriving dates from parts

Prior to the release of SQL Server 2012, you could derive dates from other values and expressions using T-SQL. While it was possible, this approach often required lots of coding and, in some cases, produced inconsistent results. As a result, in SQL Server 2012 Microsoft has included several new functions that allow you derive date and time parts.

Use the DATEFROMPARTS scalar function

1. Open the query editor in SSMS.

2. In the query editor, enter and execute the following T-SQL code:

```
SELECT
    DATEFROMPARTS ( 1972, 5, 26) AS DATEFROMPARTS,
    DATETIME2FROMPARTS ( 1972, 5, 26, 7, 14, 16, 10, 3 ) AS DATETIME2FROMPARTS,
    DATETIMEFROMPARTS ( 1972, 5, 26, 7, 14, 16, 10) AS DATETIMEFROMPARTS,
    DATETIMEOFFSETFROMPARTS ( 1972, 5, 26, 7, 14, 16, 10, 12, 0, 3 ) AS
```

```
DATETIMEOFFSETFROMPARTS,
      SMALLDATETIMEFROMPARTS ( 1972, 5, 26, 7, 14) SMALLDATETIMEFROMPARTS,
      TIMEFROMPARTS(7, 14, 16, 10, 3) TIMEFROMPARTS
```

The result for this query resembles the following image.

Now you can produce varying date and time values of different precision levels by using built-in functions instead of writing custom T-SQL code.

Differencing, modifying, and validating date values

In addition to offering the aforementioned functions, T-SQL allows you to perform calculations against date values and validate date values. For example, you can calculate the number of days between two dates, or you can add a month or year to a date. In SQL Server 2012, Microsoft introduced the *EOMONTH* function, which determines the last date of a given month.

Perform date calculations and validations

1. Open the query editor in SSMS.

2. In the query editor, enter and execute the following T-SQL code:

```
SELECT
      DATEDIFF(dd, GETDATE(), '5/26/2013') AS DaysUntilMyBirthday,
      DATEADD(y, 1, GETDATE()) AS DateAdd,
      EOMONTH(GETDATE()) AS EOMonth, --New to SQL Server 2012
      ISDATE(GETDATE()) AS IsValidDate,
      ISDATE('13/1/2122') AS InvalidDate
```

Using *DATEDIFF*, you are able to find out how many days, months, or years exist between two date values. The *datepart* argument, which is *dd*, determines which date part to return. *DATEADD* also uses a *datepart* argument; however, it can add or subtract from a date value. The *EOMONTH* function, which is new to SQL Server 2012, returns the last day of the month for a given date value. Finally, you can determine whether or not a date is valid by using the *ISDATE* function. The following figure shows the results of the previous query. Notice that 1 is returned when the date is valid, and 0 is returned for invalid dates.

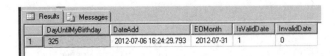

Using conversion functions

Conversion functions are divided into two categories:

- *CAST*

- *CONVERT*

The primary purpose of both types is to change a value from one data type to another. CONVERT differs from *CAST* in that it provides you with the ability to format the output of a conversion. SQL Server 2012 introduces four new conversion functions:

- *PARSE*

- *TRY_PARSE*

- *TRY_CAST*

- *TRY_CONVERT*

An example of each is provided in the upcoming "Convert dates using the new SQL Server 2012 functions" exercise.

> **Note** Regardless of the type of function, you can use the resulting value in a variable assignment or as a value in a SELECT statement. If you need a refresher on variable assignment, please refer to the "Using variables" section in Chapter 11, "Advanced data retrieval topics."

Convert data using CAST

1. Open the query editor in SSMS.

2. In the query editor, enter and execute the following T-SQL code:

```
USE AdventureWorks2012;
SELECT TOP(10)
     SalesOrderNumber,
     TotalDue,
     CAST(TotalDue AS decimal(10,2)) AS TotalDueCast,
     OrderDate,
     CAST(OrderDate AS DATE) AS OrderDateCast
FROM Sales.SalesOrderHeader;
```

The following image shows the result set for the preceding query.

	SalesOrderNumber	TotalDue	TotalDueCast	OrderDate	OrderDateCast
1	SO43659	23153.2339	23153.23	2005-07-01 00:00:00.000	2005-07-01
2	SO43660	1457.3288	1457.33	2005-07-01 00:00:00.000	2005-07-01
3	SO43661	36865.8012	36865.80	2005-07-01 00:00:00.000	2005-07-01
4	SO43662	32474.9324	32474.93	2005-07-01 00:00:00.000	2005-07-01
5	SO43663	472.3108	472.31	2005-07-01 00:00:00.000	2005-07-01
6	SO43664	27510.4109	27510.41	2005-07-01 00:00:00.000	2005-07-01
7	SO43665	16158.6961	16158.70	2005-07-01 00:00:00.000	2005-07-01
8	SO43666	5694.8564	5694.86	2005-07-01 00:00:00.000	2005-07-01
9	SO43667	6876.3649	6876.36	2005-07-01 00:00:00.000	2005-07-01
10	SO43668	40487.7233	40487.72	2005-07-01 00:00:00.000	2005-07-01

In the preceding query, the original values from the TotalDue column were stored, allowing up to four numbers after the decimal place. By using the *CAST* function, you can change the number of decimal places returned as shown in the TotalDueCast column. In addition, instead of returning a date and time value for the order date, you can use the *CAST* function to return only the date value, which you can see in the OrderDateCast column.

While the *CONVERT* and *CAST* functions perform the same primary function, the *CONVERT* function offers some added flexibility over *CAST* in that you can format the output of your result set using the *style* argument. You can apply styles to *date*, *time*, *real*, *float*, *money*, *xml*, and *binary* data types.

Note You can find a detailed list of the codes used for each type of style in the *CAST* and *CONVERT* section of SQL Server Books Online and at *http://msdn.microsoft.com/en-us/library/ms187928*.

Convert data using CONVERT

1. Open the query editor in SSMS.

2. In the query editor, enter and execute the following T-SQL code:

```
SELECT
        CONVERT(VARCHAR(20), GETDATE()) AS [Default],
        CONVERT(VARCHAR(20), GETDATE(), 100) AS DefaultWithStyle,
        CONVERT(VARCHAR(10), GETDATE(), 103) AS BritishFrenchStyle,
        CONVERT(VARCHAR(8), GETDATE(), 105) AS ItalianStyle,
        CONVERT(VARCHAR(8), GETDATE(), 112) AS ISOStyle,
        CONVERT(VARCHAR(15), CAST('111111.22' AS MONEY), 1) AS MoneyWithCommas
```

What you should notice immediately is that the *CONVERT* function accepts three arguments. The first argument is the target data type or the date type you want to convert a given value to. The second argument is the actual value that will be converted, and the final argument is the style. This final argument is optional, and if it is not provided, SQL Server will use default values. The following image shows the results of executing the previous query.

	Default	DefaultWithStyle	BritishFrenchStyle	ItalianStyle	ISOStyle	MoneyWithCommas
1	Jul 6 2012 8:24AM	Jul 6 2012 8:24AM	06/07/2012	06-07-20	20120706	111,111.23

The first five columns represent date conversions to different country styles. The last column illustrates the use of the *CONVERT* function to add commas to a value that is of the *money* data type. In the query, the *CAST* function is used in the last line of code to convert the string to *money*, and then the *CONVERT* function is used to convert that value to back to a string with commas.

New SQL Server 2012 conversion functions

SQL Server 2012 introduced four new conversion functions. *PARSE* and *TRY_PARSE* are completely new to SQL Server, while *TRY_CONVERT* and *TRY_CAST* are extensions of the existing *CONVERT* and *CAST* functions. You should use *PARSE* only when converting from strings to date/time and number data types. The other functions, which are prefixed with *TRY_*, add functionality to the base *CONVERT*, *CAST*, and *PARSE* functions. Converting a value using one of the aforementioned functions fails the entire statement. However, when you use any of the *TRY* versions of the function, a NULL value will be returned.

Convert dates using the new SQL Server 2012 functions

1. Open the query editor in SSMS.

2. In the query editor, enter and execute the following T-SQL code:

```
SELECT
        TRY_CAST('PATRICK' AS INT) TryCast,
        TRY_CONVERT(DATETIME, '13/2/2999', 112) AS TryConvert,
        PARSE('Saturday, 26 May 2012' AS DATETIME USING 'en-US') AS Parse,
        TRY_PARSE('Patricks BirthDay' AS DATETIME USING 'en-US') AS TryParse
```

The following figure illustrates the use of all the new functions.

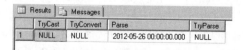

	TryCast	TryConvert	Parse	TryParse
1	NULL	NULL	2012-05-26 00:00:00.000	NULL

Instead of failing the execution of the query, the new *TRY* functions provide a more elegant approach in returning NULL values.

Using string functions

SQL Server 2012 includes 25 built-in scalar string functions, including two new functions:

- *CONCAT*

- *FORMAT*

Each function performs some operation on a provided string or numeric value. One thing to note is that if you are attempting to combine or concatenate a string and a numeric value, the numeric value must be converted to a string first.

> **Note** While numerous functions are available, this book focuses only on the most commonly used ones. If you are interested in learning about all the functions, visit the "String Functions (Transact-SQL)" page of MSDN: *http://msdn.microsoft.com/en-us/library/ms181984.*

Use SQL Server string functions

1. Open the query editor in SSMS.

2. In the query editor, enter and execute the following T-SQL code:

```
SELECT
    'LEBLANC '+', '+' PATRICK' RawValues,
    RTRIM('LEBLANC ')+', '+LTRIM(' PATRICK') TrimValue,
    LEFT('PatrickDTomorr', 7) [Left],
    RIGHT('DTomorrLeBlanc', 7) [Right],
    SUBSTRING('DTomorrPatrick',8,LEN('DTomorrPatrick')) [SubString],
    '12/'+CAST(1 AS VARCHAR)+'/2012' WithoutConcat,
    CONCAT('12/',1,'/2012') WithConcat
```

The following image shows the use of several string functions.

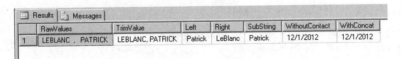

The first two columns in the result set concatenate two string values. The difference between the two is that one contains spaces before and after the comma, and the other does not. By using the *RTRIM* and *LTRIM* functions, you can remove spaces to the right (*RTRIM*) and left (*LTRIM*) of the string. The next two columns use the *LEFT* and *RIGHT* functions, which simply return the leftmost or rightmost value of the provided string value based on the second argument. In the preceding query, the *LEFT* function returns the first seven characters starting from the left, and the *RIGHT* function does the same but starting from the right.

The *SUBSTRING* function returns a part of a string based on a starting point and an end-point, which are the last two arguments provided to the function. In the preceding query, the function is used to return a value starting at character 8 and ending at the end of the string expression provided as the first argument. This ending value is derived using the *LEN* function, which returns the length of a string. In the last two columns, dates are derived from three different values. Note that in the WithoutConcat column, a *CAST* function is used to convert the integer value to a string to ensure that the concatenation succeeds. However, when you use the new *CONCAT* function, the need for *CAST* is mitigated because it converts nonstring values to strings automatically.

Using logical functions

SQL Server 2012 includes two new logical functions that allow more inline data selection with very little code:

- *CHOOSE*

- *IIF*

CHOOSE returns a value from a list based on a specified index. *IIF* returns a value based on the evaluation of a Boolean expression to true or false.

Use the CHOOSE and IIF functions

1. Open the query editor in SSMS.

2. In the query editor, enter and execute the following T-SQL code:

```
declare @choosevar int = 3
SELECT
    CHOOSE(@choosevar, 'ONE', 'TWO', 'PATRICK', 'THREE') [Choose],
    IIF(DATENAME(MONTH, GETDATE()) = 'July', 'The 4th is this month', 'No Fireworks') AS
[IIF]
```

In the preceding query, you are able to select the third item of a list of strings by using the *CHOOSE* function. If you changed 3 to 1, the function would return the first value, ONE, from the list of strings instead of the third. In the final line of code in the preceding query, the *IIF* function is used to determine which of the two strings to return. The first argument used in the *IIF* function evaluates to either true or false. In this example, an expression is used to determine if the current month is July. If the expression evaluates to true, the first string value is returned; otherwise, the second value is returned.

The following image shows the results of the previous query.

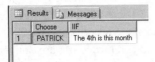

Summary

As you learned in this chapter, Microsoft SQL Server includes several types of built-in functions. In the coming chapters, you will be introduced to other types of built-in functions. While only a select set will be discussed throughout this book, you should take time to review SQL Server Books Online and explore the various capabilities of all available functions.

Creating other database objects

CHAPTER 14

Advanced T-SQL topics

After completing this chapter, you will be able to

- Perform aggregating, grouping, and windowing.

- Use SQL Server temporary objects.

- Handle T-SQL errors inside of queries.

- Add control logic around and inside T-SQL statements.

So far, the T-SQL statements and logic you have constructed have been very basic and straight-forward. In this chapter, you will learn about additional constructs to enhance the functionality of T-SQL code. First, you will examine how to perform aggregations, windowing, and grouping with T-SQL. Next, you will learn how to use temporary objects in Microsoft SQL Server. Finally, you will see examples of how to handle errors and control the flow of T-SQL queries.

Aggregating, windowing, and grouping

Typically, when data is stored in a relational database, each row represents a single value. For example, in a sales database, you may record a row for each sale that a salesperson makes. Or in a banking database, you may record a row for each transaction that occurs on a customer's account. Regardless of the data that is stored, at some point, that data will need to be aggregated in some way. In the sales example, you may want to see all the sales for each salesperson, whereas in the banking example, you may want to see the account balance for each customer. Using T-SQL syntax, you can aggregate the data with built-in aggregate scalar functions and group the data using the GROUP BY keyword to perform these operations.

In addition to aggregating the data, you can use windowing functions to perform ranking operations over a set of rows. Windowing, which will be discussed in detail later in this chapter, performs operations across a data set, typically in relation to the current row.

Performing aggregations

The most common aggregation that is performed is summation, which adds all the values of a given data set. The summation of data is supported through T-SQL's SUM function.

```
SUM( [ ALL | DISTINCT ] expression)
```

The *ALL* keyword will apply the aggregation to every value in the result, whereas *DISTINCT* will aggregate only the unique values. The *ALL* keyword is used by default; therefore, you do not need to specify it as part of the query. The supplied expression must be a numeric data type that can be a constant, variable, column, or function.

Perform a simple aggregation

1. Open the query editor in Microsoft SQL Server Management Studio (SSMS).

2. In the query editor, enter the following T-SQL code:

    ```
    USE AdventureWorks2012;
    SELECT
        SUM(poh.TotalDue) AS TotalDue
    FROM Purchasing.PurchaseOrderHeader poh
    ```

3. Execute the query and review the results.

    This query presents the total due for all purchase orders that have been placed.

4. Add three new aggregations to the query that average the total due and count the number of employees in two different ways (represented in bold).

    ```
    USE AdventureWorks2012;
    SELECT
        SUM(poh.TotalDue) AS [Total Due],
        AVG(poh.TotalDue) AS [Average Total Due],
        COUNT(poh.EmployeeID) [Number Of Employees],
        COUNT(DISTINCT poh.EmployeeID) [Distinct Number Of Employees]
    FROM Purchasing.PurchaseOrderHeader poh
    ```

5. Execute the query and review the results.

    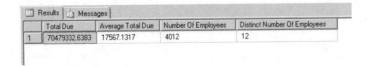

This query adds three new columns to the result set. Remember that all of the aggregations in the previous image are at the same level of granularity.

- Average Total Due uses the AVG function to calculate the average over the entire result set. It sums the total due, counts the number of rows, divides the two values, and then returns the average.

- Number Of Employees uses the *COUNT* function to every employee in the result, including duplicate values of the supplied column, EmployeeID.

- Distinct Number Of Employees uses the *COUNT* function but includes the *DISTINCT* keyword to ensure that duplicates are ignored.

You may have noticed that the syntax for each function used in the preceding query is very similar. This is the case for most of the aggregation functions. There are a few slight variations, but this syntax is standard.

Performing aggregations with groupings

Holistically aggregating the data within a result is probably not something you see in regular use. Typically, the data is broken down or grouped into categories or segments such as year, territory, country, or salesperson. Using the *GROUP BY* keyword, you can summarize the selected result set by one or more columns or expressions. To use groupings with a T-SQL query, you could start with a basic *SELECT* statement ending with a *GROUP BY* clause. The following is sample syntax:

```
SELECT
FROM
GROUP BY <column1>, <column2>,…
```

Any columns that are not used by an aggregation function that is listed in the *SELECT* statement must be included in the *GROUP BY* clause. However, a column may be included in the *GROUP BY* clause but not in the *SELECT* statement.

Perform aggregations with the GROUP BY clause

1. Open the query editor in SSMS.

2. In the query editor, enter the following T-SQL code:

```
USE AdventureWorks2012;
SELECT
    sm.Name AS ShippingMethod
    SUM(poh.TotalDue) AS [Total Due],
    AVG(poh.TotalDue) AS [Average Total Due],
    COUNT(poh.EmployeeID) [Number Of Employees],
    COUNT(DISTINCT poh.EmployeeID) [Distinct Number Of Employees]
FROM Purchasing.PurchaseOrderHeader poh
INNER JOIN Purchasing.ShipMethod sm
    ON poh.ShipMethodID = sm.ShipMethodID
```

3. Execute the query and review the results.

   You should have received the following error:

   ```
   Msg 8120, Level 16, State 1, Line 3
   Column 'Purchasing.ShipMethod.Name' is invalid in the select list because it is not
   contained in either an aggregate function or the GROUP BY clause.
   ```

   If you carefully read the error, it tells you how to correct the problem.

4. Add the *GROUP BY* clause to the end of the statement.

   ```
   USE AdventureWorks2012;
   SELECT
         sm.Name AS ShippingMethod,
         SUM(poh.TotalDue) AS [Total Due],
         AVG(poh.TotalDue) AS [Average Total Due],
         COUNT(poh.EmployeeID) AS [Number Of Employees],
         COUNT(DISTINCT poh.EmployeeID) AS [Distinct Number Of Employees]
   FROM Purchasing.PurchaseOrderHeader poh
   INNER JOIN Purchasing.ShipMethod sm
         ON poh.ShipMethodID = sm.ShipMethodID
   GROUP BY sm.Name
   ```

5. Execute the query and review the results.

	ShippingMethod	Total Due	Average Total Due	Number Of Employees	Distinct Number Of Employees
1	XRQ - TRUCK GROUND	3330909.2897	5655.194	589	12
2	ZY - EXPRESS	14874601.7677	22709.3156	655	12
3	OVERSEAS - DELUXE	8002938.997	50018.3687	160	12
4	OVERNIGHT J-FAST	11965191.1871	11027.8259	1085	12
5	CARGO TRANSPORT 5	32305691.3968	21211.8787	1523	12

   By including the *GROUP BY* clause with the Name column from the ShippingMethod table, the query was able to provide aggregations for each individual shipping method that was used. You can group by more than one column or expression.

6. Add an expression that derives the year from the OrderDate column in the PurchaseOrderHeader table:

   ```
   USE AdventureWorks2012;
   SELECT
         sm.Name AS ShippingMethod,
         YEAR(poh.OrderDate) AS OrderYear,
         SUM(poh.TotalDue) AS [Total Due],
         AVG(poh.TotalDue) AS [Average Total Due],
         COUNT(poh.EmployeeID) AS [Number Of Employees],
         COUNT(DISTINCT poh.EmployeeID) AS [Distinct Number Of Employees]
   FROM Purchasing.PurchaseOrderHeader poh
   INNER JOIN Purchasing.ShipMethod sm
         ON poh.ShipMethodID = sm.ShipMethodID
   GROUP BY
      sm.Name,
      YEAR(poh.OrderDate)
   ```

7. Execute the query and review the results.

	ShippingMethod	OrderYear	Total Due	Average Total Due	Number Of Employees	Distinct Number Of Employees
1	XRQ - TRUCK GROUND	2006	238226.7076	5672.0644	42	12
2	XRQ - TRUCK GROUND	2007	931577.2578	6128.7977	152	12
3	XRQ - TRUCK GROUND	2008	2161105.3243	5471.1527	395	12
4	ZY - EXPRESS	2005	9776.2665	9776.2665	1	1
5	ZY - EXPRESS	2006	1128598.8326	24534.7572	46	12
6	ZY - EXPRESS	2007	3657789.9952	21902.9341	167	12
7	ZY - EXPRESS	2008	10078436.6734	22853.5978	441	12
8	OVERSEAS - DELUXE	2005	81233.7049	27077.9016	3	3
9	OVERSEAS - DELUXE	2006	326145.231	36238.359	9	5
10	OVERSEAS - DELUXE	2007	1333639.9307	38103.998	35	10
11	OVERSEAS - DELUXE	2008	6261920.1304	55415.2223	113	12
12	OVERNIGHT J-FAST	2005	22539.0165	22539.0165	1	1
13	OVERNIGHT J-FAST	2006	750384.0766	10875.1315	69	12
14	OVERNIGHT J-FAST	2007	3295912.2337	11210.5858	294	12
15	OVERNIGHT J-FAST	2008	7896355.8603	10951.9498	721	12
16	CARGO TRANSPORT 5	2005	1255.8943	418.6314	3	3
17	CARGO TRANSPORT 5	2006	2226522.1526	21004.9259	106	12
18	CARGO TRANSPORT 5	2007	8073385.8419	20861.4621	387	12
19	CARGO TRANSPORT 5	2008	22004527.508	21426.0248	1027	12

The results show that by adding a second column to the group, you can even further aggregate the data. Now within each shipping method the data is aggregated by year.

Windowing

Windowing data using T-SQL is a way of providing a new perspective of data. This new perspective or new window of data is created by using an *OVER()* clause. After the new window is created, a value is generated for each row in the result set. These values are obtained by using T-SQL aggregate functions and/or ranking functions. Aggregate functions were discussed in the "Performing aggregations" section of this chapter. There are four basic ranking functions: *ROW_NUMBER*, *RANK*, *DENSE_RANK*, and *NTILE*.

- **ROW_NUMBER** Generates autoincrementing integers according to the sort in the *OVER* clause.

- **RANK** Generates a value based on the windowed sort as if the rows were competing. If there are any ties, both rows would receive the same value.

- **DENSE_RANK** Generates a value very similar to the *RANK* function. However, if there is a tie, only one value is used.

- **NTILE** Organizes the rows into some number of groups, called *tiles*.

It should be noted that windowing data can result in very complex T-SQL statements. Therefore, only a brief introduction will be provided in this chapter. See SQL Server Books Online for more details on and examples for Windowing data.

Windowing data using the ROW_NUMBER function

1. Open the query editor in SSMS.

2. In the query editor, enter and execute the following T-SQL code:

```
USE AdventureWorks2012
GO
;WITH ProductQty
AS
(
     SELECT TOP(10)
          p.ProductID,
          SUM(OrderQty) AS OrderQty
     FROM Sales.SalesOrderDetail AS sod
     INNER JOIN Production.Product AS p
          ON sod.ProductID = p.ProductID
     GROUP BY p.ProductID
)
SELECT
     p.NAME AS ProductName,
     pq.OrderQty,
     ROW_NUMBER() OVER(ORDER BY pq.OrderQty DESC) ROWNUMBER,
     RANK() OVER(ORDER BY pq.OrderQty DESC) [RANK],
     DENSE_RANK() OVER(ORDER BY pq.OrderQty DESC) [DENSERANK]
FROM ProductQty AS pq
INNER JOIN Production.Product AS p
     ON pq.ProductID = p.ProductID
```

	ProductName	OrderQty	ROWNUMBER	RANK	DENSERANK
1	Mountain-200 Silver, 38	2394	1	1	1
2	Men's Bib-Shorts, M	1616	2	2	2
3	LL Mountain Frame - Black, 44	625	3	3	3
4	Road-450 Red, 44	346	4	4	4
5	Touring-2000 Blue, 50	322	5	5	5
6	All-Purpose Bike Stand	249	6	6	6
7	LL Fork	190	7	7	7
8	ML Road Frame - Red, 52	90	8	8	8
9	Mountain Bike Socks, L	90	9	8	8
10	LL Touring Frame - Yellow, 58	36	10	10	9

As you can see in the preceding image, the *ROW_NUMBER* function generates a number for each row in sequence based on *ORDER BY*. In this case, the product with the highest OrderQty is first, and all subsequent rows are assigned a value based on the quantity. For the *RANK* and *DENSE_RANK* functions, the behavior is similar unless they encounter ties. If a tie exists, all rows are assigned the same value. However, as you can see in the image, when *RANK* is used, the number generated for the rows that are after the tie will skip a value. This depends on the number of rows included in the tie. In the case of *DENSE_RANK*, a value is not skipped in the event of a tie. This query uses a common table expression, which is explained in the "Common table expressions" section of this chapter.

New T-SQL windowing features

SQL Server 2012 introduces several new windowing arguments that can be used with the *OVER* clause. While this chapter does not provide examples of these arguments, they are definitely worth mentioning. Table 14-1 lists each argument and provides a brief description.

TABLE 14-1 New SQL Server 2012 Windowing Features

Argument	Description
ROWS/RANGE	Limits rows based on the current row
CURRENT ROW	States the starting or ending point as the current row
BETWEEN	Is coupled with *ROWS* or *RANGE* to specify starting and ending points
UNBOUND PRECEDING	States where the window will start
UNBOUND FOLLOWING	States where the window will end

Using the *HAVING* clause

The *HAVING* clause behaves similarly to a *SELECT* statement. However, it can leverage aggregation. You can use it only with a *SELECT* statement, and it is typically used with a *GROUP BY* clause.

Limit aggregated rows with a *HAVING* clause

1. Open the query editor in SSMS.

2. In the query editor, enter the following T-SQL code:

```
USE AdventureWorks2012;
SELECT
     sm.Name AS ShippingMethod,
     YEAR(poh.OrderDate) OrderYear,
     SUM(poh.TotalDue) AS [Total Due],
     AVG(poh.TotalDue) AS [Average Total Due],
     COUNT(poh.EmployeeID) AS [Number Of Employees],
     COUNT(DISTINCT poh.EmployeeID) AS [Distinct Number Of Employees]
FROM Purchasing.PurchaseOrderHeader poh
INNER JOIN Purchasing.ShipMethod sm
     ON poh.ShipMethodID = sm.ShipMethodID
GROUP BY sm.Name,YEAR(poh.OrderDate)
HAVING SUM(poh.TotalDue) > 5000000
```

3. Execute the query and review the results.

	ShippingMethod	OrderYear	Total Due	Average Total Due	Number Of Employees	Distinct Number Of Employees
1	ZY - EXPRESS	2008	10078436.6734	22853.5978	441	12
2	OVERSEAS - DELUXE	2008	6261920.1304	55415.2223	113	12
3	OVERNIGHT J-FAST	2008	7896355.8603	10951.9498	721	12
4	CARGO TRANSPORT 5	2007	8073385.8419	20861.4621	387	12
5	CARGO TRANSPORT 5	2008	22004527.508	21426.0248	1027	12

Now instead of returning every row, the result is limited to only those shipping methods whose annual total due is greater than 5 million.

Using SQL Server temporary objects

When working with T-SQL, you may often find you need to temporarily store a data set for later use. Take the preceding *GROUP BY* queries, for example. If you were to aggregate by salesperson, showing first name, middle name, last name, and address, the query could become very costly because of the number of columns in the *GROUP BY* clause and the number of *JOIN*s involved.

Therefore, instead of joining every table and grouping on all the returned columns, you can use a temporary object to store the aggregated data and join any additional tables returning the columns needed. SQL Server 2012 has three primary temporary objects:

- Common table expressions

- Table variables

- Temporary tables

When and how they should be used depends on several factors.

Common table expressions

A common table expression (CTE) is a temporary result set that is defined during the execution of a *SELECT, INSERT, UPDATE, DELETE*, or *CREATE VIEW* statement. The CTE is available only for the duration of the query and is not stored like other objects in the database. Typical uses of CTEs are to replace views, group data, perform recursion, and create multiple references to a single table. The syntax is as follows:

```
WITH <expression_name> [(column_name [,...n])]
AS
(CTE_query_definition)
```

expression_name is how the CTE will be referenced in the query, and it is required. The column listing is optional but recommended; if the column names in the query definition are not unique, you will get an error when executing the query. You can either use the column listing to correct the problem or fix it in the query definition with aliasing.

Immediately following the CTE definition, you should issue a query that references the CTE. As mentioned previously, it could be an *INSERT, UPDATE,* or *DELETE* statement.

Create and use a common table expression

1. Open the query editor in SSMS.

2. In the query editor, enter the following T-SQL code:

```
USE AdventureWorks2012;
WITH EmployeePOs (EmployeeID, [Total Due])
AS
(
    SELECT
        poh.EmployeeID,
        CONVERT(varchar(20), SUM(poh.TotalDue),1)
    FROM Purchasing.PurchaseOrderHeader poh
    GROUP BY
        poh.EmployeeID
)
SELECT *
FROM EmployeePOs
```

3. Execute the query and review the results.

	EmployeeID	Total Due
1	261	7,239,495.37
2	252	2,978,027.37
3	258	5,556,272.23
4	255	6,305,115.83
5	259	5,186,032.12
6	250	2,501,613.04
7	256	6,552,648.57
8	253	7,423,411.20
9	254	6,578,521.33
10	251	7,426,610.64
11	257	6,942,815.77
12	260	5,788,769.16

In the CTE definition, the aggregation is defined and can now be used in the *SELECT* statement that immediately follows the CTE.

4. Add a *JOIN* to the Person table to add the employees' first and last names.

```
WITH EmployeePOs (EmployeeID, [Total Due])
AS
(
    SELECT
        poh.EmployeeID,
        CONVERT(varchar(20), SUM(poh.TotalDue),1)
    FROM Purchasing.PurchaseOrderHeader poh
    GROUP BY
        poh.EmployeeID
)
SELECT
    ep.EmployeeID,
    p.FirstName,
    p.LastName,
    ep.[Total Due]
FROM EmployeePOs ep
INNER JOIN Person.Person p
    ON ep.EmployeeID = p.BusinessEntityID
```

5. Execute the query and review the results.

	EmployeeID	FirstName	LastName	Total Due
1	261	Reinout	Hillmann	7,239,495.37
2	252	Arvind	Rao	2,978,027.37
3	258	Erin	Hagens	5,556,272.23
4	255	Gordon	Hee	6,305,115.83
5	259	Ben	Miller	5,186,032.12
6	250	Sheela	Word	2,501,613.04
7	256	Frank	Pellow	6,552,648.57
8	253	Linda	Meisner	7,423,411.20
9	254	Fukiko	Ogisu	6,578,521.33
10	251	Mikael	Sandberg	7,426,610.64
11	257	Eric	Kurjan	6,942,815.77
12	260	Annette	Hill	5,788,769.16

Now you have aggregated the data for each employee without incurring the overhead of running a summation that includes multiple columns.

Table variables

Table variables behave similarly to local variables. They are typically used to store small amounts of data (fewer than 500 rows) and are available only within the scope of the batch, function, or stored procedure in which they are declared. The syntax for declaring a table variable is as follows:

```
DECLARE @local_variable [AS] table
(
    [(column_definition) [,...n])]
)
```

In the preceding script, you can replace *local_variable* with the name you prefer, but you must prefix it with an at (@) symbol. Next, you must define each column in the table. Each column will be defined in the same way you define columns when creating an actual table.

Declare and use table variables

1. Open the query editor in SSMS.

2. In the query editor, enter the following T-SQL code:

```
USE AdventureWorks2012;

DECLARE @EmployeePOs AS TABLE
(
    EmployeeID int,
    TotalDue money
)

INSERT INTO @EmployeePOs
SELECT
    poh.EmployeeID,
    CONVERT(varchar(20), SUM(poh.TotalDue),1)
```

```
FROM Purchasing.PurchaseOrderHeader poh
GROUP BY
    poh.EmployeeID
```

In the preceding query, a table variable is declared and the results of a query are inserted into the table variable.

3. In the query editor, add a *SELECT* statement that references the table variable and joins it to the Person table.

```
USE AdventureWorks2012;
DECLARE @EmployeePOs AS TABLE
(
    EmployeeID int,
    TotalDue money
)

INSERT INTO @EmployeePOs
SELECT
    poh.EmployeeID,
    CONVERT(varchar(20), SUM(poh.TotalDue),1)
FROM Purchasing.PurchaseOrderHeader poh
GROUP BY
    poh.EmployeeID

SELECT
    ep.EmployeeID,
    p.FirstName,
    p.LastName,
    ep.[TotalDue]
FROM @EmployeePOs ep
INNER JOIN Person.Person p
    ON ep.EmployeeID = p.BusinessEntityID
```

4. Execute the query and review the results.

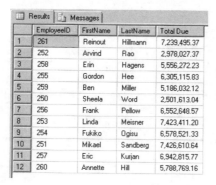

	EmployeeID	FirstName	LastName	Total Due
1	261	Reinout	Hillmann	7,239,495.37
2	252	Arvind	Rao	2,978,027.37
3	258	Erin	Hagens	5,556,272.23
4	255	Gordon	Hee	6,305,115.83
5	259	Ben	Miller	5,186,032.12
6	250	Sheela	Word	2,501,613.04
7	256	Frank	Pellow	6,552,648.57
8	253	Linda	Meisner	7,423,411.20
9	254	Fukiko	Ogisu	6,578,521.33
10	251	Mikael	Sandberg	7,426,610.64
11	257	Eric	Kurjan	6,942,815.77
12	260	Annette	Hill	5,788,769.16

Note A table variable must be aliased when you plan on referencing it in a query.

The results are exactly the same as those returned when using the CTE. However, the advantage table variables have over CTEs is that they can be accessed during the entire batch or session.

Temporary tables

You can create local and global temporary tables. Local temporary tables are available within the scope of the current session and are dropped at the end of a session. They must be prefixed with a pound (#) sign.

Global temporary tables are available for all sessions and are dropped when the session that created them and all referencing sessions are closed. They must be prefixed with two pound (##) signs.

The syntax for creating either is exactly the same as for creating a traditional table, but you must include the pound sign(s) as just specified. Unlike with the other two temporary objects, space is allocated for temporary tables. Note that table variables are not typically written to disk, but in some cases they may use resources.

Create and use temporary tables

1. Open the query editor in SSMS.

2. In the query editor, enter the following T-SQL code:

```
USE AdventureWorks2012;
CREATE TABLE #EmployeePOs
(
    EmployeeID int,
    TotalDue money
)

INSERT INTO #EmployeePOs
SELECT
    poh.EmployeeID,
    CONVERT(varchar(20), SUM(poh.TotalDue),1)
FROM Purchasing.PurchaseOrderHeader poh
GROUP BY
    poh.EmployeeID
```

This code creates the temporary table and then inserts the results of a query into the temporary table.

3. In the query editor, add a SELECT statement that references the temporary table and joins it to the Person table.

```
USE AdventureWorks2012;
CREATE TABLE #EmployeePOs
(
    EmployeeID int,
    TotalDue money
)
```

```
INSERT INTO #EmployeePOs
SELECT
      poh.EmployeeID,
      CONVERT(varchar(20), SUM(poh.TotalDue),1)
FROM Purchasing.PurchaseOrderHeader poh
GROUP BY
      poh.EmployeeID

SELECT
      ep.EmployeeID,
      p.FirstName,
      p.LastName,
      ep.[TotalDue]
FROM #EmployeePOs ep
INNER JOIN Person.Person p
      ON ep.EmployeeID = p.BusinessEntityID
```

4. Execute the query and review the results, which will be exactly the same as the results returned in the CTE steps.

If you run the query again in the same query window, you will receive an error stating that the temporary table already exists. This is because the session is still open. If you open a new query editor and rerun the query, it will succeed. Once a session that references the temporary table is closed or ended, then the temporary table is automatically dropped. This is the one disadvantage of using temporary tables as opposed to CTEs and table variables. While the latter two are automatically removed, the temporary table must be explicitly dropped within the same session or the session must be ended. It should be noted that table variables and temporary tables can be declared with primary keys and indexes to improve performance. However, indexes should not be added to temporary tables after they are created because doing so could negatively affect execution plans.

Handling T-SQL errors

As with any programming language, T-SQL provides elegant methods for handling errors and exceptions during execution. T-SQL uses *TRY...CATCH*, similar to Microsoft Visual C#. When writing T-SQL, you wrap the code in the *TRY* block, and if an error occurs, the control is sent to the *CATCH* block. Within the *CATCH* block, you should enclose T-SQL code that will handle the errors. The following is the *TRY...CATCH* syntax.

```
BEGIN TRY
     { sql_statement |statement_block}
END TRY
BEGIN CATCH
     [{ sql_statement |statement_block}]
END CATCH
```

sql_statement is any single T-SQL statement, and *statement_block* is any set or batch of T-SQL statements. This applies to both the *TRY* and *CATCH* blocks. The *TRY* and *CATCH* blocks must be constructed together.

Finally, in SQL Server 2012, Microsoft introduced the *THROW* statement, which raises an exception and transfers execution to a *CATCH* block.

```
THROW [ { error_number | @local_variable },
  { message | @local_variable },
 { state | @local_variable }
] [ ; ]
```

error_number must be between 50,000 and 2,147,483,647, and it can be a constant or variable, but it's optional when implementing error handling using T-SQL. *message* describes the error and can be a string or variable. *state* must be between 0 and 255 and can be a constant or variable. The statement preceding the *THROW* statement must end with a semicolon (;).

Implement error handing using T-SQL constructs

1. Open the query editor in SSMS.

2. In the query editor, enter the following T-SQL code:

```
BEGIN TRY
      SELECT 1/0;
END TRY
BEGIN CATCH

END CATCH
```

3. Execute the query and view the results.

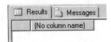

Notice that the query returned an empty set, but more important, it did not return an error. Instead of returning or displaying an error, the *CATCH* block consumes the error.

4. Within the *CATCH* block, add a *THROW* statement.

```
BEGIN TRY
      SELECT 1/0;
END TRY
BEGIN CATCH
       THROW;
END CATCH
```

5. Execute the query and view the results.

    Adding the *THROW* statement to the *CATCH* block forces the client to display the error message. *THROW* returns more accurate results and, in most cases, provides the developer with enough information to effectively handle the error.

6. If you want to customize the error that will be provided by SQL Server, replace the *THROW* statement in step 4 with the following code.

    ```
    THROW 51000, 'You divided my ZERO!!!', 1;
    ```

    Now when the query is executed, you will receive the error that you specified in the THROW statement.

Controlling flow keywords

Determining when and how code should react or work together is a pivotal part of any programming language. T-SQL includes a set of keywords that allow you to group a series of statements and make run-time decisions based on logic within the code. The keywords are as follows:

- *BEGIN...END*

- *BREAK*

- *CONTINUE*

- *GOTO*

- *IF...ELSE*

- *RETURN*

- *WAITFOR*

- *WHILE*

Technically, the *TRY...CATCH* block and the *THROW* statements are included as control flow keywords; they have been omitted from the list since they were discussed in the previous section. The following sections detail the *BEGIN...END*, *IF...ELSE*, and *WHILE* keywords.

BEGIN...END

The *BEGIN...END* keyword coupling simply encloses a group or series of T-SQL statements. *BEGIN...END* blocks can be nested.

```
BEGIN
{
  sql_Statement | statement_block
}
END
```

Use the *BEGIN...END* block

1. Open the query editor in SSMS.

2. In the query editor, enter the following T-SQL code:

    ```
    USE AdventureWorks2012;
    BEGIN
        DECLARE @StartingHireDate datetime = '12/31/2001'

        SELECT e.BusinessEntityID, p.FirstName, p.LastName, e.HireDate
        FROM HumanResources.Employee e
        INNER JOIN Person.Person p
            ON e.BusinessEntityID = p.BusinessEntityID
        WHERE HireDate <= @StartingHireDate
    END
    ```

3. Execute the query and review your results.

    In the preceding query, first a variable is declared and assigned a variable. Then the variable is used to limit the result to only employees whose hire date is less than or equal to the value assigned to that variable.

IF...ELSE

The *IF...ELSE* block simply tells the programming language to perform a T-SQL statement or a set of statements if the specified condition is met, or another T-SQL statement or set of statements if it is not. The *IF* can exist without the *ELSE*, but the *ELSE* cannot exist without the *IF*.

```
IF Boolean_expression { sql_statement | statement_block }
 [ ELSE { sql_statement | statement_block } ]
```

Use the *IF...ELSE* block

1. Open the query editor in SSMS.

2. In the query editor, enter the following T-SQL code:

   ```
   IF(DATENAME(M, GETDATE())='December')
   BEGIN
        SELECT 'Time for the holidays!!!!' Results
   END
   ELSE
   BEGIN
        SELECT 'Not sure what''s going on now :(' Results
   END
   ```

3. Execute the query and review the results.

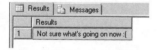

Since the month is not December, the Boolean expression returned false. Therefore, control was sent to the *ELSE* block and the statement within that block was executed.

WHILE

WHILE is a looping mechanism based on a Boolean expression. As long as the expression evaluates to true, the specified T-SQL statement or code block will execute. Two optional keywords, *BREAK* and *CONTINUE*, can be included with the *WHILE* keyword to assist in controlling logic inside the loop. If at any point during the *WHILE* loop the *BREAK* keyword causes the execution of the query to exit, any T-SQL code following the *END* keyword will be executed. The *CONTINUE* keyword, on the other hand, causes the loop to restart. Any statements after the *CONTINUE* keyword are ignored.

```
WHILE Boolean_expression
  { sql_statement | statement_block | BREAK | CONTINUE }
```

1. Open the query editor in SSMS.

2. In the query editor, enter the following T-SQL code:

```
DECLARE @count int = 0
WHILE (@count < 10)
BEGIN
    SET @count = @count + 1;
        IF(@count < 5)
        BEGIN
            SELECT @count AS Counter
            CONTINUE;
        END
        ELSE
            BREAK;
END
```

3. Execute the query and view the results.

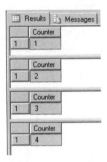

This query uses a variable in the expression of the *WHILE* loop. During each execution of the loop, the variable is incremented by 1, and once it reaches 10, the loop should exit. However, since additional logic is added that causes it to escape the loop using *BREAK* if the counter is not less than five, it results in only four iterations of the loop.

Each of the previously described keywords has the ability to logically change the flow of a T-SQL statement. While *RETURN* and *GOTO* have not been discussed, they both—when used effectively—can assist in improving how a query flows. The *RETURN* keyword immediately completes a query. For example, you could terminate the execution of a query based on logic included in the query. The *GOTO* keyword sends the execution context of the statement from its current point to the line specified in the *GOTO*.

Summary

While this chapter has skimmed only the surface of more advanced T-SQL programming constructs, you should have a solid starting point from which to build your skills as a T-SQL programmer. Logically controlling execution is essential to any programming language. The control flow keywords often offer efficiencies and performance improvements by eliminating the execution of unnecessary code.

Views

After completing this chapter, you will be able to

- Understand views.

- Create, alter, and drop views.

- Create index views.

Part IV of this book focused on the T-SQL language as a whole and many of the available constructs and keywords. All of the T-SQL code you've written so far has been *disposed*, meaning it is not reusable. In this part of the book, you are going to focus on writing code that creates reusable objects within the database. The discussion will begin with views and move on to other reusable T-SQL objects.

What are views?

A *view* is a virtual object or table whose result set is derived from a query. It is very similar to a real table because it contains columns and rows of data. The only time a view is materialized, or stored on disk, is when it is indexed. Indexed views are discussed later in this chapter. The following are some typical uses of views:

- Filter data of underlying tables

- Filter data for security purposes

- Centralize data distributed across several servers

- Create a reusable set of data

You can create views using a graphical user interface (GUI) within Microsoft SQL Server Management Studio (SSMS) or using T-SQL. Before you create any views, you should understand the following:

- Views are often used as an abstraction layer for database developers. They are also sometimes used to secure data in various ways. For example, you may create a view that exposes only specific data. In turn, instead of granting users permissions to the underlying table, you can grant them permissions to the view that exposes some of the columns.

- As a best practice, you should avoid using *SELECT* * in views. As table schemas change, so will the views column listing if *SELECT* * is used. When writing queries, you should return only those columns that are required.

- You should not use *ORDER BY* in views because they will not be valid; they are valid only when used with *TOP*. In that case, *ORDER BY* is used to determine which rows are returned.

Create views with SSMS and T-SQL

1. Open SSMS and connect to a server.

2. If the Object Explorer window is not open, open it. If you have not connected to a database server, do so.

3. Expand the server node, and then expand the Databases folder.

4. Expand the AdventureWorks2012 database.

5. Right-click the folder labeled Views and select New View from the context menu.

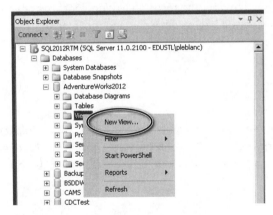

The Add Table dialog box will appear.

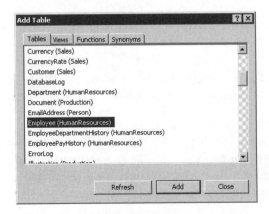

6. Scroll down the list, and locate and select the Employee(HumanResources) table. Click Add. The Employee table will appear in the Diagram pane.

7. Scroll down the list, and locate and select the Person(Person) table. Click Add and then click Close.

Your screen should resemble the following image. The two tables appear linked in the designer because of the existing foreign key relationships.

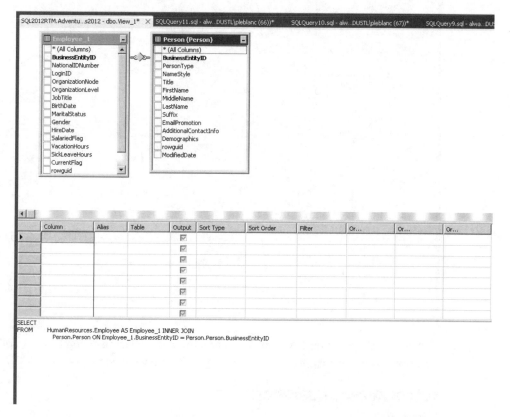

8. In the diagram pane, click the box next to the Title, FirstName, MiddleName, and LastName columns in the Person table.

9. In the diagram pane, click the box next to the JobTitle, BirthDate, and Gender columns in the Employee table.

Now your screen should resemble the following image.

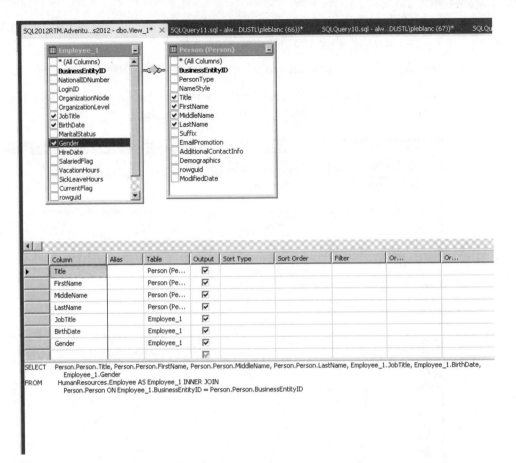

10. Click the save icon in the SSMS menu bar and the Choose Name dialog box will appear. Type **vwEmployeeInformation** in the Enter a Name for the View text box and click OK.

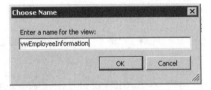

11. Click the *X* in the corner of the new view tab to close the view.

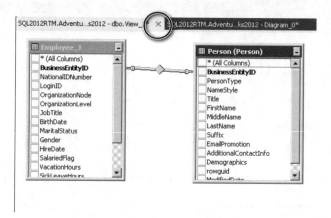

12. In Object Explorer, expand the Views folder and you will see the view you just created.

13. Open a new query window and type the following code:

```
USE AdventureWorks2012;
SELECT * FROM dbo.vwEmployeeInformation
```

14. Execute the query and view the results.

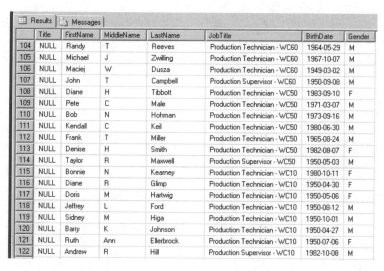

	Title	FirstName	MiddleName	LastName	JobTitle	BirthDate	Gender
104	NULL	Randy	T	Reeves	Production Technician - WC60	1964-05-29	M
105	NULL	Michael	J	Zwilling	Production Technician - WC60	1967-10-07	M
106	NULL	Maciej	W	Dusza	Production Technician - WC60	1949-03-02	M
107	NULL	John	T	Campbell	Production Supervisor - WC60	1950-09-08	M
108	NULL	Diane	H	Tibbott	Production Technician - WC50	1983-09-10	F
109	NULL	Pete	C	Male	Production Technician - WC50	1971-03-07	M
110	NULL	Bob	N	Hohman	Production Technician - WC50	1973-09-16	M
111	NULL	Kendall	C	Keil	Production Technician - WC50	1980-06-30	M
112	NULL	Frank	T	Miller	Production Technician - WC50	1965-08-24	M
113	NULL	Denise	H	Smith	Production Technician - WC50	1982-08-07	F
114	NULL	Taylor	R	Maxwell	Production Supervisor - WC50	1950-05-03	M
115	NULL	Bonnie	N	Kearney	Production Technician - WC10	1980-10-11	F
116	NULL	Diane	R	Glimp	Production Technician - WC10	1950-04-30	F
117	NULL	Doris	M	Hartwig	Production Technician - WC10	1950-05-06	F
118	NULL	Jeffrey	L	Ford	Production Technician - WC10	1950-08-12	M
119	NULL	Sidney	M	Higa	Production Technician - WC10	1950-10-01	M
120	NULL	Barry	K	Johnson	Production Technician - WC10	1950-04-27	M
121	NULL	Ruth	Ann	Ellerbrock	Production Technician - WC10	1950-07-06	F
122	NULL	Andrew	R	Hill	Production Supervisor - WC10	1982-10-08	M

Now instead of your having to writing a query that joins the two tables each time you need this information, end users and applications can use the view to quickly access the data.

Just as a view can be created using SSMS and T-SQL, it can also be altered and dropped.

Alter and drop views

1. Open SSMS and connect to a server.

2. If the Object Explorer window is not open, open it.

3. Expand the server node, and then expand the Databases folder.

4. Expand the AdventureWorks2012 database.

5. Expand the Views folder.

6. Right-click the dbo.vsEmployeeInformation view and select Design from the context menu.

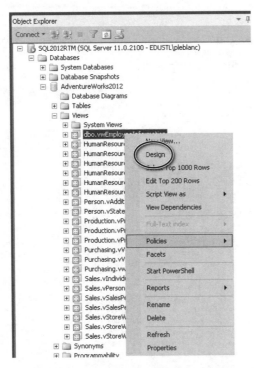

7. In the Column section, in the first available column, which should be after Gender, enter the following:

```
FirstName+' '+LastName
```

8. In the column labeled Alias, replace Expr1 with **FullName**.

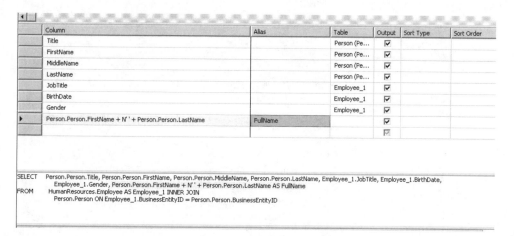

Notice that as you make changes to the column section, the T-SQL section is updated as well.

9. Click the Save button and close the view.

10. Open a new query window and execute the following query:

```
USE AdventureWorks2012;
SELECT * FROM dbo.vwEmployeeInformation
```

You will now see the FullName column added to the result set.

11. To drop the view, right-click the dbo.vwEmployeeInformation view in Object Explorer and select Delete from the context menu. The Delete Object dialog box will appear.

12. Click OK and the view will be dropped.

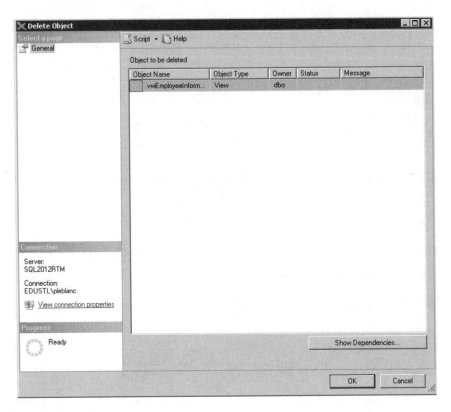

Creating indexed views

An indexed view is different from other views because it is materialized and stored on disk in the same way as a table. An interesting point about an indexed view is that the query optimizer may reference a view to improve performance even if it is not referenced in the query. This feature is available only in the Enterprise edition of SQL Server.

Referenced table requirements

Before you can create an indexed view, you need to make sure that all the referenced tables meet a few requirements. First, all referenced tables must be contained within the same database. If any computed columns in the base tables are not deterministic, they must be removed. *Deterministic* is defined as always returning the same value or result set. Since a requirement of an indexed view is that it be deterministic, all the columns in the base table must also be deterministic. You can use the following code, which leverages the *COLUMNPROPERTY* scalar function to determine if the column is deterministic:

```
USE AdventureWorks2012;
GO
SELECT COLUMNPROPERTY( OBJECT_ID('Sales.SalesOrderDetail'),'LineTotal'
,'IsDeterministic')AS 'Column Length';
GO
```

In addition to being deterministic, the computed column may also need to be marked *PERSISTED*. This depends on whether the data type is imprecise. Any *float* or *real* data type is considered imprecise and cannot be a key of an index unless it is marked *PERSISTED*.

Finally, the *ANSI_NULLS* and *QUOTED_IDENTIFIER* options must have been set to true when the referenced tables were created.

Indexed view requirements

In addition to the referenced table requirements, you need to ensure a few more things prior to creating a view and as part of view creation. The following SET options must be ON:

- *ANSI_NULLS*

- *ANSI_PADDING*

- *ANSI_WARNINGS*

- *ARITHABORT*

- *CONCAT_NULL_YIELDS_NULL*

- *QUOTED_IDENTIFIER*

The *NUMERIC_ROUNDABORT* option must be set to OFF. Prior to creating the view, you must set these options.

Next, you must verify that the view is deterministic. As previously mentioned, this means the view will return the same values each time it is queried. When you are creating the view, you must use the *WITH SCHEMABINDING* option, which binds the view to the schema of the underlying tables. Finally, the first index must be a *UNIQUE CLUSTERED* index.

Create an indexed view

1. Open the query editor in SSMS.

2. In the query editor, enter the following T-SQL code:

```
USE AdventureWorks2012;
GO
--Set the options to support indexed views
SET NUMERIC_ROUNDABORT OFF;
SET ANSI_PADDING, ANSI_WARNINGS, CONCAT_NULL_YIELDS_NULL, ARITHABORT,
  QUOTED_IDENTIFIER, ANSI_NULLS ON;
```

```
GO
--Check to see if a view with the same name already exists
IF(OBJECT_ID('Purchasing.vwPurchaseOrders')) IS NOT NULL
    DROP VIEW Purchasing.vwPurchaseOrders
GO
--Create the view
CREATE VIEW Purchasing.vwPurchaseOrders
WITH SCHEMABINDING
AS
SELECT
    poh.OrderDate,
    pod.ProductID,
    SUM(poh.TotalDue) TotalDue,
    COUNT_BIG(*) POCount
FROM Purchasing.PurchaseOrderHeader poh
INNER JOIN Purchasing.PurchaseOrderDetail pod
    ON poh.PurchaseOrderID = pod.PurchaseOrderID
GROUP BY poh.OrderDate, pod.ProductID
GO

--Add a unique clustered index
CREATE UNIQUE CLUSTERED INDEX CIX_vwPurchaseOrders_OrderDateProductID
ON Purchasing.vwPurchaseOrders(OrderDate, ProductID)
```

3. Execute the query.

Just as with the normal view, you can now write queries that will access this data. The advantage is that other queries that do not directly reference the view can be used by the optimizer to improve performance. The disadvantage is that you must maintain the index, and now this view consumes disk space. As the data in the underlying tables grows, so will the views. You are now essentially storing multiple copies of the same data.

Summary

Views offer advantages over tables, as they can be consumed in the same way as regular tables without incurring the cost, unless you are indexing the view. However, as you learned in this chapter, there are certain advantages to indexing views. On the other hand, since indexed views are materialized to disk, you can realize performance gains without making any changes to queries that use the base table. Regardless of your method, both regular views and indexed views create reusable code that can simplify query writing and improve data access.

User-defined functions

After completing this chapter, you will be able to

- Understand user-defined functions.

- Create, alter, and delete functions.

- Understand the difference between scalar and table-valued functions.

User-defined functions are similar to functions in other programming languages. Microsoft SQL Server 2012 allows you to create two types of functions: *scalar* and *table-valued*. These functions allow for a modular type of programming, where code and logic can be included inside the function. Other applications, routines, and database objects can then use the function. This approach also allows you to place standards and governance around how the code is developed and deployed.

Functions are T-SQL code that can accept parameters, perform logic and complex calculations, and return data. Scalar functions return a single value, and table-valued functions return a result set. Functions can be used as *CHECK CONSTRAINTS* in tables, by views, to define a column, in a *SELECT* statement, and in many other ways.

In this chapter, you will learn the differences between the two types of user-defined functions. You will create, alter, and drop these functions. In addition, you will use the functions in T-SQL queries. Finally, you will learn the differences between scalar and table-valued functions.

> ## Functions vs. stored procedures
>
> While functions are very similar to stored procedures, they differ in several ways. The most notable difference is that table-valued functions can be used in a *SELECT* statement, so they can be joined to tables, views, and even other functions. Stored procedures, however, cannot be used in this way.

Understanding user-defined scalar functions

A user-defined scalar function is a routine that returns a single value. These functions are often used to centralize the logic of a complex calculation that may be used by several other database or application resources. The syntax is as follows:

```
CREATE FUNCTION [ schema_name. ] function_name
( [ { @parameter_name [ AS ][ type_schema_name. ] parameter_data_type
  [ = default ] [ READONLY ] }
  [ ,...n ]
  ]
)
RETURNS return_data_type
  [ WITH <function_option> [ ,...n ] ]
  [ AS ]
  BEGIN
  function_body
  RETURN scalar_expression
  END
[ ; ]
```

Very few items are required in the preceding syntax. The only items that you must specify are *function_name*, the *RETURNS* data type, and the *BEGIN...END* code block that contains the actual T-SQL code.

Parameterizing functions

Although this section specifically discusses scalar functions, parameterizing applies to both types of functions. A parameter, in the scope of T-SQL function programming, is an input value that can be passed from the calling function into the code. A parameter can be set to a constant, a column from a table, an expression, and other values. Functions can contain three types of parameters:

- **Input** This is the value passed into the body of the function.

- **Optional** As the name indicates, this parameter is not required to execute the function.

- **Default** This parameter indicates when a value is assigned to the parameter during creation. In other words, it is a value that is specified when the function is created.

The following sample script demonstrates how to specify each parameter:

```
--Input Parameter
CREATE FUNCTION dbo.Input
@parameter1 int
…
--Optional Parameter
CREATE FUNCTION dbo.Optional
@parameter1 int = NULL
…
```

```
--Default Parameter
CREATE FUNCTION dbo.Default
@parameter1 int = 1
...
```

As you can see, if the input parameter does not have a default value, a value must be provided when the function is called. The optional parameter is set to *NULL* during creation so that when you use the function, it can be called without providing a value. Finally, the default parameter has a value assigned to it during creation, but when it is executed, you can specify *DEFAULT* in place of the parameter.

Create, alter, and drop a user-defined scalar function

1. Open Microsoft SQL Server Management Studio (SSMS) and connect to a server.

2. Open the Object Explorer window if it is not open already.

3. Expand the server node, and then expand the Databases folder.

4. Expand the AdventureWorks2012 database.

5. Expand the Programmability folder.

6. Right-click the Functions folder and select New | Scalar-valued Function.

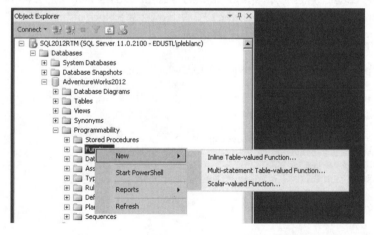

7. A query window opens with a template you can use as a starting point for creating the scalar function.

8. A few modifications have been added to the template. Open a new query window and paste in the following code.

```
USE AdventureWorks2012
-- ========================================================
SET ANSI_NULLS ON
GO
SET QUOTED_IDENTIFIER ON
GO
-- ========================================================
-- Author: Patrick LeBlanc
-- Create date: 7/8/2012
-- Description: Scalar function that will be used to return employee age
-- ========================================================
CREATE FUNCTION dbo.GetEmployeeAge
(
    @BirthDate datetime
)
RETURNS int
AS
BEGIN
    -- Declare the return variable here
    DECLARE @Age int
    -- Add the T-SQL statements to compute the return value here
    SELECT @Age = DATEDIFF(DAY, @BirthDate, GETDATE())
    -- Return the result of the function
    RETURN @Age
END
GO
```

The preceding code creates a scalar function that accepts a date value as a parameter and returns an integer that is calculated in the *BEGIN...END* code block of the code.

9. Execute the query.

10. Open a new query window and paste in the following code:

```
USE AdventureWorks2012;
SELECT TOP(10)
    p.FirstName, p.LastName, e.BirthDate,
  dbo.GetEmployeeAge(BirthDate) EmployeeAge
FROM HumanResources.Employee e
INNER JOIN Person.Person p
    ON e.BusinessEntityID = p.BusinessEntityID
```

11. Execute the query and view the result set.

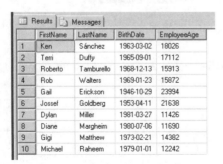

	FirstName	LastName	BirthDate	EmployeeAge
1	Ken	Sánchez	1963-03-02	18026
2	Terri	Duffy	1965-09-01	17112
3	Roberto	Tamburello	1968-12-13	15913
4	Rob	Walters	1969-01-23	15872
5	Gail	Erickson	1946-10-29	23994
6	Jossef	Goldberg	1953-04-11	21638
7	Dylan	Miller	1981-03-27	11426
8	Diane	Margheim	1980-07-06	11690
9	Gigi	Matthew	1973-02-21	14382
10	Michael	Raheem	1979-01-01	12242

User-defined scalar functions are used with the same syntax as the built-in functions discussed in Chapter 13, "Built-in scalar functions." If the parameter is optional, you can call the function without specifying a value. On the other hand, if a default value was assigned to the function, the function call would resemble the following syntax:

```
dbo.GetEmployeeAge(DEFAULT)
```

The keyword *DEFAULT* tells the SQL Server Engine to use the value that was assigned to the parameter when it was created.

A key advantage to using functions is that now instead of performing the calculation inline, a function can be used to return the age. This function can be reused by other programmers, providing a consistent mechanism for calculating the data. You may have noticed that the age is not calculated correctly—instead of returning the years, the function returns the days. Next, you'll alter the function to return years instead of days.

12. In Object Explorer, expand the Functions folder.

13. Expand the Scalar-valued Functions folder.

14. Right-click the dbo.GetEmployeeAge function and select Modify from the context menu.

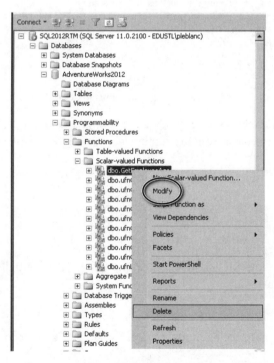

15. In the query editor, locate the *SELECT* statement and change the word *day* to **year**.

Your code will resemble the following. The bold section of the code denotes the change.

```
USE [AdventureWorks2012]
GO
/****** Object: UserDefinedFunction [dbo].[GetEmployeeAge] Script Date: 7/8/2012 1:03:20
PM
******/
SET ANSI_NULLS ON
GO
SET QUOTED_IDENTIFIER ON
GO
-- =============================================
-- Author: Patrick LeBlanc
-- Create date: 6/8/2012
-- Description: Scalar function that will be used to return employee age
-- =============================================
ALTER FUNCTION [dbo].[GetEmployeeAge]
(
    @BirthDate datetime
)
RETURNS int
AS
BEGIN
    -- Declare the return variable here
    DECLARE @Age int

    -- Add the T-SQL statements to compute the return value here
    SELECT @Age = DATEDIFF(Year, @BirthDate, GETDATE())

    -- Return the result of the function
    RETURN @Age
END
```

16. Rerun the query from step 10 and the results should display days instead of years.

17. To drop the function, execute the following T-SQL. (Alternatively, you can right-click the function in Object Explorer and select Delete from the context menu.)

```
DROP FUNCTION dbo.GetEmployeeAge
```

Executing scalar functions

Scalar functions can be called using two methods:

- Within a *SELECT* statement (as demonstrated in step 10 in the "Create, alter, and drop a user-defined scalar function" exercise)

- By using the *EXECUTE* keyword

Regardless of the method you use to select the output, if the parameter values are consistent, the results from either execution will be the same.

Calling scalar functions inline

As previously stated, a scalar function can be included in a *SELECT* statement. The parameters can be a column, constant, or expression.

```
SELECT dbo.GetEmployeeAge ('5/26/1972')
```

This is the typical use of a scalar function. This method is pretty straightforward and presents a challenge only when multiple types of parameters (input, optional, and default) are specified as parameters. If you have a single input parameter and any other combination of other types of parameters, you must ensure that the order in which they are passed corresponds to the order in which they are specified in the function. In the following function, there are two parameters:

- A default parameter

- An optional parameter

```
USE [AdventureWorks2012]
GO
IF(OBJECT_ID('dbo.GetEmployeeAge')) IS NOT NULL
    DROP FUNCTION dbo.GetEmployeeAge
GO
CREATE FUNCTION [dbo].[GetEmployeeAge]
(
    @BirthDate datetime = '5/26/1972', --DEFAULT
    @Temp datetime = NULL --OPTIONAL
)
RETURNS int
AS
BEGIN
    -- Declare the return variable here
    DECLARE @Age int
    -- Add the T-SQL statements to compute the return value here
    SELECT @Age = DATEDIFF(Year, @BirthDate, GETDATE())
    -- Return the result of the function
    RETURN @Age
END
```

In the following code snippet, the first *SELECT* statement calls the function with a single parameter. It succeeds because the second parameter is an optional input parameter. Assigning the *NULL* value to the second parameter tells SQL Server that it is optional. The second *SELECT* statement has two parameters. Since both values are provided, it succeeds. The only challenge now is to make sure that you are passing the values in the correct order.

```
--Single Input Parameter
SELECT dbo.GetEmployeeAge('5/26/1972')
--First parameter is Default and second is Input
SELECT dbo.GetEmployeeAge('5/26/1972', '1/10/1972')
```

As a best practice, you should always supply a value, regardless of the type. The following code snippet uses the function created at the beginning of this section.

```
--Input and Optional Parameters
SELECT dbo.GetEmployeeAge('5/26/1972', NULL)
--Default and Input Parameters
SELECT dbo.GetEmployeeAge(DEFAULT, '1/10/1972')
```

In the first line of code, the function accepts an input and optional parameter. Notice that an actual date is provided for the first parameter because it is an input parameter. Because the second parameter is optional, a *NULL* is specified. This tells SQL Server not to specify a value.

On the next line, the first parameter is a default parameter and the second is an input. Because *DEFAULT* is specified as the first value, SQL Server will use the value assigned to that parameter, and the date value will be assigned to the input parameter.

Calling scalar functions using the *EXECUTE* keyword

In the previous section, you learned how to call a scalar function inline. A scalar function can also be called using the *EXECUTE* keyword, which is discussed in more detail in Chapter 17, "Stored procedures." For now, it is sufficient to know that you can use this keyword to execute scalar functions. To obtain the output of a scalar function using the *EXECUTE* keyword, you must declare a variable that will hold the output:

```
USE AdventureWorks2012;
GO
DECLARE @Age int;
EXECUTE @Age = dbo.GetEmployeeAge @BirthDate = '5/26/1972'
SELECT @Age;
```

In the previous script, the *@Age* variable is declared. Then, using the *EXECUTE* keyword, the function is called, assigning the return value to the variable. Finally, a *SELECT* statement is issued to obtain the results.

Another thing to point out is that the parameter name is not required. However, if you specify multiple parameters of different types, as a best practice, you should explicitly specify the names. This ensures that the correct value is assigned to the appropriate parameter. For example, assume that a function has been created that requires two date parameters. If the parameter values are specified in the wrong order, the results could be incorrect, but the function would still successfully execute, potentially returning misleading data. Specifying the parameter names helps to mitigate that problem.

To complicate things further, assume that you have a function that has an input parameter, a parameter that is optional, and a parameter that has a default value. At a minimum, you must include the parameter name of the input parameter. If you want to override or specify a value for the other two types, you must also include the parameter names.

Regardless of the types of parameters and the method of execution, the key is to specify a value for each parameter and ensure that the order of the values corresponds to the order of the parameters.

Understanding table-valued functions

Table-valued functions come in two types:

- Inline

- Multistatement

The inline function simply returns a result set, and the multistatement function offers the ability to include logic within the body of the function. Both return a complete result, similar to selecting from a table or view, but the multistatement function can perform logic and return data. Sample syntax for both is as follows:

```
--Inline Table-Valued Function Syntax
CREATE FUNCTION [ schema_name. ] function_name
( [ { @parameter_name [ AS ] [ type_schema_name. ] parameter_data_type
 [ = default ] [ READONLY ] }
 [ ,...n ]
 ]
)
RETURNS TABLE
 [ WITH <function_option> [ ,...n ] ]
 [ AS ]
 RETURN [ ( ] select_stmt [ ) ]
[ ; ]


--Multistatement Table-Valued Function Syntax
CREATE FUNCTION [ schema_name. ] function_name
( [ { @parameter_name [ AS ] [ type_schema_name. ] parameter_data_type
 [ = default ] [READONLY] }
 [ ,...n ]
 ]
)
RETURNS @return_variable TABLE <table_type_definition>
 [ WITH <function_option> [ ,...n ] ]
 [ AS ]
 BEGIN
 function_body
 RETURN
 END
[ ; ]
```

As with the scalar function, most of the code is optional. What you should notice here is that both can return a table. The inline function returns only the result of a *SELECT* as its set, whereas the multistatement function uses a table variable that can be defined. The rows of data are added to the table as per the code and can be manipulated before the data is returned. This is unlike the inline table-valued function, where any data manipulations or filters must be done in the actual query.

Create an inline table-valued function

1. Open SSMS and connect to a server.

2. Open the Object Explorer window if it is not already open.

3. Expand the server node, and then expand the Databases folder.

4. Expand the AdventureWorks2012 database.

5. Expand the Programmability folder.

6. Right-click the folder labeled Functions and select New | Inline Table-valued Function.

   A query window opens with a template you can use as a starting point for creating the scalar function. A few modifications have been added to the template.

7. Open a new query window and paste in the following code:

```
USE AdventureWorks2012;
SET ANSI_NULLS ON
GO
SET QUOTED_IDENTIFIER ON
GO
-- =============================================
-- Author: Patrick LeBlanc
-- Create date: 6/8/2012
-- Description: Returns the line items for a given orderid
-- =============================================
CREATE FUNCTION dbo.GetOrderDetails
(
     @SalesOrderID int
)
RETURNS TABLE
AS
RETURN
(
    SELECT
        sod.SalesOrderID,
        sod.SalesOrderDetailID,
        sod.CarrierTrackingNumber,
        p.Name ProductName,
        so.Description
    FROM Sales.SalesOrderDetail sod
    INNER JOIN Production.Product p
        ON sod.ProductID = p.ProductID
    INNER JOIN Sales.SpecialOffer so
        ON sod.SpecialOfferID = so.SpecialOfferID
    WHERE
        sod.SalesOrderID = @SalesOrderID
)
GO
```

The inline table-valued function accepts one parameter, SalesOrderID. This parameter is used in the function to limit the result set to only rows that are associated with that value. Inside the function is a single T-SQL statement that is limited by the parameter.

8. Execute the query.

9. Open a new query window and paste in the following code:

```
USE AdventureWorks2012;
SELECT *
FROM dbo.GetOrderDetails(43659);
```

10. Execute the query and review the results.

Using table-valued functions

A table-valued function can be used in the same way as a table or view is used in a *SELECT* statement, as demonstrated in step 10 of the "Create an inline table-valued function" exercise. You can join to this function as if it were a table, or you can insert the results into a table variable or temporary table.

More important, the use and types of parameters are the same as those used with scalar functions. You should take care when mingling input, default, and optional parameters.

```
SELECT *
FROM dbo.GetOrderDetails(43659, DEFAULT, NULL)
```

In the preceding script, the function accepts all three parameter types—input, default, and optional—and in that order. If you tried to execute the function without specifying *NULL*, it would fail. Therefore, if you have default values, you must either supply a value or use the *DEFAULT* keyword. Also, if you have an optional parameter, you must specify a value or supply *NULL*.

You follow the same steps to alter or drop the function as when altering or dropping the scalar function.

Limitations of functions

Just as with any object inside SQL Server, user-defined functions have limitations. One limitation is that you cannot use a *TRY...CATCH* block inside a function. Therefore, you have to create your own error-handling mechanisms to elegantly handle errors. A limitation specific to scalar functions is that they cannot return *text*, *ntext*, *image*, *cursor*, or *timestamp* data types. Finally, user-defined functions cannot be used to modify the database state. Using functions in a *SELECT* statement could adversely affect the performance of the query. This is because the function will be called once for every row returned. Therefore, be cautious using complex functions when returning large result sets.

Summary

This chapter covered the two types of user-defined functions available in Microsoft SQL Server 2012: scalar and table-valued. They both offer modular programming to developers; however, their primary purposes are different. Scalar functions return a single value, whereas table-valued functions return a complete set. As you learned in this chapter, there are some limitations to using functions, but they offer clear benefits in that they are stored in the database and can be reused.

Stored procedures

After completing this chapter, you will be able to

- Understand stored procedures.

- Work with stored procedures.

- Create, alter, and delete stored procedures.

- Use different types of parameters with stored procedures.

Stored procedures are a set of SQL statements (one or more) typically grouped together to perform a specific routine. Stored procedures can be created in any user-defined database and system database except the resource database. They are comparable to multistatement functions, but they boast features and flexibilities that are not possible within functions. Some of the benefits of using stored procedures are as follows:

- They offer improved performance because of compiled code.

- They are easy to maintain because changes are central instead of inline with code.

- Since database operations can be performed inside the stored procedures, they provide a strong level of security. Instead of access being granted to the underlying object, permission can be granted only to the stored procedure. Essentially, stored procedures create a level of abstraction for permissions—instead of the user being granted *SELECT, INSERT, UPDATE,* or *DELETE* rights, the user can be granted *EXECUTE* rights to a stored procedure.

Microsoft SQL Server 2012 has four types of stored procedures:

- User-defined

- System

- Temporary

- Extended user-defined

The extended user-defined stored procedures have been replaced with common language runtime (CLR) procedures. If you want more information on CLR stored procedures, visit the "CLR stored procedure" section of SQL Server Books Online.

In this chapter, you will focus on user-defined stored procedures. The basic syntax for creating a stored procedure is follows:

```
-- Stored Procedure Syntax
CREATE { PROC | PROCEDURE } [schema_name.] procedure_name [ ; number ]
 [ { @parameter [ type_schema_name. ] data_type }
 [ VARYING ] [ = default ] [ OUT | OUTPUT ] [READONLY]
 ] [ ,...n ]
[ WITH <procedure_option> [ ,...n ] ]
[ FOR REPLICATION ]
AS { [ BEGIN ] sql_statement [;] [ ...n ] [ END ] }
[;]
<procedure_option> ::=
 [ ENCRYPTION ]
 [ RECOMPILE ]
 [ EXECUTE AS Clause ]
```

When creating a stored procedure, similar to a function, you are able to set several options. However, only the *procedure_name* and the actual *sql_statement*(s) are required.

Working with stored procedures

Basically, you can create stored procedures only by using T-SQL. However, just as with functions, Microsoft SQL Server Management Studio (SSMS) provides templates you can use as a starting point.

Create stored procedures

1. Open SSMS and connect to a server.

2. If the Object Explorer window is not already open, open it.

3. Expand the server node, and expand the Databases folder.

4. Expand the AdventureWorks2012 database.

5. Expand the Programmability folder.

6. Right-click the Stored Procedures folder and select New Stored Procedure.

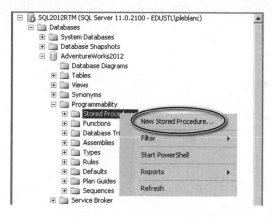

7. A query window will open with a template you can use as a starting point for creating the stored procedure. A few modifications have been added to the template.

8. Open a new query window and paste in the following code:

```
USE AdventureWorks2012;
SET ANSI_NULLS ON
GO
SET QUOTED_IDENTIFIER ON
GO
-- =============================================
-- Author: Patrick LeBlanc
-- Create date: 6/9/2012
-- Description: <Description,,> Get PurchaseOrder Information
-- =============================================
CREATE PROCEDURE dbo.PurchaseOrderInformation
AS
BEGIN
    SELECT
        poh.PurchaseOrderID, pod.PurchaseOrderDetailID,
        poh.OrderDate, poh.TotalDue, pod.ReceivedQty, p.Name ProductName
    FROM Purchasing.PurchaseOrderHeader poh
    INNER JOIN Purchasing.PurchaseOrderDetail pod
        ON poh.PurchaseOrderID = pod.PurchaseOrderID
    INNER JOIN Production.Product p
        ON pod.ProductID = p.ProductID
END
GO
```

In the preceding code, a simple stored procedure has been created that does not expect any parameters and contains a single T-SQL statement.

9. Execute the query.

10. In Object Explorer, expand the Stored Procedures folder. dbo.PurchaseOrderInformation will appear in the list of available stored procedures.

Using the EXECUTE keyword

To execute a stored procedure using T-SQL, you use the *EXECUTE* keyword. The syntax is as follows:

```
EXECUTE | EXEC procedure_name [parameter1, parameter2, n…]
```

Note that you can use *EXECUTE* or *EXEC*. This keyword has been enhanced in SQL Server 2012. In the latest release of SQL Server, you can change the names and data types of each column in the result set or redefine the result set. The syntax is as follows:

```
EXECUTE | EXEC procedure_name [parameter1, parameter2, n…]
WITH RESULT SETS
(
    ( [column_definition1, column_definition2, n…])
)
```

To change the result set, you issue the *EXECUTE* command as normal, but you add a *WITH RESULT SETS* statement, and within the parentheses you provide a new column definition for each column in the result set.

Execute stored procedures and redefine result sets

1. Open the query editor in SSMS.

2. In the query editor, enter the following T-SQL code:

```
USE AdventureWorks2012
EXEC dbo.PurchaseOrderInformation
```

3. Execute the query and review the results.

	PurchaseOrderID	PurchaseOrderDetailD	OrderDate	TotalDue	ReceivedQty	ProductName
1	1	1	2005-05-17 00:00:00.000	222.1492	3.00	Adjustable Race
2	2	2	2005-05-17 00:00:00.000	300.6721	3.00	Thin-Jam Hex Nut 9
3	2	3	2005-05-17 00:00:00.000	300.6721	3.00	Thin-Jam Hex Nut 10
4	3	4	2005-05-17 00:00:00.000	9776.2665	550.00	Seat Post
5	4	5	2005-05-17 00:00:00.000	189.0395	2.00	Headset Ball Bearings
6	5	6	2005-05-31 00:00:00.000	22539.0165	550.00	HL Road Rim
7	6	7	2005-05-31 00:00:00.000	16164.0229	468.00	Touring Rim
8	7	8	2005-05-31 00:00:00.000	64847.5328	550.00	LL Crankarm
9	7	9	2005-05-31 00:00:00.000	64847.5328	550.00	ML Crankarm
10	7	10	2005-05-31 00:00:00.000	64847.5328	550.00	HL Crankarm
11	8	11	2005-05-31 00:00:00.000	766.1827	3.00	External Lock Washer 3
12	8	12	2005-05-31 00:00:00.000	766.1827	3.00	External Lock Washer 4
13	8	13	2005-05-31 00:00:00.000	766.1827	3.00	External Lock Washer 9
14	8	14	2005-05-31 00:00:00.000	766.1827	3.00	External Lock Washer 5
15	8	15	2005-05-31 00:00:00.000	766.1827	3.00	External Lock Washer 7
16	9	16	2006-01-14 00:00:00.000	767.0528	3.00	Thin-Jam Lock Nut 9
17	9	17	2006-01-14 00:00:00.000	767.0528	3.00	Thin-Jam Lock Nut 10
18	9	18	2006-01-14 00:00:00.000	767.0528	3.00	Thin-Jam Lock Nut 1
19	9	19	2006-01-14 00:00:00.000	767.0528	3.00	Thin-Jam Lock Nut 2

This is an abbreviated result set. The query within the stored procedure actually returns all the data from the referenced tables. Typically, when you develop a stored procedure, the result is filtered down so that it returns a set that is built to solve a specific problem. This is usually accomplished using parameters and additional logic. Details on how to do this are discussed in the next section on parameters. However, before you look at parameters, you'll redefine the result set using *EXEC*.

4. Open the query editor in SSMS and enter the following T-SQL code:

```
USE AdventureWorks2012;
EXEC dbo.PurchaseOrderInformation
WITH RESULT SETS
(
    (
        [Purchase Order ID] int,
        [Purchase Order Detail ID] int,
        [Order Date] datetime,
        [Total Due] Money,
        [Received Quantity] float,
        [Product Name] varchar(50)
    )
)
```

In the preceding query, the *EXEC* keyword is used for a standard stored procedure execution. However, the columns and data types have been changed to make the column names user-friendly.

5. Execute the query and review the results.

	Purchase Order ID	Purchase Order Detail ID	Order Date	Total Due	Received Quantity	Product Name
1	1	1	2005-05-17 00:00:00.000	222.1492	3	Adjustable Race
2	2	2	2005-05-17 00:00:00.000	300.6721	3	Thin-Jam Hex Nut 9
3	2	3	2005-05-17 00:00:00.000	300.6721	3	Thin-Jam Hex Nut 10
4	3	4	2005-05-17 00:00:00.000	9776.2665	550	Seat Post
5	4	5	2005-05-17 00:00:00.000	189.0395	2	Headset Ball Bearings
6	5	6	2005-05-31 00:00:00.000	22539.0165	550	HL Road Rim
7	6	7	2005-05-31 00:00:00.000	16164.0229	468	Touring Rim
8	7	8	2005-05-31 00:00:00.000	64847.5328	550	LL Crankarm
9	7	9	2005-05-31 00:00:00.000	64847.5328	550	ML Crankarm
10	7	10	2005-05-31 00:00:00.000	64847.5328	550	HL Crankarm
11	8	11	2005-05-31 00:00:00.000	766.1827	3	External Lock Washer 3
12	8	12	2005-05-31 00:00:00.000	766.1827	3	External Lock Washer 4
13	8	13	2005-05-31 00:00:00.000	766.1827	3	External Lock Washer 9
14	8	14	2005-05-31 00:00:00.000	766.1827	3	External Lock Washer 5
15	8	15	2005-05-31 00:00:00.000	766.1827	3	External Lock Washer 7

Notice the new column names in the preceding image as compared to the image in step 3.

Parameterizing stored procedures

Similar to functions, stored procedures can include parameters as part of their code. Creating a stored procedure with parameters allows the calling programs to pass values into the procedure. Parameters in stored procedures differ from those in functions in that you can specify direction, whether it is an input or output parameter. In other words, you can specify whether the parameter will accept a value (input) or whether it will return a value (output). You can use *OUTPUT* parameters to assign a value produced by a stored procedure directly to a variable or an application in the execution context.

Stored procedures can have optional and default parameters similar to functions. How and what you assign to the values are slightly different, but the meanings and how they are syntactically specified are the same.

If your stored procedure contains a default parameter, unlike with a function you are not required to supply the *DEFAULT* keyword. If you simply execute the stored procedure using the *EXEC* keyword, the assigned value will be used at run time. The same applies if you include an optional parameter. As a best practice, it is recommended that you specify each parameter name and assign a value to each. This ensures that you are assigning the correct value to appropriate parameter, as follows:

```
EXEC [dbo].[PurchaseOrderInformation] @parameter1 = 1, @parameter2 = default, @parameter3 = null
```

The example stored procedure includes an input, default, and optional parameter. To protect against any misalignment of values and parameters, each parameter is specified with a corresponding value.

As previously mentioned, in addition to the types of parameters that functions and stored procedures share, stored procedures also can change the direction of a parameter to *OUTPUT*. This means that instead of assigning a value to the parameter when the stored procedure is executed, a value will be returned and can be accessed via that parameter.

```
USE AdventureWorks2012;
GO
--Create Proc with OUTPUT param
CREATE PROC dbo.SampleOutput
@Parameter2 int OUTPUT
as
SELECT @Parameter2 = 10
--Execute Proc with OUTPUT param
DECLARE @HoldParameter2 INT
EXEC dbo.SampleOutput
     @HoldParameter2 OUTPUT
SELECT @HoldParameter2
```

In the first part of the preceding code, a stored procedure is created that has a single output parameter. The output parameter includes the *OUTPUT* keyword. The stored procedure contains a single T-SQL statement that assigns 10 to the parameter.

In the second part of the code, a variable is declared that will hold the value of the output parameter. The *EXEC* keyword is used to execute the stored procedure. In addition, the declared variable is specified including the *OUTPUT* keyword. Finally, a *SELECT* statement is issued to display the value of the output.

Alter a stored procedure to add parameters

1. Open SSMS and connect to a server.

2. If the Object Explorer window is not open, open it.

3. Expand the server node, and then expand the Databases folder.

4. Expand the AdventureWorks2012 database.

5. Expand the Programmability folder.

6. Expand the Stored Procedures folder.

7. Locate the dbo.PurchaseOrderInformation stored procedure, right-click it, and select Modify. A new query window will open that contains the script for the stored procedure. You can then modify the stored procedure.

8. Open a new query window and enter the following T-SQL:

```
USE AdventureWorks2012;
GO
ALTER PROCEDURE [dbo].[PurchaseOrderInformation]
@EmployeeID int,
@OrderYear int = 2005
AS
BEGIN
    SELECT
        poh.PurchaseOrderID, pod.PurchaseOrderDetailID,
```

```
            poh.OrderDate, poh.TotalDue, pod.ReceivedQty, p.Name ProductName
FROM Purchasing.PurchaseOrderHeader poh
INNER JOIN Purchasing.PurchaseOrderDetail pod
        ON poh.PurchaseOrderID = pod.PurchaseOrderID
INNER JOIN Production.Product p
        ON pod.ProductID = p.ProductID
WHERE
        poh.EmployeeID = @EmployeeID AND
        YEAR(poh.OrderDate) = @OrderYear
END
```

In the preceding stored procedure, two parameters were specified: input and default. At the end of the T-SQL query, a *WHERE* clause was included that limits the result based on the values of the two parameters.

9. Execute the query.

10. Open a new query window, and enter the following T-SQL code:

```
USE AdventureWorks2012;
EXEC [dbo].[PurchaseOrderInformation]
    @EmployeeID = 258;
```

Only the input parameter has been specified, which is fine because the other parameter has a default value. While the query will succeed, as a best practice you should always specify a value for all parameters.

```
USE AdventureWorks2012;
EXEC [dbo].[PurchaseOrderInformation]
    @EmployeeID = 258,
    @OrderYear = 2006;
```

In the previous code, the default value for the OrderYear parameter has been overwritten with 2006.

11. Execute the query and review the results.

	PurchaseOrderID	PurchaseOrderDetailID	OrderDate	TotalDue	ReceivedQty	ProductName
1	11	24	2006-01-14 00:00:00.000	553.8221	3.00	Lock Nut 5
2	11	25	2006-01-14 00:00:00.000	553.8221	3.00	Lock Nut 6
3	11	26	2006-01-14 00:00:00.000	553.8221	3.00	Lock Nut 16
4	11	27	2006-01-14 00:00:00.000	553.8221	3.00	Lock Nut 17
5	31	77	2006-02-08 00:00:00.000	157.3647	3.00	Keyed Washer
6	41	95	2006-02-16 00:00:00.000	24880.9811	550.00	HL Mountain Seat/Saddle
7	51	116	2006-02-20 00:00:00.000	108.2513	3.00	LL Nipple
8	51	117	2006-02-20 00:00:00.000	108.2513	3.00	HL Nipple
9	61	136	2006-02-24 00:00:00.000	560.3312	3.00	External Lock Washer 3
10	61	137	2006-02-24 00:00:00.000	560.3312	3.00	External Lock Washer 4
11	61	138	2006-02-24 00:00:00.000	560.3312	3.00	External Lock Washer 9
12	61	139	2006-02-24 00:00:00.000	560.3312	3.00	External Lock Washer 5
13	71	161	2006-02-25 00:00:00.000	2214.0703	3.00	Chainring Bolts
14	71	162	2006-02-25 00:00:00.000	2214.0703	3.00	Chainring Nut
15	71	163	2006-02-25 00:00:00.000	2214.0703	60.00	Chainring
16	81	182	2006-03-12 00:00:00.000	618.8078	3.00	Thin-Jam Hex Nut 1
17	81	183	2006-03-12 00:00:00.000	618.8078	3.00	Thin-Jam Hex Nut 2
18	81	184	2006-03-12 00:00:00.000	618.8078	3.00	Thin-Jam Hex Nut 15
19	81	185	2006-03-12 00:00:00.000	618.8078	3.00	Thin-Jam Hex Nut 16

This is only a subset of the actual data set that is returned, but the thing to pay attention to is that the year for every OrderDate is 2006.

Dropping stored procedures

There are two ways to remove a stored a procedure from a database: using SSMS or using T-SQL. With T-SQL, you issue the following statement:

```
DROP PROCEDURE schema_name.procedure_name
```

If you want to accomplish the same task with SSMS, you'll need to follow a few steps.

Remove a stored procedure

1. Open SSMS and connect to a server.

2. Open Object Explorer if it is not already open.

3. Expand the server node, and then expand the Databases folder.

4. Expand the AdventureWorks2012 database.

5. Expand the Programmability folder.

6. Expand the Stored Procedures folder.

7. Locate the dbo.PurchaseOrderInformation stored procedure, right-click it, and select Delete.

Summary

This chapter discussed the stored procedure database object. Stored procedures are among the most robust programming tools available in the Microsoft SQL Server database. As you learned in this chapter, you can use stored procedures in several ways to accomplish many things. Typically, programmers centralize the data access of an application inside of stored procedures and include the actual logic in the code. In some cases, the two are mingled together within the stored procedure; it really is just a matter of preference.

Data manipulation triggers

After completing this chapter, you will be able to

- Explain the different types of triggers.

- Create, alter, and drop triggers.

- Explain practical uses of triggers.

Data manipulation triggers are sets of T-SQL statements that perform a specific action. They are often referred to as a special kind of stored procedure. Unlike stored procedures, triggers are executed only when a user or application attempts to modify data using Data Manipulation Language (DML). DML includes *INSERT*s, *UPDATE*s, and *DELETE*s against views and tables.

In this chapter, you will look at different types of DML triggers. You will learn how to create, modify, and drop triggers. Finally, you will walk through the steps to enable or disable an existing trigger.

Types of triggers

Triggers, like most objects contained within a Microsoft SQL Server database, have multiple types. There are three types: *AFTER*, *INSTEAD OF*, and *CLR* triggers. This chapter focuses on *AFTER* and *INSTEAD OF* triggers.

As its name suggests, the *AFTER* trigger is executed after a DML event and is the default action for a new trigger if a type is not specified. It is the most common type of trigger used. For example, suppose an application issues an *INSERT* statement that adds a single row to a table that has an *AFTER* trigger. Once the insert completes, then the code inside the trigger will execute, but within the same transaction as the triggering insert. This is a very important fact to remember. It is the reason that triggers can execute with relational integrity, but it may also reduce performance. The original transaction will not commit or roll back until the trigger has also committed or rolled back.

If an *INSERT* is executed on a table, the *INSTEAD OF* trigger will execute in place of the actual *INSERT*. In other words, the *INSERT* is not run and the code within the *DML* trigger is executed instead, as part of the triggering transaction.

You can use the following pseudocode sample script as a starting point for creating a *DML* trigger:

```
CREATE TRIGGER [ schema_name . ]trigger_name
ON { table | view }
[ WITH <dml_trigger_option> [ ,...n ] ]
{ FOR | AFTER | INSTEAD OF }
{ [ INSERT ] [ , ] [ UPDATE ] [ , ] [ DELETE ] }
[ NOT FOR REPLICATION ]
AS { sql_statement  [ ; ] [ ,...n ] | EXTERNAL NAME <method specifier [ ; ] > }
<dml_trigger_option> ::=
     [ ENCRYPTION ]
     [ EXECUTE AS Clause ]
<method_specifier> ::=
     assembly_name.class_name.method_name
```

 Note Constraints, including foreign-key cascade operations, are checked prior to executing either type of trigger. If it is an *INSTEAD OF* trigger, the constraint is checked after the trigger completes. If it is an *AFTER* trigger, the constraint is checked prior to executing the trigger. Regardless of the type of trigger, when the trigger event is rolled back, it causes a constraint violation. For *INSTEAD OF* triggers, the entire event is undone or rolled back, and in the case of *FOR* triggers, nothing is executed.

Creating triggers

As mentioned, triggers are created on tables and views. Even though they are typically considered to be special kinds of stored procedures, you will not see a folder for them under the Programmability section in Object Explorer for a given database. You need to expand a table and view the triggers there, as demonstrated in the next procedure.

View triggers on tables

1. Open SQL Server Management Studio (SSMS) and connect to a server.

2. Open Object Explorer if it is not open already.

3. Expand the server node, and then expand the Databases folder.

4. Expand the AdventureWorks2012 database.

5. Expand the Tables folder.

6. Expand the HumanResources.Employee table.

7. Expand the Triggers folder. You will see the dEmployee trigger.

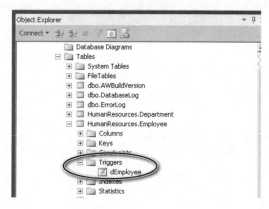

Since a trigger can be associated to a specific view and table, you will need to go to this location to find a list of triggers on an object.

Create a *FOR* trigger using T-SQL

1. Open SSMS and connect to a server.

2. Open Object Explorer if it is not already open.

3. Expand the server node, and then expand the Databases folder.

4. Expand the AdventureWorks2012 database.

5. Expand the Tables folder.

6. Expand the HumanResources.Department table.

7. Right-click the Triggers folder and select New Trigger.

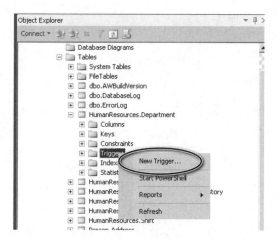

A new query window will open that contains a trigger template script. You can use this script as a good starting point for creating a trigger.

8. Open a new query window and enter the following T-SQL code:

```
USE AdventureWorks2012;
GO
CREATE TRIGGER HumanResources.iCheckModifedDate
ON HumanResources.Department
FOR INSERT
AS
BEGIN
    DECLARE @modifieddate datetime, @DepartmentID int
    SELECT @modifieddate = modifieddate, @DepartmentID = departmentid FROM inserted;

    IF(DATEDIFF(Day, @modifiedDate, getdate()) > 0)
        BEGIN
            UPDATE HumanResources.Department
            SET ModifiedDate = GETDATE()
            WHERE DepartmentID = @DepartmentID
        END
END
```

9. Execute the query.

The preceding query creates a trigger that checks the modified date. It ensures that during the insert of a new department, the modified date is the current day. If it is not, the row is updated, setting *ModifiedDate* to the current date and time.

10. Open a new query editor and enter the following T-SQL code:

```
USE AdventureWorks2012;
INSERT INTO HumanResources.Department
VALUES('Executive Marketing', 'Executive General and Administration', '2/12/2011');

SELECT *
FROM HumanResources.Department
```

11. Execute the query and review the results.

	DepartmentID	Name	GroupName	ModifiedDate
1	1	Engineering	Research and Development	2002-06-01 00:00:00.000
2	2	Tool Design	Research and Development	2002-06-01 00:00:00.000
3	3	Sales	Sales and Marketing	2002-06-01 00:00:00.000
4	4	Marketing	Sales and Marketing	2002-06-01 00:00:00.000
5	5	Purchasing	Inventory Management	2002-06-01 00:00:00.000
6	6	Research and Development	Research and Development	2002-06-01 00:00:00.000
7	7	Production	Manufacturing	2002-06-01 00:00:00.000
8	8	Production Control	Manufacturing	2002-06-01 00:00:00.000
9	9	Human Resources	Executive General and Administration	2002-06-01 00:00:00.000
10	10	Finance	Executive General and Administration	2002-06-01 00:00:00.000
11	11	Information Services	Executive General and Administration	2002-06-01 00:00:00.000
12	12	Document Control	Quality Assurance	2002-06-01 00:00:00.000
13	13	Quality Assurance	Quality Assurance	2002-06-01 00:00:00.000
14	14	Facilities and Maintenance	Executive General and Administration	2002-06-01 00:00:00.000
15	15	Shipping and Receiving	Inventory Management	2002-06-01 00:00:00.000
16	16	Executive	Executive General and Administration	2002-06-01 00:00:00.000
17	17	Payroll	Executive General and Administration	2012-08-11 12:54:13.533
18	18	International Sales	Sales and Marketing	2012-08-11 12:54:13.533
19	19	Media Control Europe	Quality Assurance	2012-09-11 14:00:12.660

In the last row of the result set, you will see the newly inserted row. Notice that the modified date is not the value that was specified in the insert. It should be the current date and time of the insert.

> **Note** In the code of the trigger, specifically the *SELECT* statement, a logical table called *inserted* is referenced. There are actually two tables of this type—the second table is deleted. These tables are available within the context of the trigger. You cannot modify the structure or contents of these tables. The inserted table stores a copy of a row or rows that were inserted, or a copy of the new values for rows that were updated. During an update, the inserted table stores the new or updated data. The second (deleted) table stores the data before an update and a row or rows that were deleted in a *DELETE* statement.

Altering triggers

As with all other programmable objects in SQL Server, a trigger can be modified only using T-SQL. A situation may arise in which you will need to change the logic inside the trigger. Instead of dropping and re-creating the trigger, you can use the *ALTER* keyword to quickly modify the trigger.

Alter an existing trigger

1. Open SSMS and connect to a server.

2. Open Object Explorer if it is not already open.

3. Expand the server node, and then expand the Databases folder.

4. Expand the AdventureWorks2012 database.

5. Expand the Tables folder.

6. Expand the HumanResources.Department table.

7. Expand the Triggers folder.

8. Right-click the iCheckModifiedDate trigger and select Modify from the context menu.

   The newly created trigger will appear in a new query window.

9. Locate the following statement:

   ```
   SET ModifiedDate = GETDATE()
   ```

10. Change the preceding statement to the following:

    ```
    SET ModifiedDate = DATEADD(day, -1, GETDATE() )
    ```

11. Execute the query.

12. Open a new query window and enter the following T-SQL code:

    ```
    USE AdventureWorks2012;
    INSERT INTO HumanResources.Department
    VALUES('Executive Purchasing', 'Executive General and Administration', '2/12/2011');

    SELECT *
    FROM HumanResources.Department
    ```

13. Execute the query and review the results.

    In the last row of the results, you should see a modified date that is set to yesterday's date.

Dropping triggers

To drop triggers, you can use either T-SQL or SSMS. To drop a trigger using T-SQL, use the following code:

```
DROP TRIGGER HumanResources.iCheckModifedDate
```

To drop a trigger using SSMS, follow the steps in this section.

Drop a trigger using SSMS

1. Open SSMS and connect to a server.

2. Open Object Explorer if it is not already open.

3. Expand the server node, and then expand the Databases folder.

4. Expand the AdventureWorks2012 database.

5. Expand the Tables folder.

6. Expand the HumanResources.Department table.

7. Expand the Triggers folder.

8. Right-click iCheckModifiedDate and select Delete from the context menu.

   This action removes the trigger from the table.

Enabling and disabling triggers

In some cases, you may not want to delete a trigger, but you want to stop it from firing during a large DML operation or for testing purposes. SQL Server provides you with the ability to disable a trigger, and once you have completed the task, you can enable the trigger again. You can do so using T-SQL or SSMS.

To disable or enable a trigger using T-SQL, use the following code:

```
USE AdventureWorks2012;
--Disable a Trigger with T-SQL
DISABLE TRIGGER HumanResources.iCheckModifedDate
ON HumanResources.Department;

--Enable a Trigger with T-SQL
ENABLE TRIGGER HumanResources.iCheckModifedDate
ON HumanResources.Department;
```

To disable or enable a trigger using SSMS, follow the steps in this section.

Disable and enable triggers using SSMS

1. Open SSMS and connect to a server.

2. Open Object Explorer if it is not already open.

3. Expand the server node, and then expand the Databases folder.

4. Expand the AdventureWorks2012 database.

5. Expand the Tables folder.

6. Expand the HumanResources.Department table.

7. Expand the Triggers folder.

8. Right-click iCheckModifiedDate and select Disable from the context menu. The Disable Triggers dialog box appears.

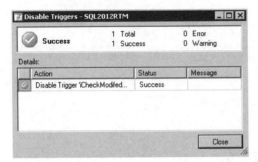

The trigger is now disabled and will not execute in the event of an insert.

9. Right-click the trigger again and select Enable to enable the trigger.

Summary

In this chapter, you learned about triggers, which are associated to a specific table or view. In the event of a DML operation on that table or view, the trigger will execute, performing some action. There are three types of triggers: *AFTER*, *INSTEAD OF*, and *CLR*. This chapter focused on the *AFTER* and *INSTEAD OF* triggers and their capabilities.

SQL Server replication

Replication

After completing this chapter, you will be able to

- Understand the different types of replication.

- Understand the different replication agents.

- Configure and monitor replication.

Moving data from one server to another or from one data center to another is something you will frequently do when working with enterprise data. The specific reasons vary, but typically there is a need to have a secondary copy for reporting, backup, and possibly disaster recovery. Regardless of the reason for moving the data, a viable solution should be available that will allow a seamless and consistent procedure.

Replication is a group of Microsoft SQL Server 2012 technologies that you can use to copy and move data and database objects from one database to another. Three primary types of replication are discussed in this chapter. The type you choose depends on several factors, which could include data size, frequency of movement, hardware, and location of computers. These are not the only factors to consider, but they are among the most important.

There are typically three types of servers in a replication topology:

- **Publisher** Database server that contains the source data.

- **Subscriber** Database server where the data and database objects are copied.

- **Distributor** Database server that stores changes. This information is stored in a database called the *distribution* database.

Consistency of the data is maintained by a replication synchronization process.

In this chapter, you will learn about the different types of replication. A brief discussion of the replication components is provided, and you will be introduced to each component at a high level. You will then walk through the process of configuring replication. Finally, you will learn how to monitor replication using native SQL Server tools.

Types of replication

There are five types of replication:

- Snapshot

- Transactional

- Merge

- Oracle Publisher

- Peer-to-peer

All five move or replicate data, but the frequency that the data is delivered and the direction can vary among them all. Throughout this chapter, you will focus on the first three: snapshot, transactional, and merge. The last two are for specialized situations and are beyond the scope of this book. Oracle Publisher is typically used when you want to move data from an Oracle database to a SQL Server database. Peer-to-peer replication is built on the foundation of transactional replication, but it is more of a scale-out and high-availability deployment.

Snapshot

Snapshot replication is exactly what the name implies: a snapshot of the data and database objects as they exist at a point in time. When snapshot replication is configured, it is generally scheduled to occur as some specific interval. An entire copy (snapshot) of the data is created and sent to the Subscriber via the Distributor. Because the entire data set is sent, tracking DML changes is not required. This has an added value because tracking changes adds overhead to the replication process. On the other hand, if the snapshot is very large, distributing the data to the destination can be a lengthy process. You can schedule the generation and deployment of the snapshot to best meet your needs.

Snapshot replication is typically used with the following:

- Small amounts of data

- High latency or intermittent network connections

- Data that changes infrequently

- Copies of data that can be an hour, day, week, or month old

Transactional

Transactional replication, like snapshot replication, begins with a snapshot. However, the initial snapshot data and schema changes at the Publisher are then asynchronously (in order) sent to the distribution database. Subscribers then receive the transactions, keeping them up to date with the Publisher.

Transactional replication is typically used in situations that require the following:

- Near real-time data on one or more subscribers

- Data that has to be incrementally loaded

- Data that is highly transactional or that changes frequently

Merge

Like the previous types, *merge* replication typically starts with a snapshot of the source database. Then the changes are tracked with triggers. This type of replication is common when users work in a disconnected manner and the data needs to be synchronized from a centralized repository to mobile devices and vice versa. When a user connects, the changes are synchronized between the two devices.

Note Since snapshot replication does not track changes, it does not rely on the distribution database. The change data within this database is actually used only by transactional and peer-to-peer replication. In the case of merge replication, it uses the repository for process history. The Distributor can reside on a Publisher or on a remote server. As a best practice, it is recommended that you use a remote Distributor, as this allows you to offload some of the processing, and the remote Distributor could act as a centralized repository for multiple Publishers. A database name distribution will also be created on this server; this is where all the metadata and the history of data changes will be stored for all types of replication.

Replication agents

Moving data and database objects between servers can be a huge undertaking. To accomplish this, SQL Server uses four agents:

- Snapshot Agent

- Distribution Agent

- Log Reader Agent

- Merge Agent

Snapshot Agent

As previously stated, all replication types leverage a snapshot to initially start the process. As a result, they all use this agent. The Snapshot Agent generates the snapshot file, which contains all the data needed to move the data and database objects that you want to replicate. This agent writes all the information to the file system. It runs on the SQL Server instance that acts as the Publisher.

Distribution Agent

This agent is primarily used by snapshot and transactional replication. Snapshot replication uses the Distribution Agent to apply the generated snapshots to all Subscribers. Transactional replication uses it to apply all subsequent changes to the Subscribers since the initial snapshot. This agent runs on the SQL Server instance acting as the Distributor for push subscriptions, and it runs on the Subscriber SQL Server for pull subscriptions.

Log Reader Agent

This agent is used only by transactional replication. It moves transactions from the transaction log to the distribution database. If you have multiple databases configured to use transactional replication, you will have multiple Log Reader Agents, one for each database. The Log Reader Agent runs on the SQL Server instance acting as the Distributor.

Merge Agent

This agent is used only by merge replication. The Merge Agent pushes the initial snapshot and successive incremental changes from the Publishers to the Subscribers. It detects changes on both the source (Publisher) and destination (Subscriber) databases since the last scheduled run of the Merge Agent. Merge replication includes a set of features that handle conflict, including conflict tables that store conflicting values. For example, assume that you have a row on the Subscriber that has a primary key of 555, and a row also exists on the Publisher that has a primary key of 555. When the synchronization happens, a conflict will occur and all the information will be logged to the conflict table. You can view this information using the Replication Conflict Viewer. Like the Distribution Agent, the Merge Agent runs on the SQL Server instance acting as the Distributor for push subscriptions, and on the SQL Server acting as the Subscriber for pull subscriptions.

Configuring replication

Now that you are familiar with the basic replication terminology and components, it's time to delve into configuring and deploying a replication topology. Typical replication topologies consist of, at a minimum, a Publisher and a Subscriber, which in most cases are two separate servers. In addition to those servers, a third server, the Distributor, may also be included to improve performance.

Configure the Distributor

1. Open SQL Server Management Studio (SSMS) and connect to an instance of SQL Server.

2. In Object Explorer, expand the Databases folder.

3. Right-click the Replication folder.

4. Select Configure Distribution from the menu.

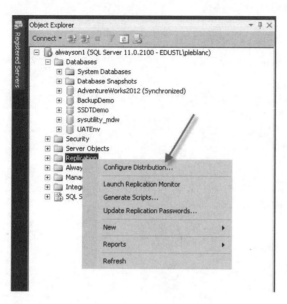

5. Click Next.

6. On the Distributor page, accept the defaults and click Next.

On the next page, Snapshot Folder, you will see a warning in reference to the location of the snapshot folder. If you are configuring a remote Distributor, you must specify a UNC path: *\\Computer Name\folder path*.

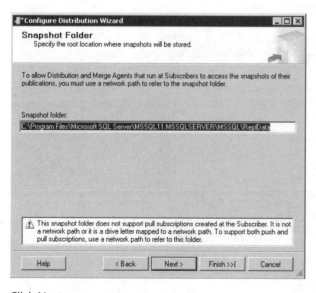

7. Click Next.

8. On the Distribution Database page, change the name of the database and specify a new location for the database and log files.

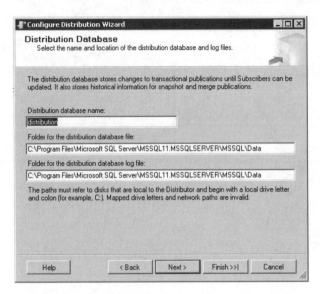

9. Accept the defaults and click Next.

10. On the Publishers page, you can enable other servers to use this server as a Distributor. By default, the current server is automatically included.

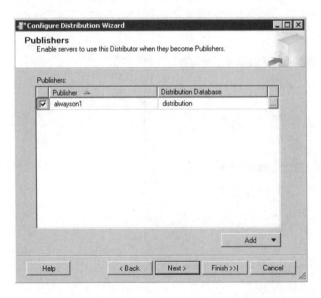

11. Accept the defaults and click Next.

12. On the final page, Wizard Actions, in addition to configuring distribution, you can generate a script that contains all the steps from the wizard. For now, accept the defaults and click Next.

13. On the Complete the Wizard page, review the summary and click Finish.

14. Configuration begins and the progress is shown on the Configuring page. Click Close.

Configure a transactional Publisher

1. Open SSMS and connect to an instance of SQL Server.

2. Expand the Replication folder.

3. Right-click the Local Publications folder and select New Publication from the menu.

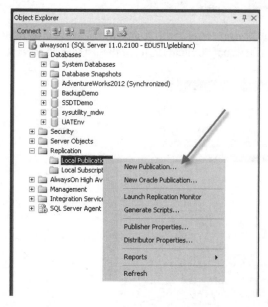

4. Click Next on the New Publication Wizard page.

5. Select the AdventureWorks2012 database on the Publication Database page and click Next.

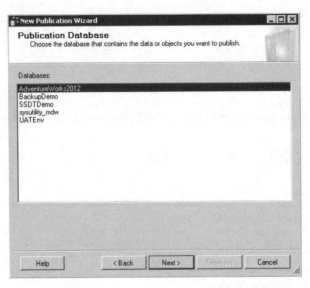

6. On the Publication Type page, you are presented with four types. The type you select depends on your requirements. Select Transactional Publication from the list and click Next.

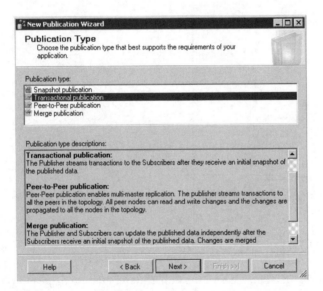

7. The Articles page is where you specify the database objects that you would like to repli-cate. As shown on the page, you can replicate several objects. You will focus primarily on tables. Each replicated object is referred to as an *article*. Expand Tables, and then expand the BusinessEntity table. You can holistically replicate the entire table or select only the columns that you want to replicate.

8. Select the box next to the BusinessEntity table.

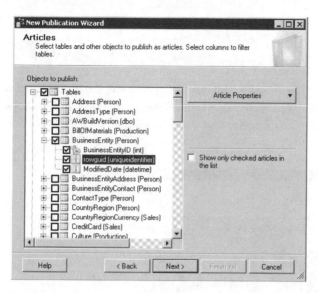

9. To the right of the list of articles is an Article Properties button. Click the drop-down arrow located on the button and select Set Properties of Highlighted Table Article.

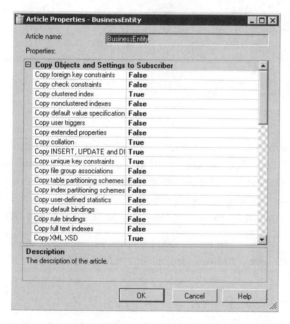

Using the Article Properties dialog box, you specify whether or not you want to copy constraints, triggers, clustered indexes, and so on. Scroll through the list and familiarize yourself with what is available.

10. Accept all the defaults for now and click OK. On the Articles page, click Next.

In some cases, you may want to replicate only certain rows from a table. By using the filter option, you can limit the rows with a *WHERE* clause.

11. You are going to replicate all the rows in the specified table, so just click Next.

As discussed earlier, prior to configuring all types of replication, a snapshot must be taken. On the Snapshot Agent page, you can specify when to create a snapshot and how often. Select the box next to the option Create a Snapshot Immediately and Keep the Snapshot Available to Initialize Subscriptions.

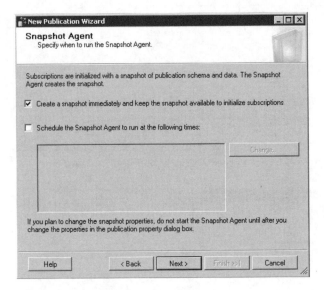

12. Click Next.

13. On the Agent Security page, you must specify under which account the Snapshot Agent and the Log Reader Agent will run. The Windows account that is used for the agents must be a member of the *db_owner* database role in the distribution database and in the publication database—in this case, AdventureWorks2012. In addition to these requirements, the Windows account that is used for the Snapshot Agent must have read, write, and modify permissions on the snapshot folder.

14. Click the Security Settings button next to the Snapshot Agent text box.

15. In the Snapshot Agent Security dialog box, select the Run Under the SQL Server Agent Service Account option. Note that the dialog box states that selecting this option is not recommended as a best practice, but for testing purposes, it will suffice. However, when going to production you should create a new Active Directory account for sole use by the Snapshot Agent.

16. In the lower section of the same dialog box, select the By Impersonating the Process Account option.

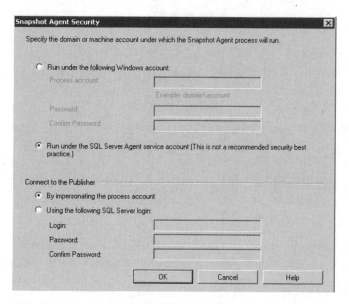

17. Click OK. Remember, these settings are not a best practice because the service account running the agent may have permissions beyond what is required by replication.

18. Back on the Agent Security page, you will see that both agents have been configured. This is because by default the wizard uses the security settings from the Snapshot Agent for the Log Reader Agent.

You can override this default by clearing the Use the Security Settings from the Snapshot Agent check box and manually configuring the settings.

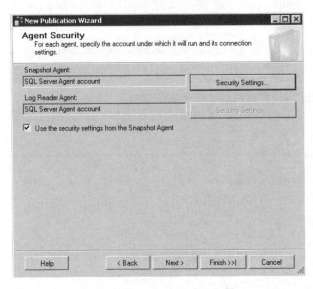

19. For now, accept the defaults and click Next.

20. On the Wizards Actions page, ensure that the Create the Publication check box is selected. If you want to generate a script, you can select the Generate a Script file with steps to create the publication also. For now, leave it cleared.

21. On the Complete the Wizard page, enter **BusinessEntity** in the Publication Name text box, review the summary, and click Finish.

    Configuration begins and the progress is shown on the Creating Publication page.

22. Click Close.

    You will see the newly created publication in Object Explorer under Replication | Local Publications. In addition, a Snapshot Agent job and a Log Reader Agent job have been created on your SQL Server instance; you can view these in Object Explorer under SQL Server Agent | Jobs.

Configure a transactional Subscriber

1. Open SSMS and connect to an instance of SQL Server.

2. Open a new query window and enter the following T-SQL code:

```
USE master;
CREATE DATABASE ADRepl;
```

3. Execute the query.

4. Expand the Replication folder in Object Explorer.

5. Right-click the Local Subscriptions folder and select New Subscriber from the menu.

6. Click Next.

7. On the Publication page of the New Subscription Wizard, ensure that the BusinessEntity publication is selected and click Next.

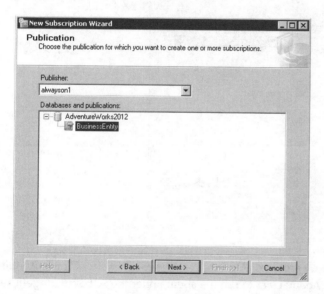

8. Now you are presented with the choice of running the Distribution Agent on the Distributor for push replication or on the Subscriber for pull replication. While running the Distribution Agent on the Subscriber does offload some of the work from the Publisher, if it is on the Subscriber, the Subscriber will bear the load. When making this choice, consider how each will be affected, and ensure that the selected choice has sufficient resources to support your decision.

   In general, place the Distributor on a more powerful machine or the machine with lowest network connection latency. For now, accept the defaults and click Next.

9. On the Subscribers page, select the box to the available choice, which will be the local machine, and select ADRepl from the Subscription Database column. You can optionally add a new subscriber by clicking the Add Subscriber button.

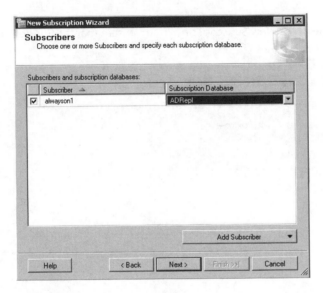

10. Click Next.

11. In the Distribution Agent Security dialog box, click the ellipsis button. Similar to the Snapshot Agent and Log Reader Agent, elect to run the agent under the SQL Server Agent services account and connect to the Distributor and Subscriber using the process account. Again, as a best practice, you should use a new Active Directory account that has been created specifically for this purpose.

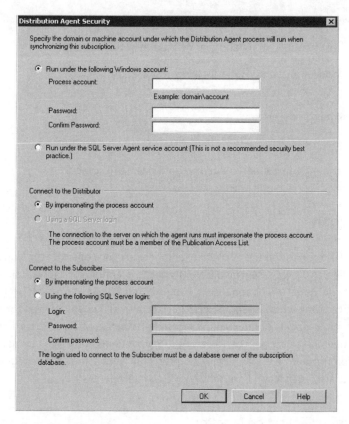

12. Click OK and click Next.

13. On the next page, Synchronization Schedule, select Run Continuously in the column labeled Agent Schedule. You can also synchronize on demand or define a schedule. Click Next.

14. On the Initialize Subscriptions page, you have two choices: Initialize Immediately or At First Synchronization. Accept the defaults and click Next.

15. On the final page, Wizard Actions, in addition to configuring distribution, you can generate a script that contains all the steps from the wizard. For now, accept the default and click Next.

16. Review the summary and click Finish.

   Configuration begins and the progress is shown on the Creating Subscriptions page.

17. Click Close.

18. Right-click the Replication folder in Object Explorer and select Refresh.

19. Expand the Local Publications folder.

20. Expand the BusinessEntity publication, and you will see the new subscription.

21. Open a new query window and enter the following T-SQL code:

```
USE ADRepl;
SELECT * FROM Person.BusinessEntity
```

22. Execute the query.

You will now see that the table is created and the data has been copied.

Monitoring replication

Having an effective method of monitoring the availability and performance of any technology is critical to its use and success. SQL Server provides several different ways to monitor replication. Using SSMS, you can start and stop each individual agent and monitor them using SQL Server Agent. In addition, you can launch Replication Monitor, which is a graphical interface that allows you to monitor replication activity. Replication Monitor reports on the health of both Publishers and Subscribers. If you are less interested in using prebuilt interfaces, you can leverage T-SQL or Replication Management Objects (RMO) to monitor replication programmatically. Finally, you can configure some of the predefined alerts for replication agents. Alerts are discussed in Chapter 27, "SQL Server Agent."

Monitor replication using Replication Monitor

1. Open SSMS and connect to an instance of SQL Server.

2. Right-click the Replication folder and select Launch Replication Monitor.

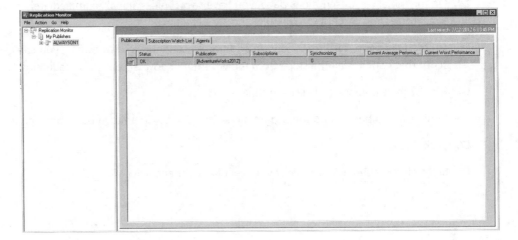

3. By default, the server that you are connected to is automatically registered and displayed. In the left section of the Replication Monitor screen, you can view that status of all publications on the selected server. You can also monitor the activity of the Subscription Watch List and all the agents that are currently running.

4. In the left navigation pane, expand your server and you will see the publication that was created earlier. If multiple publications existed on that server, you would see an entire list. Select the BusinessEntity publication and the view changes to only those items specific to that publication.

Summary

This chapter discussed the different types of replication topologies that are available within Microsoft SQL Server 2012. Each provides different techniques for solving various data movement scenarios within an organization. Selecting a type and determining how to configure it requires careful consideration and planning. The end result should provide an effective means of moving data and database objects in a consistent and effective way that meets the needs of your organization.

Database maintenance

Backups

After completing this chapter, you will be able to

- Understand the different types of backups.

- Perform a full backup.

- Perform a differential backup.

- Back up a database transaction log.

- Restore a database.

Maintenance is a vital task that should be included as part of any database administrator's (DBA's) daily workload. Database maintenance includes rebuilding indexes, updating statistics, monitoring performance and security, checking database consistency, and performing database backups. Each task should be done at regular intervals, with the intervals based on the requirements and needs of the organization. Backups are discussed in detail throughout this chapter, while the other tasks are explained later in the book.

Databases can be backed up to disk, to tape, or to a network path. Regardless of the destination, database backups should be executed regularly to protect the database from data loss and downtime. Using database backups, a DBA can restore from the last backup or to a specific point in time. In this chapter, you will learn how to back up and restore a database.

 Note The tape backup feature has been deprecated; therefore, you should avoid using this method.

Understanding backup devices

This first step in taking a database backup is to determine where you will store the files. As mentioned in the chapter introduction, backups can be stored to disk, to tape, or to a network path. In addition, to simplify the process, you can set up a *backup device*, a logical device that points to a physical location. The physical location can be either a disk location or a tape drive. So instead of explicitly typing or selecting the tape or disk location, you can specify the backup device. While doing so does simplify the backup process, it does not provide the level of flexibility that is typically needed for an effective and reliable backup strategy.

Create a backup device using SSMS

1. Open SQL Server Management Studio (SSMS) and connect to an instance of Microsoft SQL Server.

2. In Object Explorer, expand the server tree.

3. Expand the Server Objects folder.

4. Right-click Backup Devices and select New Backup Device.

5. In the Backup Device dialog box, enter **AdventureWorksFullBackups** in the Device Name text box.

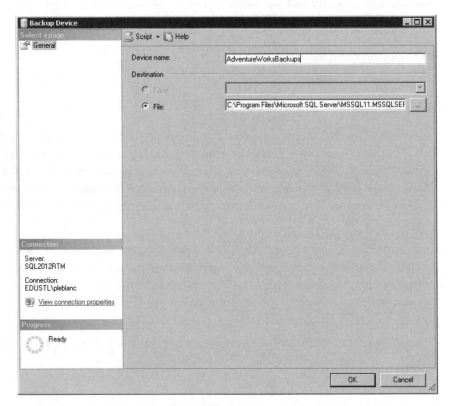

6. By clicking the ellipsis button located to the right of the File text box, you can change the physical file location. For now, accept the default.

7. Click OK.

8. Repeat steps 5–7 twice, changing the device name to **AdventureWorksDiffBackups** and **AdventureWorksTLogBackups** for each iteration.

Now when you take a backup, you can simply specify this device name instead of a disk or tape location, which will be explained in the next section. While creating a device does simplify the backup process, it is not a requirement. You can back up a database directly to the file or tape location.

> **Note** You should not place your backup files in the same location as your database and log files, as this could add additional contention on those disks that may negatively affect the performance of your database. Also, keeping the backup files separate from the database and log files protects against having a single point of failure in the event of a disaster.

Full database backups

Now that you have created a device to store database backups, you will take an actual database backup. SQL Server allows you to take a full database backup or a differential database backup. As the name suggests, a *full* database backup is a backup of the entire database. The database recovery model, as explained in Chapter 4, "Designing SQL Server databases," determines whether or not a full database backup alone is sufficient.

A single daily backup can be sufficient in some cases. If a database is in the simple recovery model, then a single full backup may suffice. (For information on recovery models, see Chapter 4.) This depends on how much data your organization can afford to lose. For example, assume that a full backup was taken at midnight of the same day. If something catastrophic occurred that affected the data at 5 p.m. the same afternoon, your recovery point would be from the last backup at midnight. Your organization would lose any data changes that occurred between midnight and 5 p.m. This may or may not be acceptable. If not, then you can put certain procedures into place to mitigate the data loss, including differential and transaction log backups. You could take multiple full backups, but depending on the database size, this could require a large amount of storage space.

SQL Server allows you to back up databases using T-SQL or SSMS. Regardless of the method you select, you have several options available. While this book discusses very few of the options explicitly, you should take time to review them. You can find more information on these options in the "BACKUP (Transact-SQL)" section of SQL Server Books Online.

Perform a full database backup using SSMS

1. Open SSMS and connect to an instance of SQL Server.

2. In Object Explorer, expand the server tree.

3. Expand the Databases folder.

4. Right-click the AdventureWorks2012 database.

5. Select Tasks | Back Up.

6. In the Back Up dialog box, you can select a different database to back up, but just accept the selected database. You can also change the backup type from Full to Differential or Transaction Log. For now, accept Full.

7. Directly below the backup type, you can specify if you want to take a Copy-Only Backup. Copy-only does not start a new backup chain, so if this option is specified, you cannot take a differential backup.

8. In the next section, Backup Set, you can specify a name and description for the database backup. For now, accept the default and enter a description if preferred.

9. Also in the Backup Set section, you can specify when the backup will expire and can be overwritten by SQL Server. It should also be noted that the backup files can be removed by using other tools and through the operating system. Accept the default of 0, which means the backup never expires.

10. In the Destination section, you can specify whether you will back up to disk or tape. The tape option will not be enabled unless you have a device attached to the server.

11. By default, the configured backup location is automatically included. If you had not created a device, the backup could have been stored directly in the location specified. Click Remove to delete that location.

12. Click Add. In the Select Backup Destination dialog box, select File Name.

13. Click the ellipsis, and in the Locate Database Files dialog box, browse to this location: C:\Program Files\Microsoft SQL Server\MSSQL11.MSSQLSERVER\MSSQL\Backup\.

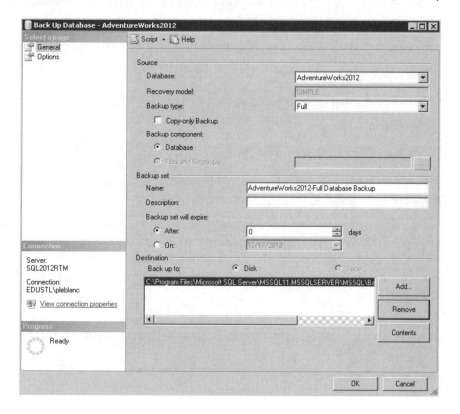

14. In the File Name text box in the Locate Database Files dialog box, type **AdventureWorks2012.bak** and click OK twice.

15. In the Select a Page pane of the Back Up Database dialog box, select Options.

16. In the first section, Overwrite Media, select the Overwrite All Existing Backup Sets option. By selecting this option, you will empty the backup set. If you accept the default choice to append, you will add a new backup file to the media set during each subsequent backup.

17. In addition to deciding whether to overwrite, you can also choose to check the media set name and backup expiration. If you select this box, you can either enter an existing media set name or leave the media set name blank to create new one. Leave this check box cleared.

18. You can also decide to back up to a new media set. Do not select this option—accept the default, Back Up to the Existing Media Set.

19. In the Reliability section, you can specify three options:

- Verify Backup When Finished

- Perform Checksum Before Writing to Media

- Continue on Error

Leave these check boxes cleared for now.

20. Since you are performing a full backup, the Transaction Log section is not enabled, and since a tape drive is not available, the Tape Drive section is also not enabled.

21. Finally, you can decide whether or not to compress a backup. If you specify to compress the backup, SQL Server will reduce the size of the backup, which ultimately saves space. The amount of space saved depends on several factors, primarily the type of data within the database. Compression can be set at the server level or individually. For now, accept the default.

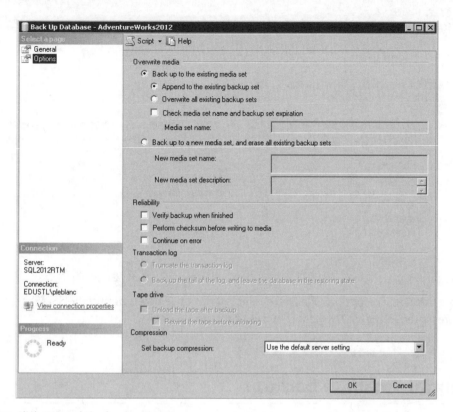

22. Click OK and the backup begins.

Once the backup is complete, browse to this directory: C:\Program Files\Microsoft SQL Server\ MSSQL11.MSSQLSERVER\MSSQL\Backup. Here you will see the backup file.

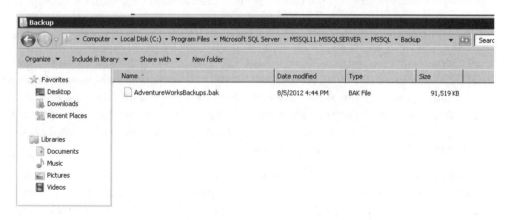

1. To perform this task with T-SQL, execute the following script:

```
BACKUP DATABASE [AdventureWorks2012]
TO DISK
=
N'C:\Program Files\Microsoft SQL Server\MSSQL11.MSSQLServer\MSSQL\Backup\
AdventureWorks2012.bak'
WITH
     NOFORMAT,
     NOINIT,
     NAME = N'AdventureWorks2012-Full Database Backup',
     SKIP,
     NOREWIND,
     NOUNLOAD,
     STATS = 10
GO
```

Note Most of the options that were selected or not selected during the SSMS steps are represented in the *WITH* section of the T-SQL statement.

Differential database backups

Differential backups are slightly different from full backups. Over time, the typical database grows, and so does the backup file. Therefore, in most cases, it is impractical to take full database backups throughout the day. This is primarily because the larger the database, the more space the backup file will require, and the longer it will take to perform the backup. In addition, the backups could potentially affect performance.

As a result, SQL Server allows you to perform incremental backups, or *differential* backups in SQL Server terminology. Differential backups are smaller than full backups because they capture only what has changed in the database since the last full backup. For this reason alone, it is a good idea to consider including them as part of your backup strategy for large databases. A large database that does not change much will generate very small differential backups. Moreover, instead of taking a full backup several times a day to protect against data loss, you can take a differential backup which, in most cases, is faster and requires less space.

To illustrate, assume that a full backup was taken at midnight, and then every four hours following the full backup, differential backups were taken. In the event of a disaster, you could restore the full backup and then the differential backup that was taken prior to the problems that occurred. As a result, your organization is exposed to only a 4-hour window of data loss, as opposed to a 24-hour window.

Note When restoring databases, you must set certain options to allow you to restore additional files. The upcoming section "Restoring databases" provides a detailed explanation.

Perform a differential backup using SSMS

1. Open SSMS and connect to an instance of SQL Server.

2. In Object Explorer, expand the server tree.

3. Expand the Databases folder.

4. Right-click the AdventureWorks2012 database.

5. Select Tasks | Back Up.

6. In the Back Up Database dialog box, select Differential from the Backup Type drop-down list. Accept all the other defaults.

7. In the Destination section, click Remove to remove any existing items.

8. Click Add and select File Name.

9. Click the ellipsis, and in the Locate Database Files dialog box, browse to this location: C:\Program Files\Microsoft SQL Server\MSSQL11.MSSQLSERVER\MSSQL\Backup\. In the File Name text box in the Locate Database Files dialog box, type **AdventureWorks2012DiffBackups.bak** and click OK twice.

10. If you browse to the directory C:\Program Files\Microsoft SQL Server\ MSSQL11.MSSQLSERVER\MSSQL\Backup, you should see two files. One is the full backup, and the other is the differential backup. Notice how much smaller the differential backup is than the full backup.

Perform a differential backup using T-SQL

1. As with a full backup, you can execute a differential backup using T-SQL:

```
BACKUP DATABASE [AdventureWorks2012]
TO   DISK
=
N'C:\Program Files\Microsoft SQL
Server\MSSQL11.MSSQLServer\MSSQL\Backup\AdventureWorks2012DiffBackups.bak'
WITH
     DIFFERENTIAL ,
     NOFORMAT, NOINIT,
     NAME = N'AdventureWorks2012-Differential Database Backup',
     SKIP, NOREWIND, NOUNLOAD,  STATS = 10
GO
```

The primary difference is the inclusion of the *DIFFERENTIAL* keyword in the *WITH* clause.

Transaction log database backups

So far, you have learned how to back up databases in simple recovery mode and restore only up until the last backup. What if your database is in full or bulk-logged recovery? What if you want to restore to a point in time? Performing transaction log backups can assist in these scenarios.

Because the transaction log contains a record of all the transactions that are performed against a specific database, you can use transaction log backups to restore to a specific point in time. You need to know about a couple of important requirements: a full backup must be taken prior to performing any transaction log backups, and the database must be in full or bulk-logged recovery mode. Also, once the database is not in simple recovery mode, the transaction log will grow until a log backup is taken. Therefore, if you do not back up the log regularly, it could consume large amounts of storage that may cause you to run out of disk space. A transaction log backup empties out committed, check-pointed transactions in the transaction log, but it does not affect the actual log file size.

Typically, transaction log backups are taken more frequently than any other backup. This is because they are usually small and require fewer resources. In rare instances, the transaction log may grow larger than the database data file. This may occur if you have a highly transactional database, like a banking system, in which most of the data in the database is changed. In this case, you will need to back up the transaction log more frequently.

Perform a transaction log backup using SSMS

1. Open SSMS and connect to an instance of SQL Server.

2. In Object Explorer, expand the server tree.

3. Right-click the AdventureWorks2012 database.

4. Select Tasks | Back Up.

5. In the Back Up Database dialog box, select Transaction Log from the Backup Type drop-down list. Accept all other defaults.

6. In the Destination section, click Remove to remove any existing items.

7. Click Add and select File Name.

8. Click the ellipsis, and in the Locate Database Files dialog box, browse to the following location: C:\Program Files\Microsoft SQL Server\MSSQL11.MSSQLSERVER\MSSQL\Backup\.
In the File Name text box in the Locate Database Files dialog box, type **AdventureWorks2012TLogBackups.trn** and click OK twice.

9. In the Select a Page pane of the Back Up Database dialog box, select Options.

10. Notice that the Transaction Log section is now enabled. Ensure that the Truncate the Transaction Log option is selected.

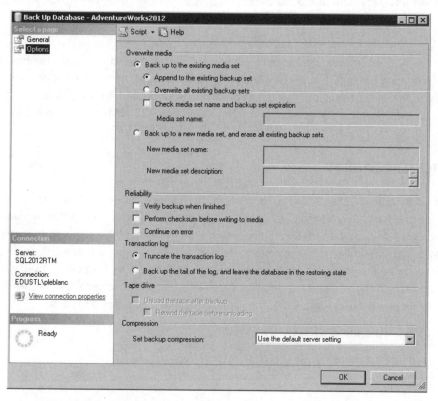

11. Click OK and the backup begins.

12. If you browse to the directory C:\Program Files\Microsoft SQL Server\ MSSQL11.MSSQLSERVER\MSSQL\Backup, you should see three files.

Perform a transaction log backup using T-SQL

1. Again, you can also replicate the previous steps with a single T-SQL statement:

```
BACKUP LOG [AdventureWorks2012]
TO Disk
=
'C:\Program Files\Microsoft SQL
Server\MSSQL11.MSSQLSERVER\MSSQL\Backup\AdventureWorks2012TLogBackups.trn'

WITH
     NOFORMAT, NOINIT,  NAME = N'AdventureWorks2012-Transaction Log  Backup',
     SKIP, NOREWIND, NOUNLOAD,  STATS = 10
GO
```

Note Have you noticed the trend with the backups using T-SQL? The main difference between this statement and a full backup is that instead of using *DATABASE* after the *BACKUP* keyword, you use *LOG*.

You have now successfully performed each type of backup. You should perform not only regular transaction log backups, but also full and differential backups. Again, the frequency of backups depends on the level of data loss that is acceptable for your organization. Building a plan to regularly back up your databases is discussed in more detail in Chapter 22, "Maintenance plans."

Restoring databases

Backing up databases is the second most important task that a DBA should perform. So what is the most important task? Recovering databases. This is why it is important that a DBA regularly take backups. However, coupled with taking the backups, the DBA should regularly test those backups. The best way to perform these tests is to restore the backups. As a best practice, a process should be put in place to ensure the validity of the backups through restoration. In most cases, a separate instance of SQL Server is configured and the databases are restored on that server. After the restore, user and application access is a good test of whether or not the data is available and valid.

Using SQL Server, you can restore the following:

- An entire database

- A page in a database

- A part of a database

- The database transaction log

- A file or filegroup in a database

As you can see, you have several options available when restoring databases, ensuring that you have the flexibility to address most scenarios that may arise. SQL Server allows you to restore databases using both T-SQL and SSMS.

Prior to restoring a database, you should always consider exactly what you are going to restore. This is especially important when restoring using T-SQL. Assume that you must restore a full backup, a single differential, and single transaction log backup, in that order. When restoring the *FULL* and *DIFFERENTIAL* backup, you must include the *NORECOVERY* keyword in the *WITH* clause.

```
RESTORE DATABASE [AdventureWorks2012]
FROM
DISK
=
' C:\Program Files\Microsoft SQL Server\MSSQL11.MSSQLServer\MSSQL\Backup\AdventureWorks2012.bak'

 WITH
      FILE = 1,
      NORECOVERY,
      NOUNLOAD,
      STATS = 5
GO
```

After this restore, the database is in an unusable state, but this allows the DBA to apply subsequent differential and transaction log backups. For this reason, most DBAs prefer to use SSMS for restoring databases. SSMS recognizes the complete backup chain and will restore all backups that you specify, and it will also place the database in a usable state when complete.

Restore a database using SSMS

1. Open SSMS and connect to an instance of SQL Server.

2. In Object Explorer, expand the server tree.

3. Right-click the AdventureWorks2012 database.

4. Select Tasks | Restore | Database.

Because you are using the GUI, it automatically recognizes all the backups that have been taken and places them in the correct restore order.

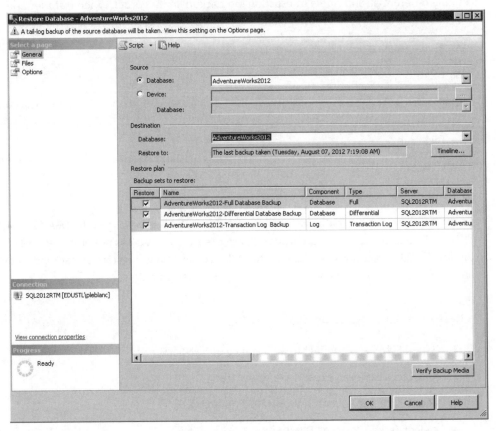

5. SQL Server 2012 introduces new functionality to the Restore Database dialog box. If you click the Timeline button next to the Restore To text box in the Source section, the Backup Timeline dialog box opens.

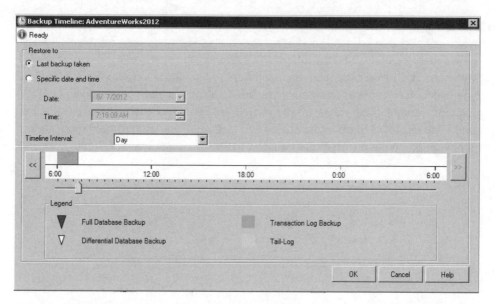

6. Using the timeline, you can easily restore to a specific point in time either by selecting the Specific Date and Time option and specifying a date or by using the slider. Click Cancel.

7. In the Select a Page pane of the Restore Database dialog box, select Files. If you want to move the database files to a new location during the restore, you can use this page.

8. Accept the defaults and select Options from the Select a Page pane.

   You can specify several options in this dialog box, but the one that you will focus on is the Recovery State. If you were restoring only a single backup file and wanted to restore additional files later in another operation, you would select RESTORE WITH NORECOVERY from the drop-down list.

9. Ensure that RESTORE WITH RECOVERY is selected from the Recovery State drop-down list.

10. Before a database can restored, all existing connections must be closed. To ensure that all connections are closed, select the Close Existing Connections to Destination Database option in the Server Connections section.

11. Click OK.

The database has been restored using a database, differential, and transaction log backup. While T-SQL offers you the ability to create reusable code, the GUI gives you a more seamless and less error-prone method for restoring a database. It should also be noted that using maintenance plans provides you with a mechanism of reusability from the GUI perspective. Maintenance plans are discussed in Chapter 22.

Summary

In this chapter, you learned the different techniques you can use to back up and restore databases. As with most SQL Server tasks, you can use either T-SQL or SSMS to perform the same tasks. The method you select often depends on whether you are doing ad hoc tasks or scheduled tasks. With regard to backups, either method works, whether scheduled or ad hoc, but as a beginner, the best approach may be to use SSMS to perform backups and restores. If you want to learn more about T-SQL, use the Script option on the corresponding window to view the script that SQL Server will run via the GUI.

Managing and maintaining indexes and statistics

After completing this chapter, you will be able to

- Understand the difference between reorganizing indexes and rebuilding indexes.

- Rebuild and reorganize indexes.

- Check index fragmentations.

- Defragment indexes.

- Create and update database statistics.

Performance is typically measured by how fast data is returned from your database to applications, reports, and end users. While several other factors should be considered when evaluating performance, most users are concerned only with how fast the data is returned. As mentioned in Chapter 6, "Building and maintaining indexes," creating indexes can help improve database performance.

As the data in the database is manipulated, the indexes can become fragmented. This means that the pages may end up out of order or the pages may have varying amounts of free space. Whatever the case, performance could be hindered. To remove fragmentation, you can either rebuild or reorganize the index, which will be discussed later in this chapter.

Performance is also improved by statistics that can be automatically created, which is a best practice. Additionally, manually created statistics help the Microsoft SQL Server query plan optimizer understand the value of the distribution of data in a table. While a detailed discussion of statistics is beyond the scope of this book, it is important to note that the statistics must be updated regularly to protect against performance degradation. Later in this chapter, you will learn about how statistics are created and updated.

Checking index fragmentation

The process of rebuilding and reorganizing an index begins with determining the fragmentation level of the index. In earlier versions of SQL Server, performing this task required a lot of work. With the recent releases of SQL Server, however, you can identify how much all the indexes in a database are fragmented by executing the following query:

```
USE AdventureWorks2012
GO
SELECT
    DB_NAME(ips.database_id) DBName,
    OBJECT_NAME(ips.object_id) ObjName,
    i.name InxName,
    ips.avg_fragmentation_in_percent
FROM sys.dm_db_index_physical_stats(db_id('AdventureWorks2012'),
default, default, default, default) ips
INNER JOIN sys.indexes i
    ON    ips.index_id = i.index_id AND
          ips.object_id = i.object_id
WHERE
    ips.object_id > 99 AND
    ips.avg_fragmentation_in_percent >= 10 AND
    ips.index_id > 0
```

This query uses a dynamic management object (DMO) to reveal vital information that assists in identifying fragmented indexes. DMOs are discussed in detail in Chapter 30, "Dynamic management objects." The results of the preceding query list all the indexes that have fragmentation greater than or equal to 10 percent. Using the results of this query, you can quickly determine which indexes are fragmented, for whatever reason. Tables can become fragmented by massive *UPDATE* or *DELETE* statements, frequent page splitting, or disk space contention. Tables can also become fragmented by *INSERT* statements if the clustered index key is not a sequential key. Fragmentation is not the only factor used to determine whether or when to perform index maintenance, but it is a good place to start. The discussion on whether to rebuild or reorganize an index is coming up later in this chapter.

You may be wondering why you filter on indexes that have more than 10 percent fragmentation. In most cases, indexes with less fragmentation should not affect performance terribly. The time spent performing maintenance on indexes with relatively small amounts of fragmentation will not be beneficial to performance. That said, every environment is different, and you should carefully evaluate index fragmentation on an index-by-index basis. If queries in your databases are performing poorly and the corresponding indexes are fragmented, addressing that fragmentation may improve query performance.

Defragmenting indexes

As previously mentioned, fragmentation can be reduced by reorganizing or rebuilding an index. When to use which method depends primarily on three factors: the fragmentation level, the size of the index, and the requirements for accessibility to the index during maintenance. Regardless of the method you use, you should always perform analysis and index maintenance on a regular basis—for example, weekly.

Reorganizing indexes

When indexes are minimally fragmented, between 10 and 30 percent, they should be reorganized. Why those values? Well, this range is typically recommended as a starting point, but as previously mentioned, you should analyze each index to determine what works best in your environment. SQL Server allows you to reorganize indexes with SQL Server Management Studio (SSMS), T-SQL, or a maintenance plan (as discussed in Chapter 22, "Maintenance plans").

If you are scheduling your index maintenance, the preferred method is to use either T-SQL or a maintenance plan. However, in some cases, you will be required to reorganize an index during an unscheduled time. In this case, the simplest and most direct approach is to use SSMS.

Reorganizing an index is not as resource intensive as rebuilding an index. Basically, this process compacts the index pages and reorders the leaf levels to match the logical order of the leaf nodes in the index B-tree. Reorganizing an index is always an online operation, meaning that the corresponding index and the associated tables are available during the entire operation.

Reorganize an index using SSMS

1. Open SSMS and connect to a server.

2. Open a new query window, and enter and execute the following T-SQL code:

```
USE AdventureWorks2012;
GO
--Create index if it does not exist
CREATE NONCLUSTERED INDEX IX_SalesOrderHeader_OrderDate
ON Sales.SalesOrderHeader
(
    OrderDate
)
INCLUDE(Status, AccountNumber)
WHERE(OnlineOrderFlag = 0)
ON AW2012FileGroup2;
GO
UPDATE Sales.SalesOrderHeader
SET OrderDate = DATEADD(day, 1, orderdate)
where orderdate <= '8/31/2006'
```

The preceding query adds an index, and then changes enough data to cause fragmentation in an index that contains the OrderDate column.

3. In Object Explorer, expand the Databases folder.

4. Expand the AdventureWorks2012 database.

5. Expand the Tables folder.

6. Expand the Sales.SalesOrderHeader table.

7. Expand the Indexes folder.

8. Right-click IX_SalesOrderHeader_OrderDate.

9. Select Reorganize from the menu.

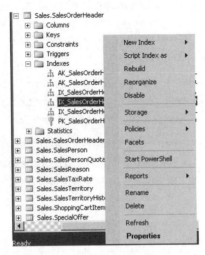

The Reorganize Indexes dialog box opens. Note the amount of fragmentation.

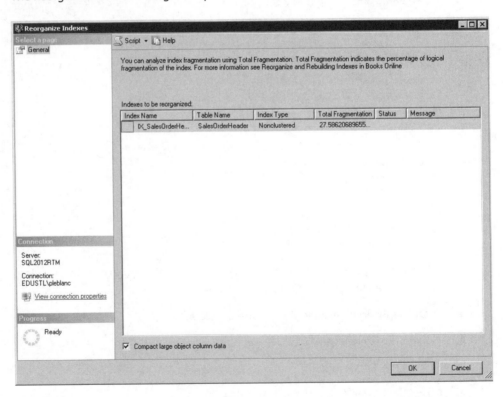

10. Click OK.

11. Repeat steps 9 and 10. Notice that the amount of fragmentation has been reduced significantly.

12. Click Cancel to close the window.

Reorganize an index using T-SQL

1. To reorganize an index using T-SQL, execute the following query:

```
USE [AdventureWorks2012]
GO
ALTER INDEX [IX_SalesOrderHeader_OrderDate] ON [Sales].[SalesOrderHeader] REORGANIZE
GO
```

 Note Just as when you create an index, when you reorganize an index you can specify several options, such as *FILL_FACTOR* and *SORT_IN_TEMPDB*.

Rebuilding indexes

For indexes with a small amount of fragmentation, reorganizing should be satisfactory. However, when fragmentation is greater than 30 percent—again, a good benchmark from which to start—you should consider rebuilding those indexes. When an index is rebuilt, it is completely dropped and re-created. Three things happen:

- Disk place is reclaimed because the pages are compacted.

- The index rows are reordered.

- Fragmentation is removed.

Rebuilding can be a resource-intensive process because the index is dropped and re-created. By default, the index and underlying table and data are not available during the index operation, as the rebuild operation is an OFFLINE operation. Other *SELECT, INSERT, UPDATE,* and *DELETE* statements will be blocked. The Enterprise edition's ONLINE feature allows *REBUILD* operations to be performed with minimal interruption of other connections. Therefore, setting the ONLINE option to ON can help to mitigate the interruption of connections. Online indexing is available only in the Enterprise edition of Microsoft SQL Server 2012.

Rebuild an index using SSMS

1. Open SSMS and connect to a server.

2. Open a new query window, and enter and execute the following T-SQL code:

```
USE AdventureWorks2012;
UPDATE Sales.SalesOrderHeader
SET OrderDate = DATEADD(day, -1, orderdate)
where orderdate <= '8/31/2006'
```

   The preceding query changes enough data to cause fragmentation in an index that contains the OrderDate column.

3. Expand the Databases folder.

4. Expand the AdventureWorks2012 database.

5. Expand the Tables folder.

6. Expand the Sales.SalesOrderHeader table.

7. Expand the Indexes folder.

8. Right-click IX_SalesOrderHeader_OrderDate.

9. Select Rebuild from the menu.

10. The Rebuild Indexes dialog box opens. Note the amount of fragmentation.

11. Click OK.

12. Repeat steps 9 and 10. Notice that the amount of fragmentation has been reduced more significantly than in the reorganization operation.

13. Click Cancel to close the window.

Rebuild an index using T-SQL

1. To rebuild an index using T-SQL, execute the following query:

```
/*This operation will work only in the Enterprise or Developer Edition*/
USE [AdventureWorks2012]
GO
ALTER INDEX [IX_SalesOrderHeader_OrderDate] ON [Sales].[SalesOrderHeader]
REBUILD WITH (ONLINE = ON)
GO
```

Rebuilding an index using SSMS does not provide the same flexibility as T-SQL. When using T-SQL, you can specify several options. As you can see in the previous query, the ONLINE operation has been specified in the *WITH* clause. This is critical for organizations that operate 24/7. In that case, index operations can be performed at almost any time. There are some restrictions to rebuilding an index online, but the process does satisfy most data needs. These restrictions could be the difference between a rebuild being feasible or not in large enterprise environments.

Checking index usage

While indexes can improve database performance, in some cases they can have an adverse effect. In addition, they require administration and consume disk space resources. Ideally, indexes provide a significant benefit to read operations on a table in exchange for a small overhead cost to *INSERT/ UPDATE/DELETE* operations. This is why having too many nonclustered indexes can be problematic. Assuring that indexes are actually used is important. You want to make sure that write operation performance is not suffering for improved read performance. For this reason, SQL Server includes a DMO (*sys.dm_db_index_usage_stats*) that can assist in identifying indexes that are not being used.

By using this DMO, you can effectively decide whether an index is needed in your database. Once you have determined an index is not needed, you should initially disable it instead of dropping it. By not removing the index, you maintain the structure of the index. If you later determine that the index is needed, you can simply enable the index instead of re-creating it. Using the index usage DMO too soon after a server restart could result in valuable indexes being dropped—perhaps indexes that are used in month-end or business cycle–end reporting.

> **Note** The information contained within DMOs is cleared when an instance of SQL Server is restarted. Therefore, before using this information to make any decisions, ensure that SQL Server has been running for a substantial amount of time. This time should span a period that is inclusive of a workload that encompasses almost every scenario that may be presented to your database.

View index usage

1. Open SSMS and connect to a server.

2. Open a new query window, and enter and execute the following T-SQL code:

```
USE AdventureWorks2012
SELECT
     DB_NAME(ius.database_id) DBName,
     OBJECT_NAME(ius.object_id) ObjName,
     i.name,
     ius.user_seeks,
     ius.user_scans,
     ius.user_lookups,
     ius.user_updates
FROM sys.dm_db_index_usage_stats ius
INNER JOIN sys.indexes i
     ON      ius.object_id = i.object_id AND
             ius.index_id = i.index_id
WHERE
     DB_NAME(ius.database_id) = 'AdventureWorks2012'
```

The preceding query includes only an abbreviated list of columns from the DMO. The last three columns return information that is a good starting point to determine index usage. All three show how many times the index was used by a query, varying only by the type of usage. Each time a query performs a seek, scan, or lookup of an index, the value in the corresponding column is incremented.

3. The results of the query will vary depending on when your instance of SQL Server was last restarted. An index will not appear in this DMO if it has never been read from or has not been updated since the last server reboot. To ensure that some data is returned, open a new query window, and enter and execute the following T-SQL code:

```
USE AdventureWorks2012;
SELECT *
FROM Sales.SalesOrderHeader
WHERE Orderdate = '2005-06-29 00:00:00.000'
```

4. Rerun the query from step 2.

5. Identify the row that contains the SalesOrderHeader table and the IX_SalesOrderHeader_OrderDate index. Make note of the number of user seeks.

6. Rerun the query from step 3.

7. Rerun the query from step 2 and notice that the value in the user_seeks column from the SalesOrderHeader table and IX_SalesOrderHeader_OrderDate index increased.

Again, the results from the query in step 2 can be used as a starting point in your determination. Always keep in mind the amount of time that has passed since your server was last restarted. The server uptime should encompass all regular business-cycle processes, reporting periods, period-end data operations, and so on.

Creating and updating database statistics

To further improve query performance, SQL Server generates statistics based on the distribution of data in a table or indexed view. These statistics are used by the query optimizer to create optimal query execution plans. You can manually create and update the statistics, or you can allow SQL Server to automatically handle the creation and updating of statistics. If an index is rebuilt, the statistics are automatically updated. However, if an index is reorganized, you should manually update the statistics. Therefore, as a best practice, you should implement a strategy that encompasses both manual and automatic statistics updates.

Viewing database statistic options

You can set two database options to automatically create statistics and update statistics: Auto Create Statistics and Auto Update Statistics. These two options are turned on by default and are recommended best practices for most database environments.

View database statistics options using SSMS

1. Open SSMS and connect to a server.

2. Expand the server tree.

3. Expand the Databases folder.

4. Right-click the AdventureWorks2012 database and select Properties from the menu.

5. Select Options from the Select a Page pane.

6. Notice that both Auto Create Statistics and Auto Update Statistics are set to True. If you decide not to allow SQL Server to perform these operations, set the options to False.

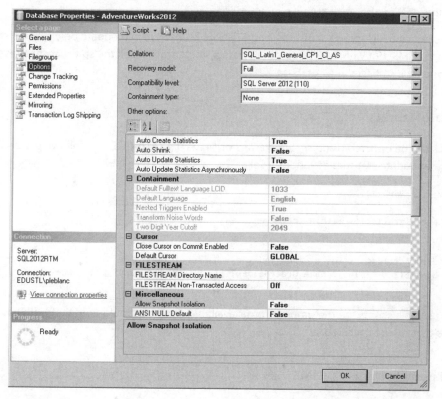

7. Click Cancel.

While you can manually create statistics, the optimizer generally does a good job at maintaining statistics on its own. With the Auto Create Statistics and Auto Update Statistics options set to True, most of the statistics work will be done for you automatically. In some isolated cases, you may find that a query has missing statistics and you have a need to manually create them. Detecting missing statistics is well beyond the scope of this book. However, manually updating statistics should be part of any regular database maintenance plan.

Updating database statistics

You may be wondering, Why should statistics be manually updated if the Auto Update Statistics option is set to True? Doesn't SQL Server do a good job at updating the statistics? In most cases, the answer is yes, and you should not manually update statistics too often. Each time statistics are updated, queries must be recompiled, requiring the optimizer to invalidate cached execution plans, so the optimizer must generate a new execution plan for the query. If this process is constantly repeated, it could negatively affect performance.

With the Auto Update Statistics option set to True, most of the statistics will be updated regularly by SQL Server. However, there will be times when you need to manually update the statistics. Very similar to indexes, statistics should be updated when query performance is slow or when there have been changes to the underlying data—more specifically, inserts. In addition, you should consider updating statistics after maintenance operations.

You can manually update statistics using SSMS or T-SQL. You can update only a single statistic at a time using SSMS, but with T-SQL you can update a single statistic, all the statistics for a given table or index, or all the statistics in a database.

Update statistics using T-SQL

Statistics can be updated using *sp_updatestats* or *UPDATE STATISTICS*. The following are sample scripts that update statistics at various levels:

```
USE AdventureWorks2012
GO
--Update all statistics within the AdventureWorks2012 database
EXEC sp_updatestats
GO
--Update all statistics for a given index on the specified table
UPDATE STATISTICS [Sales].[SalesOrderHeader] [IX_SalesOrderHeader_OrderDate]
GO
```

Both sample scripts are the simplest forms available, but you should note that both have different options that can be specified.

Update statistics using SSMS

1. Open SSMS and connect to a server.

2. Expand the Databases folder.

3. Expand the AdventureWorks2012 database.

4. Expand the Tables folder.

5. Expand the Sales.SalesOrderHeader table.

6. Expand the Statistics folder.

7. Right-click PK_SalesOrderHeader_SalesOrderID and then click Properties.

The Statistics Properties dialog box opens.

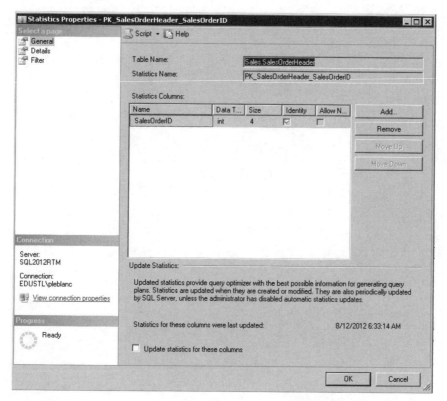

8. Toward the bottom of the screen, select the Update Statistics for These Columns check box.

9. Click OK.

The statistics are now up to date.

> **Note** While you are able to use SSMS to update statistics, it is definitely not as flexible as using T-SQL. In the event of an emergency, you could use this method to quickly update a particular statistic, but you should defer to T-SQL as a more holistic and effective approach.

Summary

This chapter covered the different techniques you can use to maintain indexes and statistics. While the techniques used for each are completely different, you should perform both on a regular basis. In the next chapter, you will learn how to create a scheduled maintenance plan that will maintain indexes and update statistics.

Maintenance plans

After completing this chapter, you will be able to

- Understand the importance of maintenance plans.

- Check for database consistency.

- Use the Maintenance Plan Wizard.

Maintenance plans are an essential part of ensuring database availability, consistency, and performance. Most plans include at least four steps:

- Database backup and backup retention policy

- Index maintenance

- Statistics maintenance

- Database consistency checking

At some point, these steps may run together on a daily basis, or they may run on an individual basis daily, weekly, monthly, or according to another schedule that satisfies the needs of your organization.

Prior chapters have focused on backups, index maintenance, and statistics maintenance, which are integral steps in the execution plan. In this chapter, you are going to add one more task to the list: database consistency checking. After a brief discussion about consistency, the focus will shift to building a complete execution plan for the databases in your environment.

Performing database consistency checks

Performing a database consistency check against a Microsoft SQL Server database involves validating the logical and physical integrity of all database objects. The schema, data allocations, page and storage consistency, and many other aspects of the database are verified for consistency. Under the hood, several individual consistency checks at various levels are executed.

After all of that, you may think that performing a consistency check is a huge undertaking. Actually, only two keywords are needed to perform an entire check: *DBCC checkdb*. Of course, you have several options that you can append to this statement to limit the results, display additional information, or even correct consistency problems. However, those two keywords alone will provide you with the fundamental tasks needed to fully accomplish the job.

1. Open SSMS and connect to a server.

2. Open a new query window, and enter and execute the following T-SQL code:

```
USE AdventureWorks2012
GO
DBCC checkdb;
```

3. Click the Messages tab in the results pane.

```
Messages
DBCC results for 'AdventureWorks2012'.
Service Broker Msg 9675, State 1: Message Types analyzed: 14.
Service Broker Msg 9676, State 1: Service Contracts analyzed: 6.
Service Broker Msg 9667, State 1: Services analyzed: 3.
Service Broker Msg 9668, State 1: Service Queues analyzed: 3.
Service Broker Msg 9669, State 1: Conversation Endpoints analyzed: 0.
Service Broker Msg 9674, State 1: Conversation Groups analyzed: 0.
Service Broker Msg 9670, State 1: Remote Service Bindings analyzed: 0.
Service Broker Msg 9605, State 1: Conversation Priorities analyzed: 0.
DBCC results for 'sys.sysrscols'.
There are 1775 rows in 21 pages for object "sys.sysrscols".
DBCC results for 'sys.sysrowsets'.
There are 328 rows in 3 pages for object "sys.sysrowsets".
DBCC results for 'sys.sysclones'.
There are 0 rows in 0 pages for object "sys.sysclones".
DBCC results for 'sys.sysallocunits'.
There are 374 rows in 5 pages for object "sys.sysallocunits".
DBCC results for 'sys.sysfiles1'.
There are 2 rows in 1 pages for object "sys.sysfiles1".
DBCC results for 'sys.sysseobjvalues'.
There are 0 rows in 0 pages for object "sys.sysseobjvalues".
DBCC results for 'sys.syspriorities'
```

Any found consistency errors will be displayed in this listing.

Creating maintenance plans

Now that all the tasks that make up the maintenance plan have been discussed, the final step is to create a maintenance plan that executes on a regular schedule. You have two options when creating your plans: T-SQL or the Maintenance Plan Wizard. Note that the actual scheduling of the maintenance plan is done using SQL Server Agent, which is discussed at length in Chapter 27, "SQL Server Agent." The important thing to remember for now is that SQL Server Agent can be used to schedule tasks.

Using the Maintenance Plan Wizard

The Maintenance Plan Wizard is probably the easiest way to develop maintenance plans in SQL Server. However, it does lack flexibility compared to T-SQL. For example, you cannot limit what indexes are rebuilt; it's either all or nothing. As a beginner, you should start with the wizard, and as your skills increase, you can begin building more plans using T-SQL.

Use the Maintenance Plan Wizard

1. Open SSMS and connect to a server.

2. In Object Explorer, expand the server tree.

3. Expand the Management folder.

4. Right-click the Maintenance Plans folder and select Maintenance Plan Wizard.

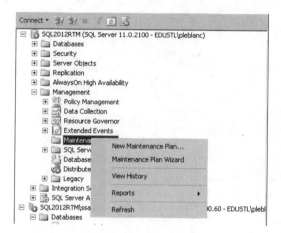

5. Click Next on the Maintenance Plan Wizard Introduction page.

6. On the Select Plan Properties page, type **AdventureWorks Maint Plan** in the Name text box.

7. Ensure that the Single Schedule for the Entire Plan or No Schedule option is selected.

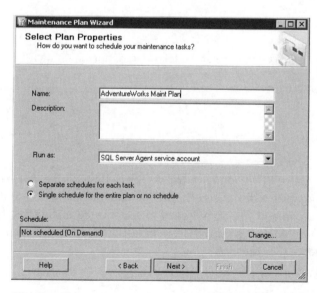

8. Click the Change button to create a schedule. The New Job Schedule dialog box appears.

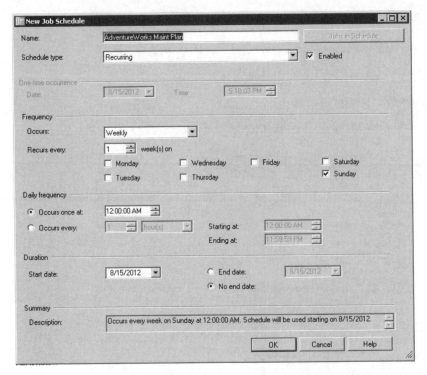

9. In the New Job Schedule dialog box, type **Nightly AW Maint Schedule** in the Name text box.

10. In the Frequency section, change the Occurs drop-down list to Daily. Several further options are available, and you should review each section, but for now accept all the other defaults.

11. Click OK.

12. Click Next.

13. On the Select Maintenance Tasks page, select the following options:

    • Check Database Integrity

    • Rebuild Index

    • Back Up Database (Full)

> **Note** You may have noticed that you have two choices with regard to indexes: Rebuild Index or Reorganize Index. If you choose Rebuild Index, then the statistics are automatically updated and you do not need to select Update Statistics. However, if you select Reorganize Index, then you must select Update Statistics because that process does not update the statistics.

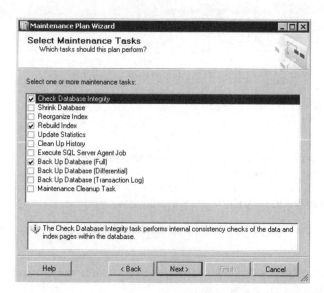

You have several options to choose from, but for the sake of brevity, only a few are selected. You can create additional maintenance plans to perform other tasks. For example, you can create a new maintenance plan to perform differential or transaction log backups.

14. Click Next.

On the Select Maintenance Task Order page, you can order the tasks.

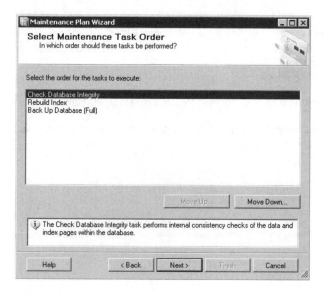

15. Change the order to the following:

    - Back Up Database (Full)

    - Rebuild Index

    - Check Database Integrity

16. Click Next.

17. On the Define Back Up Database (Full) Task page, select AdventureWorks2012 from the Database(s) drop-down list. Click OK.

18. Accept all the other defaults and click Next.

19. On the Define Rebuild Index Task page, select AdventureWorks2012 from the Database(s) drop-down list.

20. In the Advanced Options section, select the Keep Index Online While Reindexing check box, and select the Rebuild Indexes Offline option.

21. Click Next.

22. On the Define Database Integrity Task page, select AdventureWorks2012 from the Database(s) drop-down list.

23. Click Next.

24. On the Select Report Operations page, you can specify if and where you want to create a log file. Also, if you have any operators created, you can have the report emailed. (Operators are discussed further in Chapter 27.)

25. Accept the defaults and click Next.

26. Review your selected options on the Complete the Wizard page and click Finish.

    The Maintenance Plan Wizard Progress page appears, and each action should successfully complete.

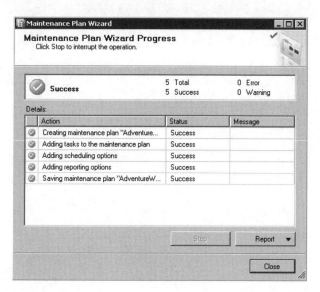

27. Click Close.

28. Finally, to verify that a job was created, in Object Explorer expand the SQL Server Agent Jobs folder.

29. Right-click the job and select Properties to view the details.

Note You will learn more about SQL Server Agent jobs in Chapter 27.

Summary

This chapter discussed database consistency checking, which is the final task involved in building a complete database maintenance plan. You learned how to build a maintenance plan using a wizard that covers a broad scope of items. What you select and when you schedule it to run depends on your environment. Regardless, you should always ensure that you are maintaining your database at all the levels discussed in this chapter.

Database management

SQL Server Profiler

After completing this chapter, you will be able to

- Understand how and when to use SQL Server Profiler.

- Create a trace.

- Understand the advantages of running a server-side trace.

At the core of most enterprise applications is a relational database. Unfortunately, when the database is experiencing performance issues, so will any system that depends on it. Identifying the cause of a slowdown and correcting the associated issues can be problematic. When it comes to relational databases, there can be any number of problems, including but not limited to high CPU usage, memory limitations, high disk activity, or slow queries.

For a new database administrator (DBA), identifying these problems can be like looking for a needle in a haystack. To make matters somewhat simpler, Microsoft SQL Server includes a tool, SQL Server Profiler, that has the ability to capture almost any type of activity that can be executed against an instance of the SQL Server database engine.

In this chapter, you'll learn what SQL Server Profiler is and how and when to use it. You'll go through the steps to create, run, pause, and stop a trace. In addition, you will learn how to create a trace template that you can reuse. Finally, you will learn how to create a server-side trace that captures information in a less intrusive manner than interactively running the SQL Server Profiler GUI.

Understanding SQL Server Profiler

SQL Server Profiler can capture any event, from blocking to long-running queries. Over time, it may become one of the most used tools in your DBA toolbox. SQL Server Profiler can be run interactively or as a server-side operation. If you plan to run SQL Server Profiler for only a short period of time, using the GUI is a good option. However, if you plan to run it for an extended period of time, you should avoid using the GUI because it can degrade the performance of your SQL Server instance. Instead, create a server-side T-SQL trace using a T-SQL script on the server. Both methods are explained later in this chapter.

Typical uses of SQL Server Profiler

SQL Server Profiler has become a popular tool. However, with the release of SQL Server 2012, it has been placed on the deprecated list and will eventually be removed from the product altogether.

 Note SQL Server Profiler is being replaced by the SSMS-embedded Extended Events (XEvents) tool, which is discussed in Chapter 24, "Extended Events."

Even though SQL Server Profiler is going to be removed, as a beginner you should consider using it as a precursor to Extended Events. Most of the information that can be collected in SQL Server Profiler will be available with Extended Events, and you will be able to duplicate the typical uses of SQL Server Profiler with Extended Events. Some of these uses are as follows:

- Performance tuning

- Detecting deadlocks

- Auditing

- Detecting blocking

Again, these are only a few of the tasks that can be performed with either, and as time goes on and your skills improve, you will find several other uses for SQL Server Profiler.

Creating traces

Before you begin to use SQL Server Profiler, you will need to understand a few terms. The first term to become familiar with is *trace*. The SQL Server Profiler GUI creates a trace to capture server and database activity. The activity that is captured is stored in a *trace file*, which you can use to diagnose problems that may exist. No matter if you are using the GUI or running the trace on the server, all the events are written to a trace file.

Trace files are composed of *events*, which could be the execution of a query or stored procedure, a successful or failed login, a database data or log file growth event, or the acquisition of locks, to mention a few. The trace file contains rows, and each row equates to a trace event, with complete information on the connection, the start and end time of the event, the application and host origin and, in many cases, the actual T-SQL text executed against the server. The events are grouped into event categories such as the following:

- Locks

- Security audit

- Stored procedures

- T-SQL

This is a very short list of the event classes available via SQL Server Profiler. It is unlikely that you will ever use all the events that are included, but as time goes on, you will identify those that can be useful as situations arise.

Create, filter, and run a trace using SQL Server Profiler

1. Click Start | All Programs | SQL Server 2012 | Performance Tools | SQL Server Profiler.

2. Select File | New Trace from the SQL Server Profiler menu.

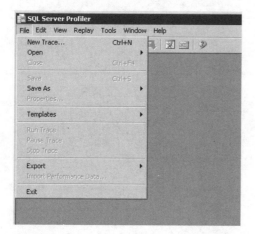

3. In the Connect to Server dialog box, enter your server name in the Server Name text box.

4. Click Connect.

5. In the Trace Properties dialog box, enter **Long Running Stored Procedures** in the Trace Name text box.

6. Ensure that Standard (Default) is selected in the Use the Template drop-down list.

    Other templates are available. Selecting a different template will configure a predetermined list of events on the Events Selection tab, which will be discussed later. You can always change these events later.

7. In the next section, you can save the trace to either a file or a table. This is important when you plan on analyzing the data later. You can always save the trace to a file or table. For now, don't select either. The trace will be displayed in the GUI only for now, but later you can save it to another location.

8. The final option is to enable a trace stop time. While this is not a requirement if you are going to run the trace interactively, you should definitely consider including a trace stop time. This will ensure that the trace stops capturing information and does not affect the performance of your server.

    Select the Enable Trace Stop Time check box. By default, the time in the box is one hour from the current time. You can change it to the time that meets your requirements.

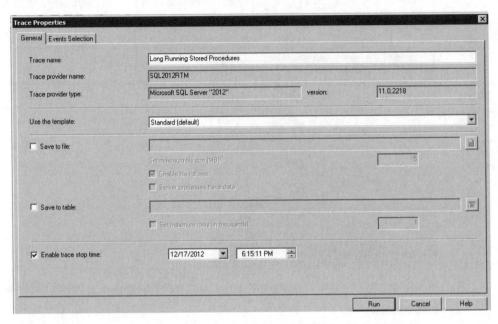

9. Click the Events Selection tab at the top of the Trace Properties dialog box.

    This is where you select the different events that will be captured by the trace. Each event is grouped by event category.

10. Clear all events in the Events list.

11. Select the Show All Columns check box.

12. Select the Show All Events check box.

13. Scroll down to the Stored Procedures event category and select the box next to the SP:Completed event. Scroll down further to the T-SQL event category and select the box next to the SP:StmtCompleted event.

14. Clear the Show All Events check box.

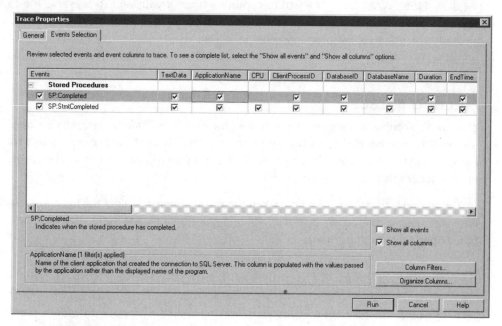

15. Click the Organize Columns button.

16. Scroll down the list until you locate TextData. Select it and click the Up button until it is at the top of the list.

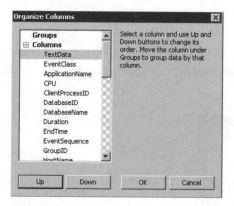

17. Click OK.

18. Click the Run button.

Depending on what is currently using your SQL Server instance, you may or may not see any events being generated.

19. In the menu bar, select File | Stop Trace. Do not close this trace; you will use it in the upcoming sections.

Note When using the GUI to capture a trace, if you want to preserve the captured information, do not stop the trace. Instead, pause and restart the trace. If you stop the trace, all captured information will be lost.

Filtering a trace

You can do a couple of things to minimize the amount of information captured by a trace. The first is to limit the number of data columns included in a trace event. A data column is an attribute of an event class that can be stored in a trace file. The availability of a data column depends on whether or not it is applicable to the selected event.

The second is to include trace filters. You can specify filters that limit the trace to a specific database, to a specific connection, by the duration of a query, or by application name. Trace filters can be based upon several other criteria.

Specify trace criteria

1. If you closed the trace that you were working on in the previous procedure, please repeat the steps in that section. If the trace is open, skip this step and go to step 2.

2. If the trace is running, stop or pause it. Then select File | Properties.

3. Click the Events Selection tab.

4. Click the Column Filters button.

5. In the left pane, select DatabaseName.

6. Expand the Like tree, and type **AdventureWorks2012** into the blank text box that appears below Like.

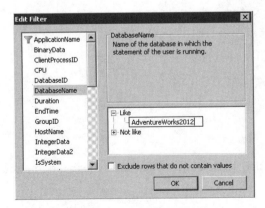

7. Select Duration from the left pane.

8. Expand the Greater Than or Equal To tree and type **5000** into the blank text box that appears below Like.

> **Note** When filtering by duration, you must enter the value in milliseconds or one thousandths (5000 ms is 5 seconds) of a second.

9. Click OK.

10. Open SSMS, connect to a server, and then open a new query window.

11. Type and execute the following T-SQL code in the new query window:

```
USE AdventureWorks2012;
IF(OBJECT_ID('dbo.uspGetDepartments')) IS NOT NULL
    DROP PROC dbo.uspGetDepartments
GO
CREATE PROC dbo.uspGetDepartments
AS
SET NOCOUNT ON
    WAITFOR DELAY '00:00:07'
    SELECT * FROM HumanResources.Department
SET NOCOUNT OFF
```

12. If SQL Server Profiler is stopped or paused, select File | Run Trace.

13. Open a new query window in SSMS, and type and execute the following T-SQL code:

```
USE AdventureWorks2012;
EXEC dbo.uspGetDepartments;
```

14. Return to SQL Server Profiler, and in about seven seconds, two events will be captured.

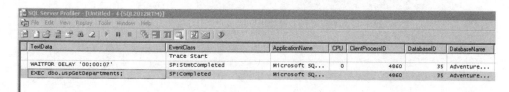

Notice that the first row that has TextData contains a T-SQL command, which causes the query to essentially pause execution for the amount of time specified—seven seconds, in the case of this stored procedure. If you return to the stored procedure and remove that statement, and rerun the query while the trace is running, you should not see any events captured. Do not modify the query, as you will use it as is later.

15. From the SQL Server Profiler menu, select File | Stop Trace.

16. Select File | Save As | Trace File.

17. If a Long Running Stored Procedures trace already exists, select it and click Save. If not, type **Long Running Stored Procedures** in the File Name text box and click Save.

You can browse to the directory where you saved the file and open it with SQL Server Profiler to analyze the trace.

Do not close SQL Server Profiler, as you will use it in the next section.

Creating trace templates

By default, SQL Server Profiler includes several trace templates. Some can be useful at times; however, you may find that you are running custom-configured traces repeatedly. Instead of configuring the trace each time you run it, SQL Server Profiler allows you to save the trace as a template.

Create a trace template

1. If you closed the trace that you were working on in the previous procedure, repeat the steps in that section. If the trace is open, skip this step and go to step 2.

2. Ensure that the trace is stopped.

3. Select File | Save As | Trace Template.

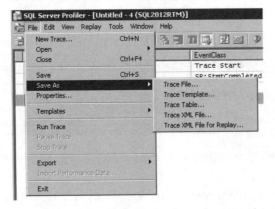

4. In the Template Name text box, type **AW Long Running Stored Procedures**.

5. Click OK. You will get a successful save.

6. Click OK.

7. Select File | New Trace.

8. Connect to your server.

9. In the Trace Properties dialog box, expand the Use the Template drop-down list and scroll down. You will see the newly created template.

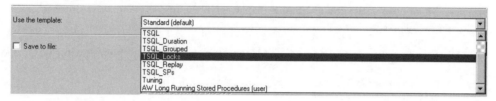

Now instead of configuring the trace each time you want to capture long-running stored procedures, you can leverage the template and quickly start the trace.

Running server-side traces

The GUI offers a quick method for gathering events and viewing the information. However, if you capture an excessive number of events, you could adversely affect the performance of your server. As an option, you can instead run the trace on the server side, which is less intrusive and has less of an effect on the server.

Create and run a server-side trace

1. Click Start | All Programs | SQL Server 2012 | Performance Tools | SQL Server Profiler.

2. Select File | New Trace from the SQL Server Profiler menu.

3. In the Trace Name text box in the Properties dialog box, type **Long Running**.

4. From the Use the Template drop-down list, select AW Long Running Stored Procedures (users).

5. Select the Enable Trace Stop Time check box and specify a date and time.

6. Click Run.

7. Select File | Stop Trace.

8. Select File | Export | Script Trace Definition | For SQL Server 2005 - SQL11.

9. In the Save As window, in the File Name text box, type **serverSide** and then click Save.

10. Open SSMS.

11. Select File | Open | File.

12. Browse to the location where the trace was exported and select the file.

13. Click Open.

14. Locate InsertFileNameHere in the script and replace it with **C:\Program Files\ Microsoft SQL Server\MSSQL11.SQL2012\MSSQL\Log\LongRunning**.

15. Execute the query.

    Make note of the TraceID that is displayed in the results pane. If no other traces are running, the value should be 2.

16. Open a new query window in SSMS, and type and execute the following T-SQL code:

```
USE AdventureWorks2012;
EXEC dbo.uspGetDepartments;
```

17. When the query completes, browse to C:\Program Files\Microsoft SQL Server\MSSQL11. SQL2012\MSSQL\Log. You will see a new trace file, LongRunning.trc.

18. To stop the trace, open a new query window, and type and execute the following query:

```
USE master;
exec sp_trace_setstatus 2, 0
exec sp_trace_setstatus 2, 2
```

    Stopping the trace is a two-step process. First, by using the system stored procedure *sp_trace_setstatus*, you stop the trace. Then, in the next call of the procedure, you delete the trace definition from the server. The first parameter is the *traceid*, which you should have remembered from step 15. The second parameter sets the status of the trace, 0 stops the trace, and 2 deletes it from the server.

19. Open the trace file with SQL Server Profiler and you should see information about the stored procedure execution.

Summary

In this chapter, you learned some of the many uses of SQL Server Profiler. Even though SQL Server Profiler will not be included in future releases of Microsoft SQL Server, it still remains a viable performance-tuning option. Since this tool has a very intuitive GUI, it is a good starting point for any DBA, and it should still be considered for use in modern troubleshooting.

Extended Events

After completing this chapter, you will be able to

■ Create and configure Extended Events sessions.

■ Use an Extended Events session to monitor system performance.

■ Analyze captured Extended Events data in SQL Server Management Studio.

Extended Events (or XEvents) is the next-generation tracing and troubleshooting architecture for SQL Server. If you've never heard of Extended Events before Microsoft SQL Server 2012, don't worry, this chapter will provide a solid introduction to this highly flexible, user-configurable monitoring tool.

SQL Server Profiler is deprecated in SQL Server 2012, and SQL Trace will be replaced by the Extended Events system in a future version of SQL Server. Extended Events offers many advantages over the older tools, including much less overhead, better performance at scale, and the ability to capture details that were previously not observable.

The most immediate advantage you may enjoy is that the default system Extended Events session that is already passively running on SQL Server 2012 captures deadlocks. This means that for the first time, you can diagnose a deadlock that happened in the past without setting up and catching a SQL trace. This is a crucial advantage for DBAs!

This chapter will introduce you to Extended Events at a high level and run through a pair of example scenarios that use the tool's powerful monitoring capabilities.

Understanding the Extended Events architecture

Extended Events is the all-purpose monitoring tool for SQL Server, from basic error capturing to advanced troubleshooting. Let's go over some basic Extended Events architecture terminology:

■ Extended Events is organized around *sessions*, which capture a configurable collection of *events*, which are organized in *categories*. Events as they occur on SQL Server are sent to *targets* to collect the data. The most basic and fastest data storage target is an event_file or .xel file.

■ *Actions* or *global fields* describe basic information that will be familiar to you from SQL trace fields: database id, hostname, session id, object name, and statement. *Event filters* or *predicates* allow you to refine the scope—for example, by filtering requests only in the AdventureWorks2012 database.

- A *package* is a container of the previously described objects that are collectible from a *module*, which is provided by a Windows process (such as the main executable of SQL Server, sqlservr.exe).

Creating and configuring an Extended Events session

You'll get started by using Extended Events to monitor query activity on the database, much in the same way you would use SQL Server Profiler to monitor database activity.

Create and configure an Extended Events session

1. Open SQL Server Management Studio (SSMS) and connect to a server.

2. Open Object Explorer if it is not already open.

3. Expand the server node, and expand the Management folder.

4. Expand the Extended Events folder, and then expand the Sessions folder.

   You'll see two sessions already set up, one for AlwaysOn_health and one for system_health (you'll use this later in the chapter).

 Note See Chapter 31, "AlwaysOn," for more information about AlwaysOn.

5. Right-click the Sessions folder and click New Session Wizard.

6. Skip the Introduction page by clicking Next.

7. Type **Query Monitoring** in the Session Name text box. If you are attempting to troubleshoot a startup issue, selecting the Start the Event Session at Server Startup check box may come in handy on this page. For now, leave it cleared. Click Next.

8. On the next page, select the Use This Event Session Template option, and then select Query Detail Tracking from the drop-down list.

 Note You will find each of the built-in templates already provided and their extensive descriptions here. If you want to only manually add events and fields, select the Do Not Use a Template option.

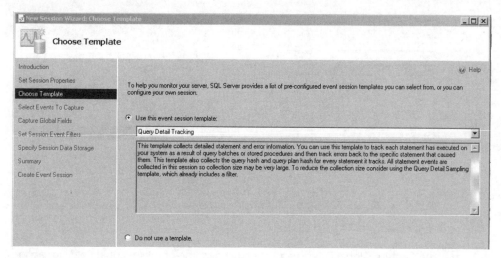

9. Click Next.

   On the Select Events to Capture page, note that the template has already selected a half-dozen events to capture in this Extended Events session. These events are in the Selected Events box on the right side of the page.

10. On the left side of the Select Events to Capture page, type **login** into the Event Library search text box.

    Notice how the library is quickly filtered, allowing you to search for commands easily.

11. Click the results row for login.

    Note that below the search results window, a detailed description of the event is provided, as well as fields predetermined for this event.

12. Click the > arrow to move the login event into the Selected Events window.

13. Click module_end in the Selected Events window.

14. Click the < arrow to remove the module_end event from the Selected Events window. Now the module_end event will not show up in your session data.

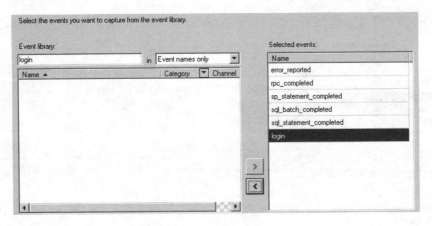

15. Click Next.

16. The Capture Global Fields page already has some of these global fields (or actions) selected for you, based on the template. Scroll down in this window and select the box next to database_name. Click Next.

17. The Set Session Event Filters page allows you to limit the activity returned by the session. In this case, you'll add a filter to show only activity in the AdventureWorks2012 database.

In the white text box located in the Additional Filters (Applied to All Events) section, click the Click Here to Add a Clause area.

18. In the Field drop-down box, select sqlserver.database_name.

19. You can change the selection in the Operator drop-down to any of a variety of comparison choices. For now, leave this selection as equals (=).

20. Type **AdventureWorks2012** in the text box under Value.

This will filter session data to include only events where the request's database_name equals AdventureWorks2012. You could just as easily have set up a filter on the database_id of the AdventureWorks2012 database, the user name, or the client host_name.

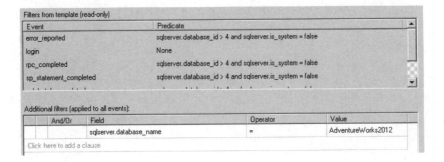

21. Click Next.

On the Specify Session Data Storage page, you'll see two of the three primary targets. The ring_buffer Target check box is enabled by default—this allows for continuous, rolling, in-memory storage of event data. However, the fastest and most versatile target is event_file.

22. Select the box next to Save Data to a File for Later Analysis, and then clear the box next to Work with Only the Most Recent Data.

By default, the location of event_file is *<instance path>*\MSSQL\Log\Query Monitoring.xel. You can also limit the file size and have the file roll over to prevent one file from becoming too large. This behavior is very similar to the SQL Server Profiler setting with the same name.

23. Change the Maximum File Size setting to 50 MB, and then clear the Enable File Rollover option.

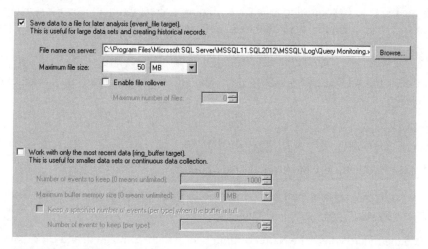

24. Click Next and then click Finish.

25. On the Create Event Session page, despite the appearance of a large green circle with a check mark in it, you're not done yet. The session has not yet been created.

26. Select the Start the Event Session Immediately After Session Creation check box.

27. Select the Watch Live Data on Screen As It Is Captured check box.

This is the third main way to access data, and it will open a new screen for the SSMS streaming data provider. This is the easiest way to access data, but it should be used only briefly—it also has the most overhead of the three Extended Events targets.

28. Click Close.

You will see the Query Monitoring: Live Data window is already running, and you may see it showing some activity in your database. Keep this window open so you can perform the next set of steps in the section that follows.

Using an Extended Events session to monitor system performance

Now that you have an Extended Events session running on the server, you'll give it some activity to capture. If you are familiar with tracing server activity using the SQL Server Profiler tool from any previous version of SQL Server, you'll notice similar behaviors in this modern interface.

You'll be pleasantly surprised to see dramatic improvements in the ability to view captured data, all done with less overhead on your database server. The Extended Events Live Data window uses less I/O and CPU to display events than the SQL Server Profiler tool.

Use an Extended Events session to monitor system performance

You should see the Query Monitoring: Live Data window is already running, and you may see it showing some activity in your database. To generate some activity, you'll run a simple *SELECT* statement.

1. In Object Explorer, expand the Databases folder.

2. Right-click the AdventureWorks2012 database, and then click New Query. Execute the following query:

```
USE AdventureWorks2012;
select * from [Production].[TransactionHistory]
```

3. In SSMS, click the Query Monitoring: Live Data tab.

   You should see a set of events just generated by yourself. Because this buffer reads the data asynchronously, there may be as much as a five-second delay.

4. Locate the record where the Name column is sql_batch_completed, and click that record. Information about that event will appear in the Details tab.

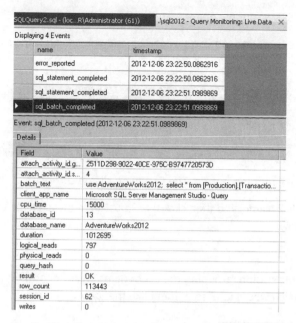

Field	Value
attach_activity_id.g...	2511D298-9022-40CE-975C-B9747720573D
attach_activity_id.s...	4
batch_text	use AdventureWorks2012; select '' from [Production].[Transactio...
client_app_name	Microsoft SQL Server Management Studio - Query
cpu_time	15000
database_id	13
database_name	AdventureWorks2012
duration	1012695
logical_reads	797
physical_reads	0
query_hash	0
result	OK
row_count	113443
session_id	62
writes	0

5. On the Details tab, locate the row with a Field value of batch_text. This will show the query you executed in the other tab, as it was captured by the Extended Events session.

6. Close the Query Monitoring: Live Data tab. Note that this does not stop the Extended Events session; it is still running on SQL Server.

   Now you'll stop the Extended Events session back in Object Explorer.

7. If it's not already open, expand the server folder, expand Management, expand Extended Events, and expand Sessions. Right-click the Query Monitoring session and then click Stop Session.

   Note that the icon changes from a green arrow pointing right to a red arrow pointing down.

8. Navigate to the operating system folder where you stored the .xel file, which should be *<instance path>*\MSSQL\Log\.

   Note that the actual file name has a uniquely identifying string appended to it—for example, Query Monitoring_0_129993306334000000.xel.

9. Double-click the file. A new SSMS window opens with this file in the tab.

   This interface is similar to the Live Data tab you saw earlier, and you can view the same details for each recorded event.

10. In the SSMS toolbar, click the Grouping button. The Grouping dialog box opens.

11. Under Available Columns, click Name, and then click the > button to move Name to the Columns Grouped On window.

12. Click OK.

    On a lengthy Extended Events session, grouping the event name will offer additional insight into the recorded events, which would look something like the following image.

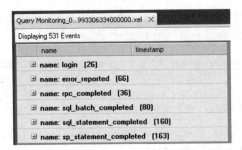

13. On the toolbar located above the tab, click the Filters button.

14. In the Filters window, click the Set Time filter.

15. Use the sliders to restrict the current display of events to a time frame precise to the second. You can add other filters here to help you make sense of a large Extended Events event_file data set.

16. Click OK to accept your settings and to close the Filters window.

17. On the toolbar located above the tab, click the Choose Columns button.

    In the Choose Columns window, you can add more fields to the dataset.

18. Locate database_name, duration, batch_text, and session_id in the Available Columns screen, and use the > arrow button to move each to the Selected Columns window. Use the up and down arrows to arrange the columns in any order.

19. Click OK.

20. Back in the Query Monitoring tab, expand the sql_batch_completed group.

    You can now see more data for each event, including the statement you executed earlier that begins with "use AdventureWorks2012".

name	timestamp	database_name	duration	session_id	batch_text
sql_batch_completed	2012-12-06 23:19:57.2510825	AdventureWorks2012	1124023	62	use AdventureWorks2012; select * from [Production].[TransactionHistory]

Summary

This chapter reviewed the basics of the state-of-the-art monitoring and troubleshooting Extended Events feature of Microsoft SQL Server 2012. While Extended Events has been part of SQL Server since the 2008 version, it now includes a GUI to manipulate and view the sessions. You learned about the architecture of Extended Events and how to set up, tune, stop, and analyze a basic Extended Events session.

SQL Server security

After completing this chapter, you will be able to

- Understand the SQL Server security model.

- Understand principals.

- Create SQL Server logins and users.

- Create user-defined server roles.

- Create database users.

- Create built-in database roles.

- Configure a contained database.

No matter if you work for a university, a bank, or a retail store, securing data is always a database administrator's (DBA's) top priority. Who can access the data, what data they can access, and how to access the data are often main topics of conversation inside and outside the information technology (IT) department. Data access needs will vary across applications, departments, and individuals, but the underlying requirement of governing permissions persists for every aspect of the data.

Microsoft SQL Server 2012 provides a very robust security structure that allows DBAs to control access from the server down to a specific object within the database. For example, a DBA could be given server-level permission without being granted any data-level access. Or an application or individual could be given access to a database or database objects without being granted any server-level permissions.

The topic of SQL Server security could fill an entire book itself because there are so many items to consider. The following are just a few of the questions that should be asked and addressed with regard to SQL Server security:

- Should SQL Server be network accessible?

- What port should SQL Server use?

- Who has access to backup files?

- Who can interactively log on to SQL Server?

- How should the SQL Server files be secured?

- How should SQL Server encryption keys and backups be configured and maintained?

Most of these questions are well beyond the scope of this book, and as a result this chapter focuses primarily on instance-level and data-level access. This chapter's more limited focus is not meant to discount the importance of addressing the other questions and considerations surrounding SQL Server security. Instead it is meant to provide a solid starting point and foundation for those new to SQL Server Security.

Understanding principals

A *principal* is an entity that has access to SQL Server resources. There are generally three levels of principals:

- Windows

- SQL Server

- Database

A Windows account or group, whether local to the server or from Active Directory, can be a principal. A Windows principal can be granted access to a SQL Server instance as a Windows authenticated login. Active Directory can then handle activation or deactivation, password policy, and security workflows. As an alternative to Active Directory, SQL Server can handle authentication itself with SQL Server logins, where activation, deactivation, and security workflows must be handled by a DBA inside SQL Server. You can, however, enforce Active Directory policy on a SQL Server login by specifying an option, as you'll learn later in this chapter. You must have enabled Mixed Mode Authentication on the server for SQL Server authentication. In previous releases of SQL Server, server logins mapped to database users. Logins handled authentication and server-level permissions. However, with the release of SQL Server 2012, an alternative connection method is available with the concept of contained databases, which is discussed in the last section of this chapter. Depending on the selected authentication mode, which was discussed in Chapter 2, "Installing, configuring, and upgrading Microsoft SQL Server 2012," you may or may not be able to create SQL Server principals. You must have configured Mixed Mode Authentication to do this. Finally, for databases, you will have a user or role.

 Note In earlier releases of SQL Server, you must have already created a SQL Server login before a database user could be created. With the release of SQL Server 2012, that procedure has changed with the concept of contained databases, which is discussed in the last section of this chapter.

Creating server logins

A *login* is a security principal that is based on a Windows account or group. In addition, a login can be an account that is created on SQL Server. Server-level permissions, such as CREATE DATABASE or BACKUP DATABASE, can be granted to logins. If a login needs to access a database, it must be mapped to a database user, as discussed in the "Creating database users" section of this chapter.

By default, the sa login principal is created when SQL Server is installed. If you did not configure Mixed Mode Authentication, the account will be disabled. The sa account is an administrator account that has access to every SQL Server resource. As a best practice, avoid sharing the password for this account, and ensure that the password is changed on a regular basis.

Create a Windows-based login using SSMS

1. Open SQL Server Management Studio (SSMS) and connect to a server.

2. Open Object Explorer if it is not already open.

3. Expand the server tree.

4. Right-click the Security folder and select New | Login.

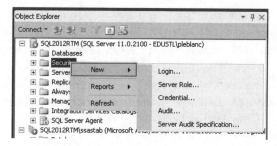

You must have an existing Windows account created in Active Directory or on your local machine to continue.

5. On the General page, enter a Windows account in the Login Name text box. You must enter the account in the following format: *domain\username*. For example, if the Windows account alias is jdoe, you will type **domain\jdoe**. Alternatively, you can click the Search button to find the Windows entity that you want to enter.

6. Since this is a Windows-based account, ensure that the Windows Authentication option is selected.

   If this was a SQL Server login, you would select the SQL Server Authentication option. With this option selected, a password must be entered and confirmed using the Password and Confirm Password text boxes.

7. You have the choice to enforce Windows Active Directory password polices and password expiration policies on this account by selecting the Enforce Password Policy and Enforce Password Expiration check boxes. This means that whatever polices have been configured for passwords and password expirations by your Active Directory administrator will be enforced for SQL Server login.

8. Finally, you can specify that the password must be changed when the account is initially used by selecting the User Must Change Password at Next Login option. For now, ensure that the Windows Authentication option is selected.

9. Leave the next options, Mapped to Certificate and Mapped to Asymmetric Key, cleared. You can select only one or the other.

Note Certificates and asymmetric keys are specific to encryption. You can learn more about these topics in SQL Server Books Online.

10. Selecting the Map to Credential check box allows you to map this login to the credential of another account. This option allows a SQL Server login to access resources external to SQL Server under the context of the login specified in the credential. For now, leave the box cleared.

11. When creating an account that will have database-level access, you should specify a default database using the Default Database drop-down list. When first authenticated to the SQL Server instance, a new connection will be in the default database's context. For example, if a new query window is opened by SSMS, the current database displayed will be the default database. If this is a login that will be used for data access, as a best practice always select a user-created database and not a system database. Assume the person who owns this account will be the DBA for this instance, so the default database can remain master.

12. The final drop-down list, Default Language, by default uses the default language configured on the server. Alternatively, you can select a language. For the purposes of this exercise, use the default.

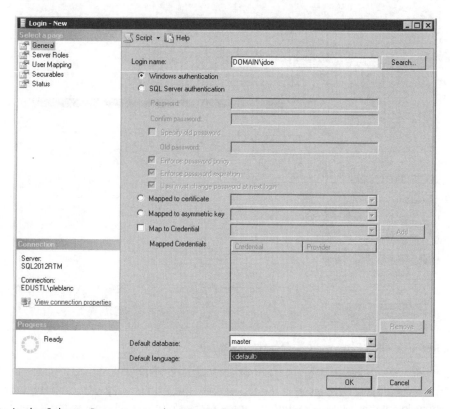

13. In the Select a Page pane, select Server Roles.

14. A list of built-in server roles is displayed on this page. The public role is selected by default. A description of each server role is provided in the "Creating user-defined server roles" section of this chapter. For now, select the box next to the sysadmin server role, which allows the system administrator to execute any task against the server.

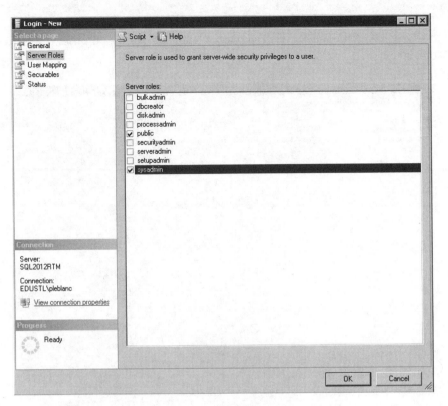

15. In the Select a Page pane, select User Mapping.

16. If you want to explicitly grant this user access to a specific database, you can select that database from the list displayed at the top of the page. Additionally, you can assign the user to built-in database roles. Creating database users is discussed further in the "Creating database users" section of this chapter. For now, do not select anything.

 Note The sysadmin role has unrestricted permissions to all databases without the need to create database users. Therefore, think carefully before adding anyone to this role.

17. In the Select a Page pane, select Securables.

This page lists items that can be secured and their corresponding permissions or the permissions that can be assigned to that login. Security is typically set at the server or database level. However, SQL Server provides you with the ability to set a much finer level of security.

18. Click the Search button. You are presented with three choices:

    a. You can add access to specific server-level items or you can provide access to every item by choosing the following option: The Server 'Your Server Name'.

    b. If you select the Specific Objects option, you can add items of different types.

    c. If you select All Objects of the Types option, you can holistically grant permissions to all objects of a specific type.

19. For the purposes of this exercise, click Cancel.

20. In the Select a Page pane, select Status. On this page, you have the ability to grant or deny the login permission to connect to the server. Ensure that the Grant option is selected.

21. Ensure that the Enabled option is selected.

22. Finally, if this was a SQL Server account, you could lock out the account, just as you can with Active Directory. Click the OK button and the login will be created.

You can also use T-SQL to perform these steps. In the following procedures, the first exercise repeats the steps outlined previously; the second exercise creates a SQL Server login. The main differences between the two are that in the second query you must provide a password and you can mimic Active Directory by explicitly including the MUST_CHANGE option and enabling both the CHECK_EXPIRATION and CHECK_POLICY options.

Create a Windows-based login using T-SQL

1. To create a Windows-based login using T-SQL, execute the following query:

```
USE [master]
GO
CREATE LOGIN [DOMAIN\jdoe] FROM WINDOWS WITH DEFAULT_DATABASE=[master]
GO
ALTER SERVER ROLE [sysadmin] ADD MEMBER [DOMAIN\jdoe]
GO
```

1. To create a SQL-based login using T-SQL, first ensure that the password provided meets the Windows policy for your domain, and then execute the following query:

```
USE [master]
GO
CREATE LOGIN [JDOE] WITH PASSWORD=N'password'
    MUST_CHANGE,
    DEFAULT_DATABASE=[master],
    CHECK_EXPIRATION=ON,
    CHECK_POLICY=ON
GO
ALTER SERVER ROLE [sysadmin] ADD MEMBER [JDOE]
GO
```

Creating user-defined server roles

In addition to the built-in server roles, in SQL Server 2012 you have the ability to create user-defined server roles. Now you can create server roles that combine the capabilities of existing server roles, or you can grant explicit permission to specific securables and create a more fine-grained server role.

Create a user-defined server role using SSMS

1. Open SSMS and connect to a server.

2. Open Object Explorer, if it is not already open.

3. Expand the server tree.

4. Expand the Security folder.

5. Right-click the Server Roles folder and select New Server Role from the menu.

6. In the New Server Role dialog box, type **BulkAdminAndDBCreator**.

7. In the Owner text box, type **sa** or click the ellipsis button and search for a login.

8. In the Securables section, select the box next to Servers.

9. In the Explicit section, select the box in the Grant column for both the Administer Bulk Operations and Create Any Database permissions.

10. Select Members in the Select a Page pane.

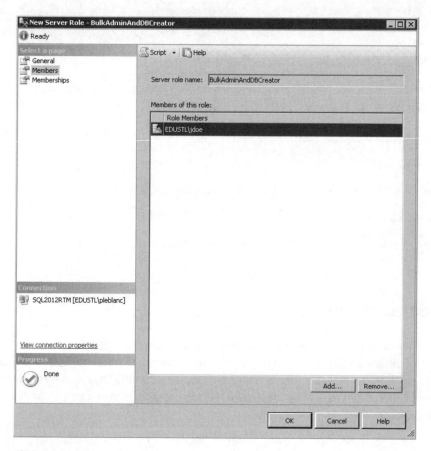

11. Click Add.

12. In the Enter the Object Names to Select text box, type *domain***\jdoe**, where *domain* is your domain.

13. Click the Check Names button to verify the login.

14. Click OK.

15. Select Memberships in the Select a Page pane.

16. If you wanted to add this role to one of the built-in server roles, you could do so here. Leave all boxes cleared and click OK.

1. To create a user-defined server role using T-SQL, execute the following query:

```
USE [master]
GO
CREATE SERVER ROLE [BulkAdminAndDBCreator]
GO
ALTER SERVER ROLE [BulkAdminAndDBCreator] ADD MEMBER [DOMAIN\jdoe]
GO
use [master]
GO
GRANT ADMINISTER BULK OPERATIONS TO [BulkAdminAndDBCreator]
GO
use [master]
GO
GRANT CREATE ANY DATABASE TO [BulkAdminAndDBCreator]
GO
```

Creating database users

Prior to SQL Server 2012, you created a SQL Server login before creating a database user. However, with the latest release and the inclusion of SQL Server contained databases, that best practice has been modified. With the new feature, you can create a user without a login and have user connections authenticate straight to the user database. This topic is discussed in detail in the "Configuring contained databases" section of this chapter.

For now, you'll focus on creating a user based on an existing login. A user can be based on a SQL Server or Windows login. During or after the creation of a user, you can grant access to specific objects such as tables, views, and stored procedures; access to all objects of a specific type; or access to all objects within a schema.

Two database-level principals will appear in every database:

- By default, every user belongs to the public database role. The user will inherit all the permissions of this role if explicit permissions have not been granted to any objects within the database.

- A guest user is disabled by default. The guest user is inherited by any login that has access to the database. As a result, any permissions granted to this account are also inherited by those users. Since data access will vary by user, you should avoid granting permissions to the guest account.

In addition, there will be two schemas, which are not principals and cannot be modified or dropped:

- sys contains all the system-related objects. It is often referred to as the *system catalog*.

- INFORMATION_SCHEMA contains views, which display METADATA about SQL Server internals.

Create a user using SSMS

1. Open SSMS and connect to a server.

2. Open Object Explorer if it is not already open.

3. Expand the server tree.

4. Expand the Databases folder.

5. Expand the AdventureWorks2012 database.

6. Right-click the Security folder and select New | User from the menu. The Database User dialog box opens.

7. In the User drop-down list, select Windows User.

8. In the User Name and Login Name text box, type **domain\jdoe**.

9. In the Default Schema text box, type **dbo**.

10. In the Select a Page pane, select Owned Schemas. Specifying a user as an owner of a schema gives that user full control. Do not select any schemas.

11. In the Select a Page pane, select Membership. Selecting a role from the list grants the user all the permissions of that role. Do not select any roles.

12. In the Select a Page pane, select Securables.

13. On the Securables page, click the Search button. Very similar to when you created a database user, you can grant or deny access at the same levels.

14. With the Specific Objects option selected, click OK.

15. In the Select Objects dialog box, click the Object Types button.

16. In the Select Object Types dialog box, select Tables and click OK.

17. Click the Browse button.

18. Select the boxes next to the dbo.AWBuildVersion and dbo.DatabaseLog tables and click OK twice.

19. In the Securables section, select the AWBuildVersion table.

20. In the Explicit section, select the boxes in the Grant section for the following permissions: Delete, Insert, Select, and Update.

21. Repeat steps 19 and 20 for the DatabaseLog table.

22. In the Select a Page pane, select Extended Properties. If you want to include any metadata about the login, you can do so here. For now, don't add anything.

23. Click OK.

Create a database user using T-SQL

1. To create a user using T-SQL, execute the following query:

```
USE [AdventureWorks2012]
GO
CREATE USER [domaim\jdoe] FOR LOGIN [domaim\jdoe] WITH DEFAULT_SCHEMA=[dbo]
GO
use [AdventureWorks2012]
GO
GRANT DELETE ON [dbo].[DatabaseLog] TO [domaim\jdoe]
GO
use [AdventureWorks2012]
GO
GRANT INSERT ON [dbo].[DatabaseLog] TO [domaim\jdoe]
```

```
GO
use [AdventureWorks2012]
GO
GRANT SELECT ON [dbo].[DatabaseLog] TO [domaim\jdoe]
GO
use [AdventureWorks2012]
GO
GRANT UPDATE ON [dbo].[DatabaseLog] TO [domaim\jdoe]
GO
use [AdventureWorks2012]
GO
GRANT DELETE ON [dbo].[AWBuildVersion] TO [domaim\jdoe]
GO
use [AdventureWorks2012]
GO
GRANT INSERT ON [dbo].[AWBuildVersion] TO [domaim\jdoe]
GO
use [AdventureWorks2012]
GO
GRANT SELECT ON [dbo].[AWBuildVersion] TO [domaim\jdoe]
GO
use [AdventureWorks2012]
GO
GRANT UPDATE ON [dbo].[AWBuildVersion] TO [domaim\jdoe]
GO
```

To deny permission, replace the *GRANT* keyword with *DENY*. Also, if you want to *not GRANT* or *DENY*, you can replace either with *REVOKE*. Remember that *DENY* will take precedence over *GRANT*. To remove an existing *GRANT* or *DENY* permission on an object, use *REVOKE* in a T-SQL script.

Creating built-in database roles

In addition to the four previously mentioned principals, each database includes built-in database roles. Table 25-1 lists and describes each role.

TABLE 25-1 Built-in database roles

Role	Description
db_accessadmin	These users control access to the database.
db_backupoperator	These users can back up the database.
db_datareader	These users have permissions to read all data within the database.
db_datawriter	These users have permissions to insert, update, or delete from the database.
db_ddladmin	These users have the ability to create, alter, and drop objects from the database.
db_denydatawriter	These users cannot read any data within the database.
db_denydatareader	These users cannot modify any data within the database.
db_owner	In addition to having unrestricted access to all objects in the database, these users can execute maintenance and configurations activities on the database. Most important, they can also drop the database. Therefore, carefully consider which users should be assigned this role.
db_securityadmin	These users control role membership.

Create a built-in database role using SSMS

1. Open SSMS and connect to a server.

2. Open Object Explorer if it is not already open.

3. Expand the server tree.

4. Expand the Databases folder.

5. Expand the AdventureWorks2012 database.

6. Expand the Security folder.

7. Right-click the Roles folder and select New | New Database Role from the menu.

8. The Database Role dialog box opens.

9. In the Role Name text box, type **DBControlTable_reader**.

10. In the Owner text box, type **dbo**.

11. Click Add.

12. The Select Database User or Role dialog box opens.

13. In the Enter the Object Names to Select text box, type *domain***jdoe**, where *domain* is your domain and **jdoe** is a user in the database.

14. Click OK.

15. Select Securables from the Select a Page pane.

16. Click Search.

17. In the Add Objects dialog box, ensure that the Specific Objects option is selected and click OK.

18. In the Select Objects dialog box, click Object Types.

19. Select Tables from the list and click OK.

20. Click Browse.

21. In the Browse for Objects dialog box, select the boxes next to the dbo.AWBuildVersion, dbo.DatabaseLog, and dbo.ErrorLog tables and click OK.

22. Click OK again.

23. With the AWBuildVersion table selected in the Securables section, in the Grant column of the Explicit section, select the box on the Select row.

24. Repeat step 23 for the DatabaseLog and ErrorLog tables.

25. Click OK.

Now instead of explicitly granting read access to each table, you can add a login as a member of this role and it will have the ability to view the contents of those tables.

Create a built-in database role using T-SQL

1. To create a built-in database role using T-SQL, execute the following query:

```
USE [AdventureWorks2012]
GO
CREATE ROLE [DBControlTable_reader] AUTHORIZATION [sa]
GO
USE [AdventureWorks2012]
GO
ALTER ROLE [DBControlTable_reader] ADD MEMBER [edustl\jdoe]
GO
use [AdventureWorks2012]
GO
GRANT SELECT ON [dbo].[DatabaseLog] TO [DBControlTable_reader]
GO
use [AdventureWorks2012]
GO
GRANT SELECT ON [dbo].[AWBuildVersion] TO [DBControlTable_reader]
GO
use [AdventureWorks2012]
GO
GRANT SELECT ON [dbo].[ErrorLog] TO [DBControlTable_reader]
GO
```

Configuring contained databases

As mentioned earlier, contained databases are a new feature introduced in SQL Server 2012. The concept of containment means that the database is isolated from the instance of SQL Server on which it is hosted. Certain information within the database is specific to the database and does not depend on any features outside the database. In SQL Server 2012, databases can be only partially contained. In other words, a database may use features that are available outside the database.

There are several levels of containment, but you will focus only on user authentication in this section. A contained user can be created from a Windows login or a database user with a password. If you base a database user on an existing login, it will not be contained. Before you can create any contained users, you must enable Contained Database Authentication at the server and database level.

Configure Contained Database Authentication using SSMS

1. Open SSMS and connect to a server.

2. Open Object Explorer if it is not already open.

3. Right-click the server name and select Properties from the menu.

4. Select Advanced from the Select a Page pane.

5. In the Containment section, set the Enable Contained Databases option to True.

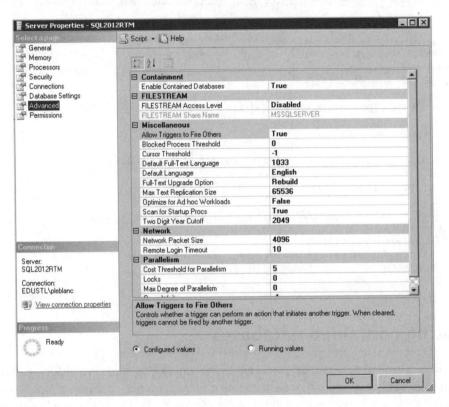

6. Click OK.

7. Open a new query window in SSMS.

8. Type and execute the following T-SQL statement:

```
USE master;
GO
CREATE DATABASE SBSContained;
```

9. In Object Explorer, expand the server.

10. Expand the Databases folder.

11. Right-click the SBSContained database and select Properties from the menu.

12. In the Select a Page pane, select Options.

13. Select Partial from the Containment Type drop-down list.

14. Click OK.

Configure Contained Database Authentication using T-SQL

1. To configure Contained Database Authentication using T-SQL, execute the following query:

```
use master
go
exec sp_configure 'contained database authentication', '1';
go
reconfigure;
USE [master]
GO
ALTER DATABASE [SBSContained] SET CONTAINMENT = PARTIAL
GO
```

Creating a contained user

The steps for creating a contained user are similar to those for creating an uncontained database user. The primary difference is on the General page when creating a new database user.

Create a contained user using SSMS

1. Open SSMS and connect to a server.

2. Open Object Explorer if it is not already open.

3. Expand the server tree.

4. Expand the Databases folder.

5. Expand the AdventureWorks2012 database.

6. Right-click the Security folder and select New | User. The Database User window opens.

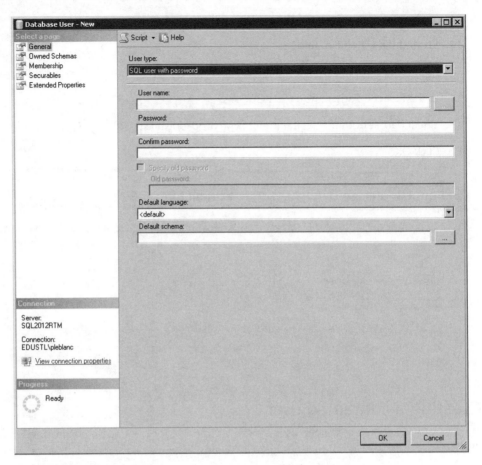

7. Select SQL User with Password from the User Type drop-down list.

8. Type **SBS** in the User Name text box.

9. Enter a valid password in the Password and Confirm password text boxes.

10. Select Owned Schemas in the Select a Page pane, and select the box next to db_owner.

11. Click OK.

Benefits and limitations of contained databases

As with most features, there are benefits and limitations to contained database security. Most of the limitations are specific to containment's operability with other SQL Server features. If database containment is enabled, you cannot use change data capture, change tracking, and replication.

The benefits of containment solve a problem that has been a thorn in the side of many DBAs for a long time. Since user information was stored at the server level prior to containment, moving a database posed certain challenges. The main challenge was that vital login information about the user, which is stored at the server level, would not be available when the database was moved from one SQL Server instance to another. As a result, several steps would have to be completed prior to the user working properly.

With the advent of contained databases, this problem can be easily mitigated. Since all the information is contained with the database, moving will not cause a problem. For example, if you have configured AlwaysOn, in the event of a failover, a user can connect to the newer server without any security issues.

 Note AlwaysOn is discussed in Chapter 31, "AlwaysOn."

Summary

This chapter provided an explanation of several security concepts, including creating logins at the server and database level. Security is important to most organizations, and having the proper mechanisms and governance in place is vital to any application and database deployment. Microsoft SQL Server 2012 provides flexible and effective security mechanisms that allow for fine-grained control of the server, database, and database objects.

Resource Governor

After completing this chapter, you will be able to

- Use Resource Governor.

- Enable and disable Resource Governor.

- Create resource pools.

- Configure Resource Governor to manage workload and resource consumption.

- Create, register, and test classifier functions.

- Modify Resource Governor configurations.

Similar to most relational database management systems (RDBMs), Microsoft SQL Server uses memory and CPU to handle its workloads. In some cases, a particular workload may or should have access to more of these resources than other workloads. For example, the CEO of an organization may run a memory-intensive report first thing in the morning. At the same time, other users may be running other workloads that are not as important. As a result, the workloads executed by the CEO will require more memory. This is where Resource Governor comes into play.

By using the Resource Governor, you can create a workload group mapped to a resource pool that governs how the resources are allocated. Resource pools and workload groups are explained in detail in the following sections. For now, understand that these two concepts are at the core of Resource Governor and assist in assigning minimum and maximum values to the CPU and memory available to an instance of SQL Server.

Minimum vs. maximum values

In some cases, assigning minimum values can be counterproductive. For example, one group may require additional resources, but it can't access them because another group has allocated the resources but is not using them. In this case, the minimum is detrimentally affecting the group that needs the resources by holding the resources without using them. Therefore, think carefully before assigning minimums.

This chapter provides a complete overview of how and when to use Resource Governor. You will learn how to enable, configure, and disable Resource Governor, and you'll explore how to set up each Resource Governor component. Finally, you will learn how to test and validate the Resource Governor configuration.

Enabling and disabling Resource Governor

Before you can start using Resource Governor, you must enable it. You have three ways to enable it, two with SQL Server Management Studio (SSMS) and one with T-SQL. The following steps demonstrate an SSMS method and a single T-SQL method.

Enable Resource Governor using SSMS

1. Open SSMS and connect to a server.

2. Open Object Explorer if it is not already open.

3. Expand the server tree.

4. Expand the Management folder.

5. Right-click Resource Governor and select Enable from the menu.

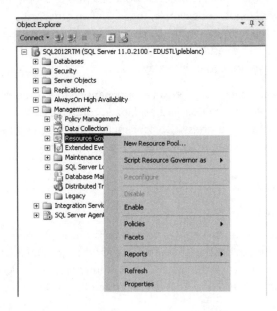

Enable Resource Governor using T-SQL

1. To enable Resource Governor using T-SQL, execute the following query:

```
USE [master]
GO
ALTER RESOURCE GOVERNOR RECONFIGURE;
GO
```

The *RECONFIGURE* statement in the preceding script not only enables Resource Governor, but also applies any T-SQL changes that have been made prior to the execution of the statement. With Resource Governor enabled, you can now start using it to manage workloads and system resources.

Disable Resource Governor using SSMS

1. Open SSMS and connect to a server.

2. Open Object Explorer if it is not already open.

3. Expand the server tree.

4. Expand the Management folder.

5. Right-click Resource Governor and select Disable from the menu.

Disable Resource Governor using T-SQL

1. To disable Resource Governor using T-SQL, execute the following query:

```
USE [master]
GO
ALTER RESOURCE GOVERNOR DISABLE;
GO
```

Note Keep this script handy, as it may be necessary for you to disable Resource Governor in the case of an accidental misconfiguration on a production system. In addition, SQL Server includes a dedicated administrator connection (DAC) you can use to connect if a misconfigured classifier function renders the server inaccessible. The DAC connection is not governed.

Creating resource pools

A *resource pool* represents the amount of system resources (memory or CPU) available to the server. Two predefined pools exist by default:

- The *internal* pool cannot be dropped or altered. It represents the pool that critical SQL Server functions workloads are placed in, and it has priority over all other pools.

- The *default* pool is a user-defined pool that cannot be dropped, but it can be altered. In addition, user-defined workload groups can be mapped to it.

Creating a resource pool is the first step in configuring Resource Governor to control workload resource usage. When configuring a resource pool, you can specify the minimum and maximum server memory and CPU. When specifying a minimum value for either, you must consider that the sum of all minimums for the pools cannot be greater than 100 percent. Also, if the minimum value is greater than zero for a given pool, the maximum value is adjusted. Calculating the new maximum is beyond the scope of this book; if you are interested in learning more, visit the "Resource Governor" section of SQL Server Books Online.

Create a resource pool using SSMS

1. Open SSMS and connect to a server.

2. Open Object Explorer if it is not already open.

3. Expand the server tree.

4. Expand the Management folder.

5. Expand Resource Governor.

6. Right-click the Resource Pools folder and select New Resource Pool.

7. The Resource Governor Properties dialog box opens.

8. In the Resource Pools table, click in the column labeled Name on the row with the red-highlighted exclamation point.

9. In the Name column, type **sbsPool**.

10. In the Minimum CPU% column of the same row, type **20**.

11. In the Maximum CPU% column of the same row, type **50**.

12. In the Minimum Memory % column of the same row, type **20**.

13. In the Maximum Memory % column of the same row, type **50**.

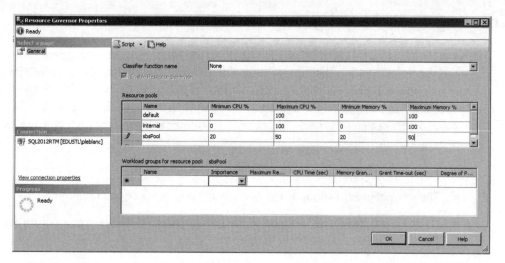

14. Click OK.

15. Right-click the Resource Pools folder and select Refresh.

16. Expand the Resource Pools folder and you will see the new pool, sbsPool.

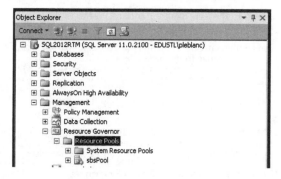

Create a resource pool using T-SQL

1. To create a resource pool using T-SQL, execute the following query:

```
Use master;
CREATE RESOURCE POOL [sbsPool] WITH(min_cpu_percent=20,
        max_cpu_percent=50,
        min_memory_percent=20,
        max_memory_percent=50)


GO
ALTER RESOURCE GOVERNOR RECONFIGURE;
GO
```

Creating a workload group

After the pool is created, the next step is to create a workload that will be mapped to that pool. A *workload group* catches a database request with commonalities defined by a set of filters. The filters are defined using a classifier function, which is explained in the next section. A workgroup applies a uniform policy to all the requests in the group. Each connection in a workgroup is individually capped, for example. The resource pool divides resources among requests and applies caps to requests as a whole.

Similar to resource pools, there are two default workload groups:

- The *internal* group cannot be modified in any way, but it can be monitored.

- Some modifications can be made to the *default* group. By default, requests are assigned to this group when a session cannot be classified.

When creating a workload group, you can set six arguments, and you must map the group to a resource pool. Table 26-1 describes the arguments.

TABLE 26-1 Workload group arguments

Argument	Description	Default value
importance	Request the level of importance relative to all requests. The value can be High, Medium, or Low.	Medium
request_max_memory_grant_percent	Maximum amount of memory provided to a given request relative to the group. Must be greater than zero. The memory grant should not be changed, and note that it is for a single query in a group.	25
request_max_memory_grant_timeout_sec	Amount of time a request can wait for memory.	0
request_max_cpu_time_sec	Maximum amount of CPU time provided to a given request relative to a group. A zero value means it defaults to the global maximum degree of parallelism.	Global value
max_dop	Maximum degree of parallelism for each request.	0
group_max_requests	Maximum number of concurrent requests that are permitted to execute within a workgroup.	0 (unlimited)

Workload groups can be created using SSMS or T-SQL. If all the defaults are accepted, creating a group and assigning it to a pool is simple. The following T-SQL query illustrates this:

```
use master;
CREATE WORKLOAD GROUP sbsTSQLdefaults
     USING sbsPool;
GO
ALTER RESOURCE GOVERNOR RECONFIGURE;
GO
```

When the group is created, all the default values are assigned to the arguments.

Create a workload group using SSMS

1. Open SSMS and connect to a server.

2. Open Object Explorer if it is not already open.

3. Expand the server tree.

4. Expand the Management folder.

5. Expand Resource Governor.

6. Expand the Resource Pools folder.

7. Expand the sbsPool resource pool.

8. Right-click the Workload Groups folder and select New Workload Group from the menu.

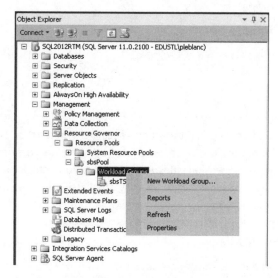

The Resource Governor Properties dialog box opens.

9. In the Workload Groups for Resource Pool table, click in the column labeled Name on the row with the red-highlighted exclamation point.

10. In the Name column, type **sbsSSMSgroup**.

11. In the Importance column, select Medium.

12. In the Maximum Requests column, accept 0.

13. In the CPU Time (Sec) column, enter **50**.

14. In the Memory Grant % column, enter **25**.

15. Accept the default for Grant Time-out (Sec) and Degree of Parallelism.

16. Click OK.

17. Right-click the Workload Groups folder and select Refresh. You will now see the new group.

Create a workload group using T-SQL

1. To create a workload group using T-SQL, execute the following code:

```
USE [master];
CREATE WORKLOAD GROUP [sbsSSMSgroup] WITH(group_max_requests=0,
        importance=Medium,
        request_max_cpu_time_sec=50,
        request_max_memory_grant_percent=50,
        request_memory_grant_timeout_sec=0,
        max_dop=0) USING [sbsPool]
GO
ALTER RESOURCE GOVERNOR RECONFIGURE;
GO
```

Using classifier functions

As mentioned earlier, requests are grouped or classified based on specific characteristics. These characteristics are defined in a user-defined function. This function is referred to as the *classifier function*, and it contains logic that assists in grouping the sessions. Resource Governor uses the logic to place requests into existing workload groups. As sessions are created, they are classified into a group. When your system is under heavy CPU and/or memory pressure, Resource Governor may cap requests that have been sorted into a workgroup by the classifier function. This helps protect other requests on the server from being starved for CPU or memory.

The classifier function should be created in the master database, and only one function at a time can be specified as the Resource Governor classifier function. Typically, prebuilt system functions are used to assist the classifier function with identifying requests. For example, if you want to identify a request based on who is logged in, use the *SUSER_NAME()* function, which returns the login of the user. On the other hand, if you want to classify requests by application name, use the *APP_NAME()* function. In addition to those two functions, you can use the *HOST_NAME()* function to identify the computer or server source of the session.

After the function is created, you will need to update the Resource Governor configurations. The detailed steps for this are provided in the following section.

1. Open the query editor in SSMS.

2. In the query editor, enter and execute the following T-SQL code:

```
USE master
GO
CREATE FUNCTION sbsClassifier()
RETURNS SYSNAME WITH SCHEMABINDING
BEGIN
      DECLARE @Group sysname

      IF(SUSER_SNAME()) = 'jdoe'
      BEGIN
            SET @Group = 'sbsSSMSgroup'
      END

      RETURN @Group
END
GO
```

In the preceding function, the *SUSER_NAME* function is used to determine who the user is. If the user is jdoe, then all sessions for that user are sent to the sbsSSMSgroup workload group.

3. Open another query window and execute the following T-SQL code:

```
USE MASTER
GO
ALTER RESOURCE GOVERNOR with (CLASSIFIER_FUNCTION = dbo.sbsClassifier)
ALTER RESOURCE GOVERNOR RECONFIGURE
GO
```

This code registers the function with Resource Governor, and then Resource Governor is reconfigured so that it can begin using the function.

Testing classifier functions

Now that all the pieces are in place, how can you verify that functions are being used as expected? Well, unless your system is under duress, you will not be able to observe pools or workgroups being restricted. However, you can verify if the classification of incoming requests is working as you intended.

Test a classifier function using T-SQL

1. Open the query editor in SSMS.

2. In the query editor, execute the following T-SQL code:

```
USE [master]
GO
CREATE LOGIN [jdoe]
     WITH PASSWORD=N'pass@word1',
     DEFAULT_DATABASE=[AdventureWorks2012],
     CHECK_EXPIRATION=OFF,
     CHECK_POLICY=OFF
GO
USE [AdventureWorks2012]
GO
CREATE USER [jdoe] FOR LOGIN [jdoe]
GO
USE [AdventureWorks2012]
GO
ALTER ROLE [db_datareader] ADD MEMBER [jdoe]
GO
```

The preceding code creates a SQL Server login and a database user within the AdventureWorks2012 database that can read all the contents of that database.

3. Open a new query window and connect as the user jdoe.

4. In the query editor, execute the following T-SQL code:

```
USE AdventureWorks2012;
SELECT *
FROM HumanResources.Department
```

5. Return to the first query window where the user was created and delete all the contents. In the query editor, execute the following query:

```
USE AdventureWorks2012;
SELECT
     s.group_id,
     CAST(g.name as nvarchar(20)) ResourceGroup,
     s.session_id,
     s.login_name,
     s.login_time,
     CAST(s.host_name as nvarchar(20)) HostName,
     CAST(s.program_name AS nvarchar(20)) ProgramName
FROM sys.dm_exec_sessions s
INNER JOIN sys.dm_resource_governor_workload_groups g
     ON g.group_id = s.group_id
WHERE
     g.name = 'sbsSSMSgroup'
ORDER BY
     g.name
GO
```

The results will include at least one row, which references the session that is connected as jdoe.

If you opened additional sessions connected as that user, you will see more rows when the query is executed. Finally, note that group_id is not one (the default workgroup). This column identifies which Resource Governor workgroup the session was placed in.

Modifying Resource Governor configurations

If you ever find the need to change any of the Resource Governor configurations, you can do so easily with SSMS or T-SQL. In addition, you can remove a pool, workload, or classifier. Before removing a pool, you must first remove any workload groups that are associated with it. If you want to remove a classifier function, you must first disassociate it from Resource Governor.

Alter an existing workload group using T-SQL

1. Open the query editor in SSMS.

2. In the query editor, execute the following T-SQL code:

```
USE [master];
ALTER WORKLOAD GROUP [sbsTSQLdefaults]
WITH (REQUEST_MAX_MEMORY_GRANT_PERCENT = 50);
GO
ALTER RESOURCE GOVERNOR RECONFIGURE;
GO
```

Now the requests classified to this workload will have access to additional memory. New sessions would, but existing sessions would not. Existing sessions will continue to be governed even if you DISABLE Resource Governor; they will remain in their workgroup for a period of time.

Drop existing workload groups and resource pools using SSMS

Note Prior to following these steps, ensure that any connections that were open using the jdoe user are closed.

1. Open SSMS and connect to a server.

2. Open Object Explorer if it is not already open.

3. Expand the server tree.

4. Expand the Management folder.

5. Expand Resource Governor.

6. Expand the Resource Pools folder.

7. Expand the sbsPool resource pool.

8. Expand the Workload Groups folder.

9. Right-click the sbsTSQLDefaults workload group and select Delete.

10. Repeat the steps, but instead delete sbsSSMSgroup.

11. Right-click sbsPool and select Delete from the menu. If any sessions are open that reference the pool, you may receive an error.

Drop a classifier function using T-SQL

1. Open the query editor in SSMS.

2. In the query editor, execute the following T-SQL code:

```
USE [master]
ALTER RESOURCE GOVERNOR with (CLASSIFIER_FUNCTION = null)
ALTER RESOURCE GOVERNOR RECONFIGURE
GO
USE [master]
DROP FUNCTION dbo.sbsClassifier
GO
```

You must first set the classifier function for Resource Governor to a new function or null. Then you will be able to drop the function.

Summary

This chapter provided an overview of the Resource Governor feature of Microsoft SQL Server. You walked through the steps to properly configure Resource Governor, and you learned about certain situations where controlling your system resources can benefit from Resource Governor. When performing the configurations, carefully consider the impact that Resource Governor's restrictions will have on users and applications. Carefully monitor Resource Governor after implementation to ensure the desired effect of limiting heavy performance impacts.

SQL Server Agent

After completing this chapter, you will be able to

- Understand the components of SQL Server Agent.

- View SQL Server Agent Configuration Manager options.

- Configure SQL Server Agent properties.

- Create operators.

- Configure alerts and jobs.

- Create proxies.

As discussed in Chapter 22, "Maintenance plans," regularly scheduled tasks must be performed to ensure that disaster recovery, retention policies, index performance, and monitoring goals are maintained. To ensure that all of these tasks are accomplished via a single technology, Microsoft SQL Server includes a Windows service known as SQL Server Agent. SQL Server Agent can execute and schedule tasks or jobs. The scheduled tasks should not be confused with Windows scheduled tasks in Task Scheduler. SQL Server Agent can execute the following:

- SQL Server Integration Services (SSIS) packages

- T-SQL scripts

- PowerShell scripts

- ActiveX scripts

- Replication tasks

- Analysis Services tasks

- Operating system tasks (CmdExec)

Within a job, each of the aforementioned items can be executed as a step. The details relating to creating and scheduling jobs are provided later in the chapter. First, you'll learn about SQL Server Agent components.

SQL Server Agent components

As previously mentioned, SQL Server Agent executes jobs, and these jobs are one component used by SQL Server Agent to execute the defined tasks. In addition to jobs, SQL Server Agent includes other components. Table 27-1 lists and describes each component.

TABLE 27-1 SQL Server Agent components

Component	Description
Job	A sequential list of actions.
Schedule	A description of when a job will run. A schedule is created for each job, but a new job can copy the schedule of an existing job.
Operator	The person to be notified when a certain action or event occurs on SQL Server or SQL Server Agent.
Alert	A notification or response to a certain event. Alerts are based on SQL Server events, SQL Server performance conditions, or WMI events. An operator may be notified if an alert is fired.
Proxy	The context in which the job is executed.

As you may have noticed from the component descriptions, they typically work together as a single unit of work. While this is not a requirement, it is something you will encounter over and over again as you create each component. For example, a job may use a schedule to run automatically, an operator may be notified if a job succeeds or fails, or an operator may be notified if an alert is fired. You will learn how to create and manage each component later in this chapter.

Viewing SQL Server Agent Configuration Manager options

Certain aspects of SQL Server Agent are configurable. For example, which security account it should start as, where the error log should be stored, and whether it should start automatically. You may also want to start, stop, or pause SQL Server Agent. Some tasks can be configured using only SQL Server Configuration Manager, whereas others can be configured using SQL Server Management Studio (SSMS).

View SQL Server Agent configuration options using SSMS

1. Click Start | All Programs | Microsoft SQL Server 2012 | Configuration Tools | SQL Server Configuration Manager. SQL Server Configuration Manager opens.

2. Select SQL Server Services from the left navigation pane.

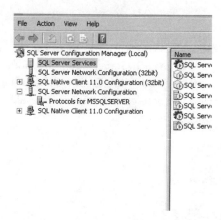

3. In the right section, right-click SQL Server Agent and select Properties from the menu.

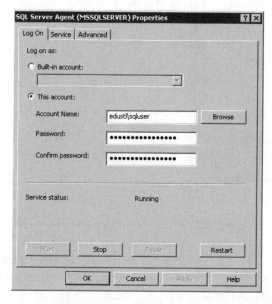

4. On the Log On tab, you can stop SQL Server Agent by clicking Stop. You can also start, pause, or restart it in other scenarios. In addition, you can specify which account the service logs on as.

> **Important** It is very important to make any service account changes here in SQL Server Configuration Manager. Making these changes in the Control Panel's Local Services console could result in SQL Server permissions becoming broken.

5. Click the Service tab.

   The only configurable option here is Start Mode. In most cases, you should set the value to Automatic. However, if you are not using any of the SQL Server Agent functionality, you should set it to Manual or Disabled. If you set the value to Manual, SQL Server Agent can still be started; however, if you set the value to Disabled, you cannot start it. That said, there is no good reason it should be stopped on a production server.

6. Click the Advanced tab.

   On this tab, you can configure three options. The first is whether or not you want to provide a customer feedback report. The second and probably the most important option you can specify is where you want to place the SQL Server Agent error logs. You can accept the default or you can move the logs to another location. To ensure that you have sufficient disk space and you don't run out of space on your local C drive, you should consider relocating the error logs to another location.

7. Click Cancel.

Configuring SQL Server Agent properties

While SQL Server Configuration Manager provides some very important configurable options for a Windows service, SSMS exposes other options that you should definitely examine. Since SQL Server Agent is typically a mechanism used to regularly execute critical tasks or tasks that could be resource dependent or intensive, using SSMS you have the ability to control properties such as the following:

- Executing jobs based on resource availability

- When to restart SQL Server Agent

- How much information to persist in the error log

- Alerts and notifications

These properties are available via SSMS and are easily configured.

View and configure SQL Server Agent properties with SSMS

1. Open SSMS and connect to a server.

2. Open Object Explorer if it is not already open.

3. Expand the server.

4. Right-click SQL Server Agent and select Properties from the menu.

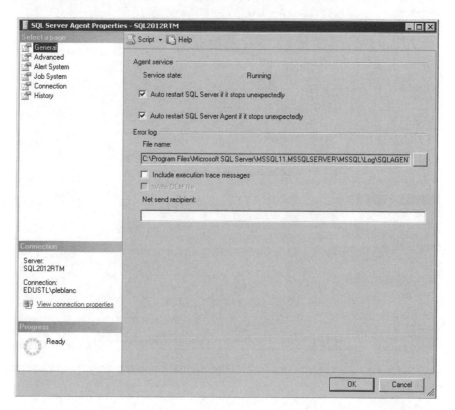

On the General page in the Agent Service section, you can control how SQL Server Agent behaves if the server or SQL Server Agent stops.

It is highly recommended that you keep the first two check boxes selected at all times. In addition, when you select the Include Execution Trace Messages check box in the Error Log section, SQL Server Agent will send more information to the error log. If you decide to select this box, ensure that you have sufficient disk space to accommodate the change. If you are working with older technologies, you can also send messages via net send by entering the user in the Net Send Recipient text box.

 Note In future versions of SQL Server, the net send option will be removed. Therefore, you should avoid using this feature.

5. Click OK to accept the defaults.

6. In the Select a Page pane, click Advanced.

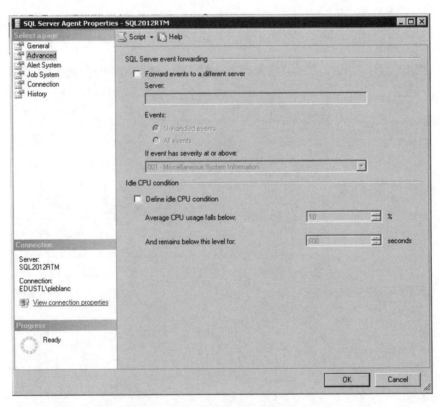

On the Advanced page, you can control the events and where they should be stored, locally or remotely.

7. Click OK to accept the defaults.

8. In the Idle CPU Condition section, select the Define Idle CPU Condition check box. You now have the ability to control when a job actually runs based on CPU usage.

9. In the Average CPU Usage Falls Below text box, enter **40**.

10. In the And Remains Below This Level For text box, enter **30**.

    Specifying the preceding two values tells SQL Server Agent to execute jobs only when the average CPU is below 40 percent for 30 seconds.

11. In the Select a Page pane, select History.

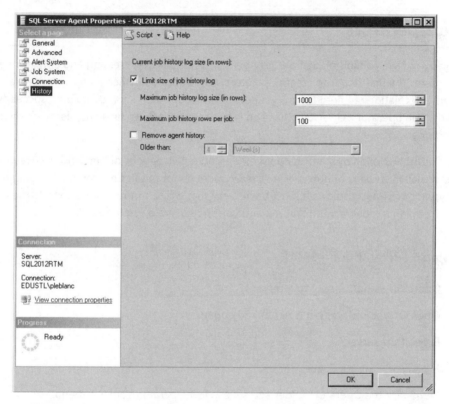

On this page, you can configure how much history to maintain about jobs and when to purge log information.

12. Enter **5000** in the Maximum Job History Log Size (in Rows) text box. This setting limits the log size to 5,000 rows for all jobs.

13. Enter **500** in the Maximum Job History Rows per Job text box. This setting tells SQL Server Agent to store only 500 rows of log information for each job.

14. Select the Remove Agent History check box, enter **1** in the Older Than text box, and accept the value Week(s) from the drop-down list.

    This setting is a bit misleading; it is not a scheduled reoccurring process. Instead, it removes the data within the specific values when OK is clicked.

15. Click OK.

Note You may have noticed that three pages were skipped: Alert System, Job System, and Connection. This is because the Alert System page is discussed in Chapter 28, "Database Mail," and discussion of the Job System and Connection pages is beyond the scope of this book.

Creating operators

Now that you have configured SQL Server Agent, it is time to start creating and configuring your environment. The first step is to create operators. As mentioned earlier, an *operator* contains all the pertinent information required to notify a person or group when a job completes, succeeds, or fails. In addition, an operator may also be notified when an alert is fired. Jobs and alerts are discussed later in the chapter.

The notification of an operator is conducted using email, pagers, or net send. To use the email database, mail must be configured—you'll learn more about this in Chapter 28. If paging is used, some type of third-party software must be in place that will send the notifications. However, similar to net send, paging is a deprecated feature, and you should avoid using both.

Create an operator using SSMS

1. Open SSMS and connect to a server.

2. Open Object Explorer if it is not already open.

3. Expand the server.

4. Expand SQL Server Agent.

5. Right-click the Operators folder and select New Operator from the menu.

6. The New Operator window opens.

7. On the General page, type **WeekdayDBA** in the Name text box.

8. Enter an email address in the E-mail Name text box.

   In the Pager on Duty Schedule section, you can specify the availability of a person or group. In this section, you have the flexibility to select certain days and times as needed.

9. Select all the weekday check boxes, but leave Saturday and Sunday cleared, because this person is off on the weekends. Enter **7:00:00 AM** in the Workday Begin text box.

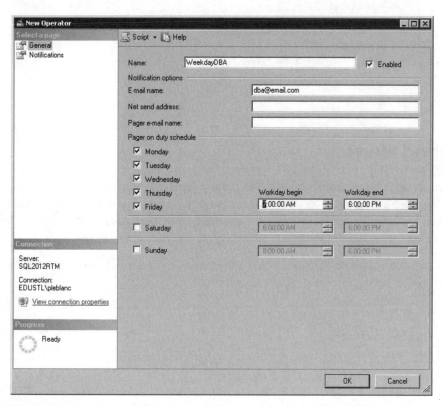

10. Click OK.

 Note You may have noticed the Notification page in the Select a Page pane. You will revisit that page once you have created an alert.

Create an operator using T-SQL

1. To create an operator using T-SQL, execute the following script:

```
USE [msdb]
GO
EXEC msdb.dbo.sp_update_operator @name=N'WeekdayDBA',
        @enabled=1,
        @weekday_pager_start_time=70000,
        @weekday_pager_end_time=180000,
        @pager_days=62,
        @email_address=N'jdoe@email.com',
        @pager_address=N'',
        @netsend_address=N''
GO
```

Configuring alerts

As a SQL Server database administrator (DBA), maintaining and monitoring your SQL Server environment is an integral part of the job. Being a reactive DBA instead of a proactive DBA could determine if you are an employed or unemployed DBA, depending upon the situation. By using SQL Server Agent alerts, you can proactively monitor SQL Server events and performance conditions.

Alerts are automated notifications that are fired when certain events are triggered. You can configure alerts to fire for the following types of events:

- SQL Server

- SQL Server performance

- Windows Management Instrumentation (WMI)

With each option, SQL Server provides very granular configuration choices. For example, when configuring a performance condition, you can specify a threshold that determines when the alert should be fired. In the next procedure, you'll create an alert based on SQL Server's built-in counters that look for use of deprecated features, including deprecated T-SQL code.

Create a SQL Server alert using SSMS

1. Open SSMS and connect to a server.

2. Open Object Explorer if it is not already open.

3. Expand the server.

4. Expand SQL Server Agent.

5. Right-click the Alerts folder and select New Alert from the menu. The New Alert dialog box opens.

6. In the Name text box, type **Deprecated Usage**.

7. Select SQL Server Performance Condition Alert from the Type drop-down list.

8. Select Deprecated Features from the Object drop-down list.

9. Select Usage from the Counter drop-down list.

10. Select SET ROWCOUNT from the Instance drop-down list.

11. Select Rises Above from the Alert If Counter drop-down list.

12. Leave 0 in the Value text box.

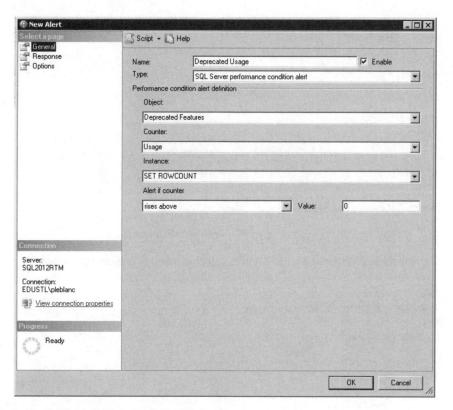

13. In the Select a Page pane, select Response.

14. Select the Notify Operators check box.

15. In the Operator List section, select the check box in the E-mail column.

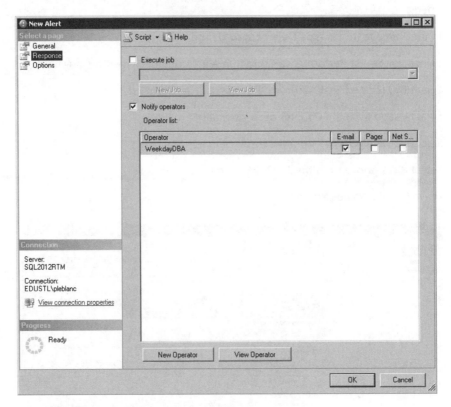

16. Select Options in the Select a Page pane.

You can add additional messages to the alert by using this page.

17. In the Include Alert Error Text In section, select the E-mail box and then click OK.

Create a SQL Server alert using T-SQL

1. To create a SQL Server alert using T-SQL, execute the following script:

```
USE [msdb]
GO
EXEC msdb.dbo.sp_add_alert @name=N'Deprecated Usage',
        @enabled=1,
        @delay_between_responses=0,
        @include_event_description_in=0,
        @performance_condition=N'Deprecated Features|Usage|SET ROWCOUNT|>|0',
        @job_id=N'00000000-0000-0000-0000-000000000000'
GO
EXEC msdb.dbo.sp_add_notification
    @alert_name=N'Deprecated Usage', @operator_name=N'WeekdayDBA', @notification_method
= 1
GO
```

The first stored procedure, *sp_add_alert*, creates the alert, and the second stored procedure, *sp_add_notification*, adds a notification for the specified operator.

Configuring jobs

SQL Server Agent jobs are typically used to automate maintenance tasks such as backups and index rebuilds. While these are the most common uses, SQL Server Agent jobs can be used to automate other tasks such as running an extraction, transformation, and loading (ETL) process for a data warehouse. Not only does a job include steps or tasks that it may execute, but it also may include a schedule, alert, and notification.

A job usually contains a series of steps scheduled to run by SQL Server Agent. You can configure the job to send a notification when it completes, succeeds, or fails. Finally, you can include alerts as part of a job.

Note If a user is not part of the sysadmin role, the user must be added to the SQLAgentUserRole, SQLAgentReaderRole, or SQLAgentOperatorRole in the msdb database in order to create, modify, or delete jobs.

Create a job using SSMS

1. Open SSMS and connect to a server.

2. Open Object Explorer if it is not already open.

3. Expand the server.

4. Expand SQL Server Agent.

5. Right-click the Jobs folder and select New Job from the menu.

6. The New Job dialog box opens.

7. Type **AdventureWorks2012 Nightly Full Backup** in the Name text box.

8. Type **sa** in the Owner text box.

Note sa is used only for demonstration purposes here. You should not use it in production scenarios. As a best practice, you should create a dedicated SQL Server service account that will be used to execute jobs.

9. Select Database Maintenance from the Category drop-down list.

10. In the large Description text box, type **Nightly full backup of the AdventureWorks database that runs at midnight every day including weekends**.

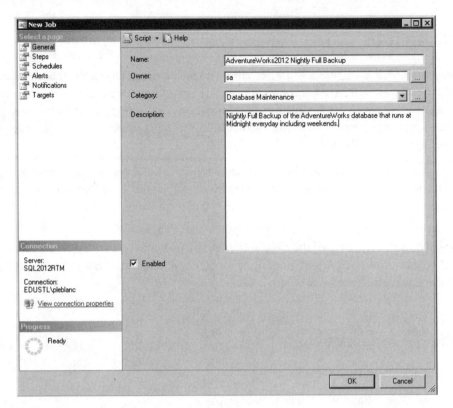

11. Select Steps from the Select a Page pane.

12. On the Steps page, click New.

13. In the Step Name text box, type **Nightly Backup**.

14. In the Type drop-down list, accept the default, Transact-SQL Script (T-SQL).

15. Accept the default for the Run As drop-down list, which is blank. You will return to this later.

16. Accept the default, master, in the Database drop-down list.

17. Execute the following T-SQL code in the Command text box:

```
use master
go
BACKUP DATABASE AdventureWorks2012
TO C:\Program Files\Microsoft SQL Server\MSSQL11.MSSQLSERVER\MSSQL\Backup\
AdventureWorks2012.bak
```

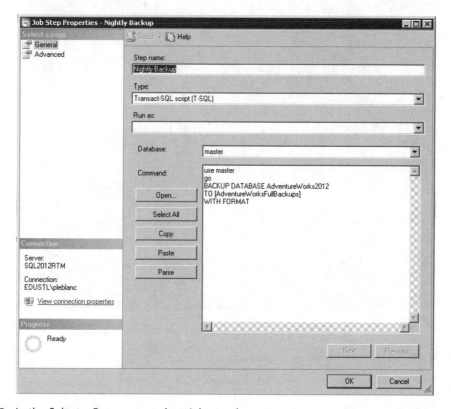

18. In the Select a Page pane, select Advanced.

On this page, you can configure several settings. Review the options on this page. If there are multiple steps in the job, you can specify which step to run depending upon the success or failure of this step. You can also enter the number of retry attempts. You can log additional information about the step and run a specific step as a different user.

19. Accept the defaults for now and click OK.

20. In the Select a Page pane, select Schedules. On the Schedules page, click the New button.

21. Type **Nightly Midnight** in the Name text box.

22. Select Daily from the Occurs drop-down list in the Frequency section.

23. Accept all the defaults for the other items and click OK.

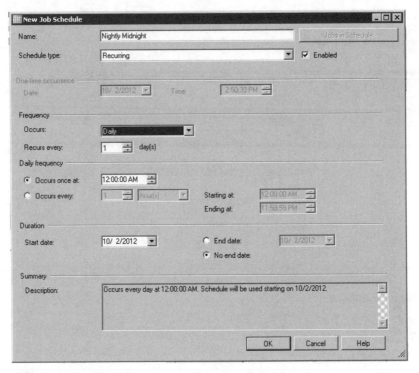

24. In the Select a Page pane, select Notifications.

25. Select the E-mail check box.

26. Select WeekdayDBA from the drop-down list.

27. Click OK.

 Note Two pages were omitted during this discussion: Alerts and Targets. If you want to include an alert with the job, you can specify it on the Alert page. If you want to set up multiserver administration, you can use the Target page to do so.

Creating proxies

In some cases, you may need to execute a job as an account that has access to objects external to SQL Server. To accomplish this, you use a proxy. A *proxy* is the security context that a job can impersonate at run time for a specific and limited purpose. For example, you may use a proxy when executing an SSIS package or to run a PowerShell script. Proxies depend on credentials. The *credential* is what provides the proxy access to the external objects. A credential typically contains the security information of a Windows account: the user name and password. This account may be a system administrator with network drive privileges. Prior to creating a proxy, you must create a credential.

> **Note** The Windows user that is used when creating the credential must be granted the Logon as Batch Job permission on the server that hosts the SQL Server instance.

Create a credential using SSMS

1. Open SSMS and connect to a server.

2. Open Object Explorer if it is not already open.

3. Expand the server.

4. Expand the Security folder.

5. Right-click the Credentials folder and select New Credential. The New Credential dialog box opens.

6. Enter a name in the Credential Name text box.

7. Enter the Windows user name in the Identity text box. Alternatively, click the ellipsis button to search for the account.

8. Enter the password for that account in both the Password and Confirm Password text boxes.

> **Note** The Encryption Provider section is disabled because this section is intended for use with an Enterprise Key Management (EKM) provider.

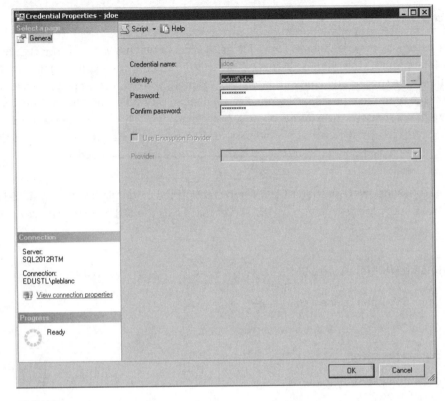

9. Click OK.

   With the credential created, you can create a proxy that can use the permissions of this Windows account.

Create and use a proxy with SSMS

1. Open SSMS and connect to a server.

2. Open Object Explorer if it is not already open.

3. Expand the server.

4. Expand SQL Server Agent.

5. Right-click the Proxies folder and select New Proxy from the menu. The New Proxy Account dialog box opens.

6. Type **BackupAccount** in the Proxy Name text box.

7. Type a credential in the Credential Name text box, or click the ellipsis button and select from a list of available credentials.

8. In the Active to the Following Subsystems section, select the box next to PowerShell.

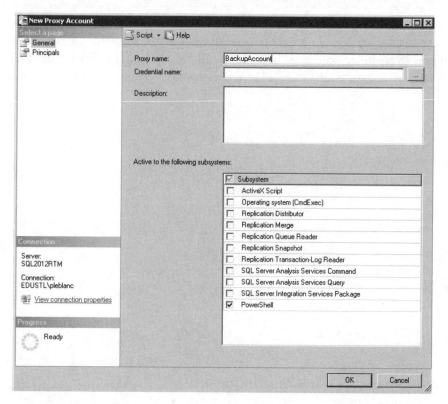

9. In the Select a Page pane, select Principals. This is where you grant any additional accounts access to this proxy.

10. Click OK.

11. Expand the Jobs folder.

12. Right-click the AdventureWorks2012 Nightly Full Backup job and select Properties.

13. Select Steps from the Select a Page pane.

14. Click New.

15. Select PowerShell from the Type drop-down list.

16. Select Backup Account from the Run As drop-down list. This forces SQL Server Agent to execute the step under the context of this proxy.

17. Click Cancel.

Summary

In this chapter, you learned about the various SQL Server Agent components, and you explored how to use SQL Server Configuration Manager to change SQL Server Agent properties. You learned how to create operators and alerts that can be used as a means of notification. Finally, you learned how to create jobs that can assist in streamlining and automating daily tasks.

Database Mail

After completing this chapter, you will be able to

- Understand Database Mail components.

- Configure Database Mail.

- Send email using Database Mail.

- Monitor Database Mail.

Microsoft SQL Server 2005 released the dependency of installing a Messaging Application Programming Interface (MAPI) client to send email from an instance of SQL Server. Now email can be sent using a Simple Mail Transfer Protocol (SMTP) email server, such as a Microsoft Exchange Server. Not only are you relieved from the MAPI client, but also SQL Server will continue to queue messages even if there is a problem with the SMTP server. When the problem is resolved, SQL Server will start to send messages.

In addition, since sending mail is external to SQL Server, performance degradation is highly unlikely. Log information is stored for each mail event that is performed and readily available to administrators. This log information includes successful events in addition to errors that may be used to solve any Database Mail or SMTP errors that occur. Finally, as a precautionary measure, you can restrict or limit file sizes to mitigate any performance problems that may arise on the mail server due to sending large files.

In this chapter, you'll learn about the various Database Mail components. You'll configure each component and discover how use Database Mail for sending email and configuring alerts and operators. Finally, you'll see how to monitor Database Mail using built-in features of SQL Server.

Database Mail components

For Database Mail to work, you need to create and configure certain objects. Other items are installed and set up during the SQL Server installation:

- **msdb** The msdb database stores all the configuration and security information. In addition, this database hosts all the objects needed to send email. For example, several system stored procedures exist in the msdb database that are specific to Database Mail.

- **Configuration objects** As mentioned, the msdb database stores configuration objects. These objects consist of Database Mail accounts and profiles. The Database Mail accounts contain the information needed to send email, such as the email address and sender name. Database Mail profiles are actually containers of mail accounts. An account can be assigned to one or many profiles. There are two types of profiles: public and private. Members of the DatabaseMailUserRole in the msdb database have access to the public profiles. Any user that is a member of that role has the ability to send email with the public profile using Database Mail. The private role is more restrictive. A user must be given access to this profile and granted EXEC permissions on *sp_send_dbmail* before the user can send email using that profile. When sending email with Database Mail, you must specify a mail profile. Therefore, if you need to reconfigure a Database Mail account that is assigned to a profile, you can do so without affecting the email of other accounts that are assigned to that same profile.

- **Messaging objects** Similar to the configuration objects, the messaging objects are stored in the msdb database. The objects consist of several views and stored procedures, including the *sp_send_dbmail* procedure, which can be used to send email programmatically with T-SQL. An example of how to use the procedure is provided later in this chapter.

- **Logging and auditing** When mail events are executed, information is stored in the msdb database and the Windows event log.

- **Database Mail executable** This executable is used to obtain the information from the queue in msdb and to send the email to the mail servers.

Configuring Database Mail

You can configure Database Mail using T-SQL or the Database Mail Configuration Wizard; the method you use is a matter of preference. If you decide to use T-SQL, you must enable the Database Mail extended stored procedures. However, the extended stored procedures will be automatically enabled if you choose to use the wizard, so you will use the wizard in this chapter. If you decide that you don't want to use the wizard and you want to use T-SQL instead, use the following script to enable the extended stored procedures:

```
EXEC sp_configure 'show advanced options', 1;
GO
RECONFIGURE;
GO
EXEC sp_configure 'Database Mail XPs', 1;
GO
RECONFIGURE
GO
```

A server restart is not required after executing this script. Once it is completed, you can begin to configure Database Mail.

Note You can configure Database Mail to use local or remote SMTP servers. As a result, you can use your Microsoft (Live) account or Gmail account as the SMTP server for your Database Mail configuration. For a Live account, the server is smpt.live.com, port 587, and you must use Secure Sockets Layer (SSL).

Configure Database Mail using the Configuration Wizard

1. Open SSMS and connect to an instance of SQL Server.

2. Expand the Management folder.

3. Right-click Database Mail.

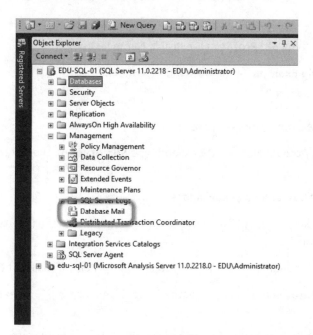

4. Select Configure Database Mail from the menu that appears.

5. Click Next on the Welcome to Database Mail Configuration page.

6. Ensure that the Set Up Database Mail by Performing the Following Tasks option is selected on the Select Configuration Task page.

7. Click Next.

   If you have not enabled the database extended stored procedures, you will be prompted to enable Database Mail.

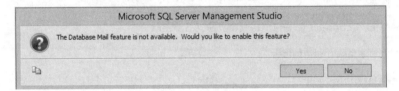

8. Click Yes.

9. On the New Profile page, type **SBSProfile** in the Profile Name text box.

10. Type **Step by Step Profile Example** in the Description text box.

11. Click Add.

    The New Database Mail Account window opens.

12. Type **SBSAccount** in the Account Name text box, and type **SBS Account example** in the Description text box.

13. In the Email Address text box, enter an email address.

14. Enter the display name that you would like to use when sending email in the Display Name text box, which is optional.

15. The Reply E-mail option is optional. Therefore, you can leave the Reply E-mail text box blank.

16. Type the SMTP that will be used to send email in the Server Name text box—for example, **smtp.live.com**.

17. If the port is not 25, enter the correct port in the Port text box. This is usually required only to change if SSL will be used.

18. If the SMTP server requires a secure connection, select the This Server Requires a Secure Connection (SSL) check box.

19. Finally, you have three choices for SMTP authentication. If you can authenticate using Windows with the database engine service account, select the first option. If you are using a remote server, as in this example, select Basic Authentication, and then provide a user name and password. Finally, if your SMTP server accepts anonymous authentication, select Anonymous Authentication. Many internal SMTP servers will accept anonymous authentication for servers within a private corporate network.

> **Note** Sensitive information has been protected in the following image.

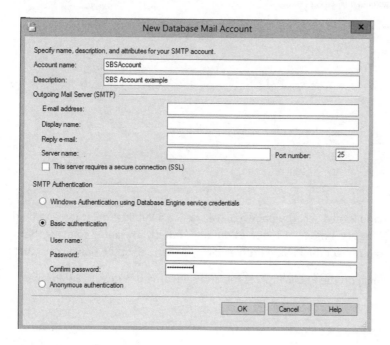

20. Click OK.

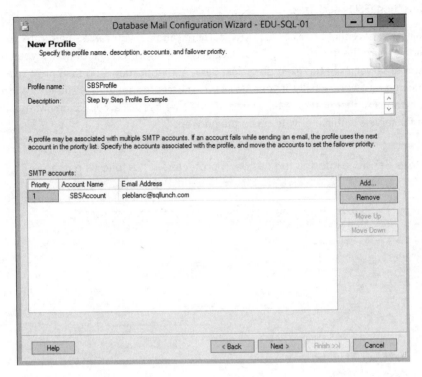

21. Click Next.

22. On the Manage Profile Security page, you will notice a Public Profiles tab and a Private Profiles tab. You will focus on the Public Profiles tab now, but if you wanted to make this profile private, you would select the Private Profiles tab and then select the box next to that profile.

For now, remain on the Public Profiles tab and select the box next to SBSProfile.

23. Click in the Default Profile column and select Yes from the drop-down list.

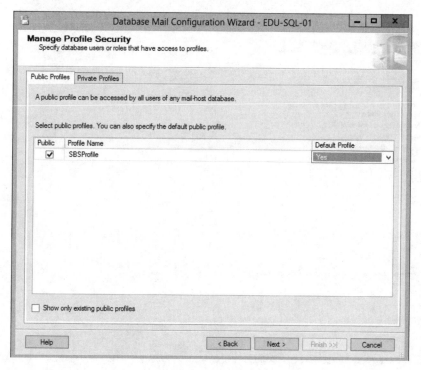

24. Click Next.

On the Configure System Parameters page, you can set options that control several advanced parameters.

25. Review the description of each option by clicking in the Value column for each parameter.

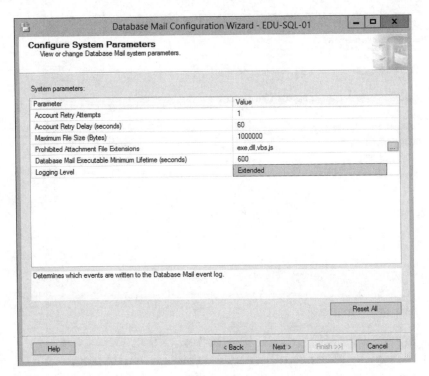

26. Accept the default values for now and click Next.

The Complete the Wizard page provides a summary of the actions that are about to be performed.

27. Review the summary and click Finish.

On the final page, a list of the actions performed is displayed.

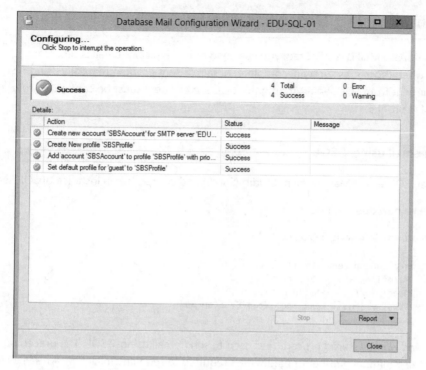

28. Click Close.

Note If you want to send a test email, right-click Database Mail in Object Explorer and select Send Test E-mail from the menu. Enter a valid email address in the To text box and click Send Test E-mail. If everything is configured correctly, you should receive an email shortly. If not, you can check the Database Mail log for errors, as discussed later in this chapter.

Sending email using Database Mail

Now that Database Mail is configured, you can send email. Typically, email is sent from SQL Server Agent jobs when those jobs succeed, complete, or fail, or sent programmatically using T-SQL. Before email can be sent from SQL Server Agent jobs, SQL Server Agent must be configured to use a Database Mail profile.

Send an email using T-SQL

1. Open SQL Server Management Studio (SSMS) and connect to an instance of SQL Server.

2. Open a new query window.

3. Execute the following T-SQL code:

```
EXEC msdb.dbo.sp_send_dbmail
      @profile_name = 'SBSProfile',
      @recipients = 'email@email.com',
      @body = 'Email test from Step-By-Step Book.',
      @subject = 'Test From SQL Server' ;
```

The *sp_send_dbmail* stored procedure is used to send email using T-SQL. The preceding sample script uses the minimum number of parameters required to send an email. You can see a complete list of all parameters in SQL Server Books Online.

Configure SQL Server Agent to send Database Mail

1. Open SSMS and connect to an instance of SQL Server.

2. Right-click SQL Server Agent in Object Explorer and select Properties from the menu.

3. On the SQL Server Agent Properties window, select Alert System from the Select a Page pane.

4. Select the Enable Mail Profile check box.

5. Select SBSProfile from the Mail Profile drop-down list.

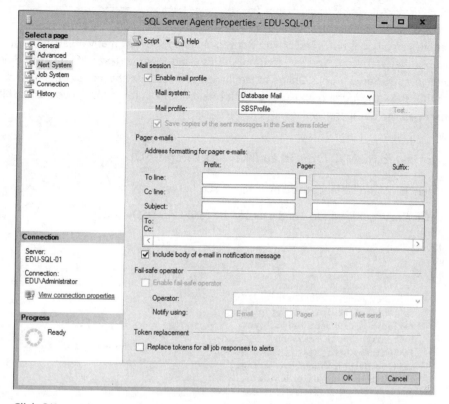

6. Click OK.

In Chapter 27, "SQL Server Agent," you created a job and configured notifications to be sent to an operator when the job fails. Recall that in the event that the jobs fails, the operator will be notified of the failure via email.

Monitoring Database Mail

Now that you've completed the steps to configure Database Mail, you may encounter a scenario in which sending email does not work, or you want to check to see how many email messages were sent and to whom they were sent. You can accomplish this using SSMS or T-SQL. If you use T-SQL, you will need to review SQL Server Books Online to familiarize yourself with the views contained in the msdb database that show the logging and auditing information for Database Mail. If you use SSMS, you need only open the Database Mail log.

View the Database Mail log and audit events using T-SQL

1. Open SSMS and connect to an instance of SQL Server.

2. Open a new query window and execute the following T-SQL code:

```
USE msdb ;
GO
SELECT
      profiles.name ProfileName,
      accounts.name AccountName,
      faileditems.recipients Recipients,
      faileditems.subject MailSubject,
      faileditems.body EmailBody,
      faileditems.sent_status SentStatus,
      maillog.description EventMessage,
      faileditems.sent_date SentDate
FROM dbo.sysmail_faileditems faileditems
INNER JOIN dbo.sysmail_allitems allitems
      ON faileditems.mailitem_id = allitems.mailitem_id
INNER JOIN dbo.sysmail_profile profiles
      ON faileditems.profile_id = profiles.profile_id
INNER JOIN dbo.sysmail_profileaccount profileaccounts
      ON profiles.profile_id = profileaccounts.profile_id
INNER JOIN dbo.sysmail_account accounts
      ON profileaccounts.account_id = accounts.account_id
INNER JOIN dbo.sysmail_event_log maillog
      ON faileditems.mailitem_id = maillog.mailitem_id
```

The preceding query returns a list of only the failed email attempts. Using T-SQL, you can quickly view information about failed email using the EventMessage column from the previous query. Looking at this column, you can then diagnose what caused the failure.

View the Database Mail log and audit events using SSMS

1. Open SSMS and connect to an instance of SQL Server.

2. Expand the Management folder.

3. Right-click Database Mail and select View Database Mail Log from the menu.

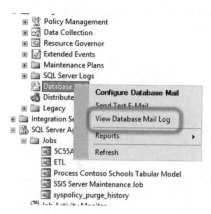

4. Database Mail opens. You can quickly see a consolidated view of all Database Mail activity.

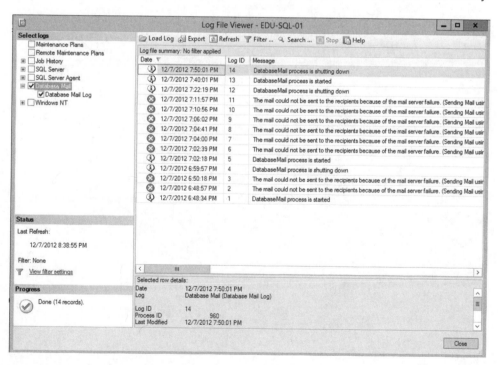

You can export, search, or filter the contents of the Log File Viewer using the menu located at the top of the window.

Summary

This chapter provided an overview of SQL Server Database Mail. It is important to remember that Database Mail does not require a MAPI client. First, you reviewed the components that make up Database Mail. Then you learned how to enable and configure Database Mail, and how to send email using T-SQL and also from SQL Server Agent jobs. Finally, you explored the different ways to view Database Mail audit and log information to research and solve potential problems.

Data definition triggers

After completing this chapter, you will be able to

- Explain the different types of triggers.

- Create, alter, and drop triggers.

- Explain practical uses of triggers.

Data definition triggers, which differ from data manipulation triggers, fire based on events that occur at the server and database level. For example, you can create a data definition trigger that will fire when a database or table is created. These triggers are commonly used for auditing the creation of databases on a server or objects within a database. In addition, they can be used as a means of governing when tables, views, procedures, and other objects are created and for controlling naming conventions for particular objects and object types. Moreover, data definition triggers can also be used to control who can log on to a server. Data manipulation triggers, on the other hand, are attached to a specific object, table, or view in a database. Unlike data definition triggers, data manipulation triggers fire based only on a change in a table or view.

In this chapter, you will be introduced to the different types of database definition triggers available. You will then learn how to create, modify, enable, and disable the triggers. Finally, you will walk through the steps to remove or drop a trigger from a database.

Types of triggers

Triggers, like most objects contained within a Microsoft SQL Server database, have multiple types. There are essentially two types of data definition triggers: CLR and T-SQL. CLR triggers are compiled managed code written in one of the .NET programming languages such as Visual Basic or C#. T-SQL triggers are written in T-SQL and execute statements similar to stored procedures.

> **Note** In this chapter, you will focus on T-SQL triggers. If you are interested in CLR triggers, you can reference SQL Server Books Online, which provides details on how to create them.

As mentioned earlier, data definition triggers are primarily used to audit the creation or dropping of server and database objects and control server access. They are fired when the specified SQL

Server data definition events such as *CREATE_DATABASE*, *CREATE_TABLE*, *DROP_TABLE*, and so on are executed. A complete listing of these events is provided in SQL Server Books Online.

The T-SQL programming language is used to create data definition triggers. The following pseudo-code represents templates that you can use to create either type:

```
---Audit server or database object creation (CREATE, DROP, ALTER, etc...)
CREATE TRIGGER trigger_name
ON { ALL SERVER | DATABASE }
 [ WITH <ddl_trigger_option> [ ,...n ] ]
{ FOR | AFTER } { event_type | event_group } [ ,...n ]
AS
{ sql_statement [ ; ] [ ,...n ] }
<ddl_trigger_option> ::= [ ENCRYPTION ] [ EXECUTE AS Clause ]

---Trigger to control logon events
CREATE TRIGGER trigger_name
ON ALL SERVER [ WITH <logon_trigger_option> [ ,...n ] ]
{ FOR| AFTER } LOGON
AS
{ sql_statement [ ; ] [ ,...n ] }
<logon_trigger_option> ::= [ ENCRYPTION ] [ EXECUTE AS Clause ]
```

Note Data definitions are scoped at the database or server level. For example, a trigger on the *CREATE_VIEW* event could be created for one or many databases on the server. However, if you want to create a login trigger, this event is at the server level and must be created using the ON ALL SERVERS syntax.

Creating triggers

Similar to data manipulation triggers, data definition triggers are typically considered to be special kinds of stored procedures. On the other hand, data definition triggers are not associated with a specific table or view; instead, they are considered server objects. Also, data definition triggers do not have the ability to reference the logical inserted and deleted tables. (Details about these tables are provided in Chapter 18, "Data manipulation triggers.") Instead, there is an *EventData()* function that exposes details about the event of the data definition trigger. This function returns an XML value; therefore, you must use XQuery view the results.

Note Coverage of the XML data type and XQuery is beyond the scope of this book. To learn more, visit SQL Server Books Online.

Create a trigger using T-SQL

1. Open SSMS and connect to a server.

2. Open Object Explorer if it is not already open.

3. Expand the server node, and then expand the Databases folder.

4. Expand the AdventureWorks2012 database.

5. Expand the Programmability folder.

6. Right-click the Database Triggers folder, and then choose New Database Trigger.

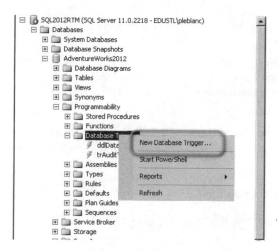

A new query window opens that contains the Trigger Template script. You can use this script as a good starting point for creating a trigger.

7. Open a new query window and execute the following T-SQL code:

```
USE AdventureWorks2012
GO
IF(OBJECT_ID('dbo.TableAudits')) IS NOT NULL
    DROP TABLE dbo.TableAudits
CREATE TABLE dbo.TableAudits
(
    UserName nvarchar(100),
    AuditEvent nvarchar(100),
    TSQLStateent nvarchar(2000),
    AuditDate datetime
)
GO
```

The preceding script creates a table that will store information captured by a data definition trigger.

8. Open a new query window and execute the following query:

```
USE AdventureWorks2012;
  GO
  IF EXISTS (SELECT * FROM sys.triggers
      WHERE parent_class = 0 AND name = 'trAuditTableChanges')
  DROP TRIGGER trAuditTableChanges
  ON DATABASE;
GO
CREATE TRIGGER trAuditTableChanges
ON DATABASE
FOR ALTER_TABLE
AS
DECLARE @Data XML
SET @Data = EventData()
INSERT TableAudits (AuditDate, UserName, AuditEvent, TSQLStateent)
VALUES
  (GETDATE(),
  CONVERT(NVARCHAR(100), CURRENT_USER),
  @Data.value('(/EVENT_INSTANCE/EventType)[1]', 'nvarchar(100)'),
  @Data.value('(/EVENT_INSTANCE/TSQLCommand)[1]', 'nvarchar(2000)') ) ;
GO
```

In the preceding script, a record will be written to the TableAudits table in the event someone attempts to alter an existing table. XQuery is used to capture the event type and the actual SQL statement.

Next, you'll add a column to the Employee table.

9. Open a new query window and execute the following query:

```
USE AdventureWorks2012
GO
ALTER TABLE HumanResources.Employee
ADD Age int;
```

10. Open a new query window and execute the following query:

```
USE AdventureWorks2012
GO
SELECT *
FROM dbo.TableAudits
```

The results show what was inserted into the audit table by the trigger.

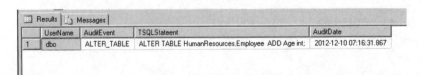

As you can see, the event and the entire T-SQL statement are written to the table. This is an example of a simple, homemade schema-change-auditing data definition trigger.

View a trigger on a server using SSMS

1. Open SSMS and connect to a server.

2. Open Object Explorer if it is not already open.

3. Expand the server node, and then expand the Databases folder.

4. Expand the AdventureWorks2012 database.

5. Expand the Programmability folder.

6. Expand the Database Triggers folder. If necessary, right-click Database Triggers and choose Refresh.

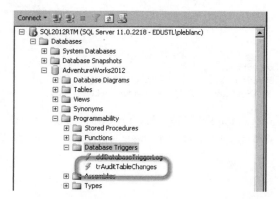

Because triggers are associated with a specific database, you will need to go to this location to find a list of triggers on a database. On the other hand, if you created a login trigger using the ALL SERVER option, you would view the triggers by expanding the server, clicking Server Objects, and then clicking the Triggers folder in Object Explorer.

Altering triggers

As with all other programmable objects in SQL Server, you can modify a trigger by using T-SQL. For example, if you need to change the logic that was initially developed in the trigger, you can use ALTER to quickly change the trigger without dropping it from the associated object.

1. Open SSMS and connect to a server.

2. Open Object Explorer if it is not already open.

3. Open a new query window and execute the following T-SQL statement:

```
USE AdventureWorks2012
GO
ALTER TRIGGER trAuditTableChanges
ON DATABASE
FOR ALTER_TABLE
AS
DECLARE @Data XML
SET @Data = EventData()
INSERT TableAudits (AuditDate, UserName, AuditEvent, TSQLStateent)
VALUES
    (GETDATE(),
    CONVERT(NVARCHAR(100), SYSTEM_USER),
    @Data.value('(/EVENT_INSTANCE/EventType)[1]', 'nvarchar(100)'),
    @Data.value('(/EVENT_INSTANCE/TSQLCommand)[1]', 'nvarchar(2000)') ) ;
```

In the bold line of the preceding code, the *SYSTEM_USER* function is used instead of the *CURRENT_USER* scalar function. *SYSTEM_USER* returns the actual login; *CURRENT_USER* returns the database user.

Enabling and disabling triggers

In some cases, you may not want to delete a trigger but instead want to stop it from firing during a large data definition operation or for testing purposes. SQL Server provides you with the ability to disable a trigger, and once you have completed the task, you can enable the trigger. You can do this using T-SQL or SSMS.

Disable a trigger using T-SQL

1. To disable a trigger with T-SQL, execute the following code:

```
USE AdventureWorks2012
GO
DISABLE TRIGGER trAuditTableChanges ON DATABASE;
GO
```

Enable a trigger using T-SQL

1. To enable a trigger with T-SQL, execute the following code:

```
USE AdventureWorks2012
GO
ENABLE TRIGGER trAuditTableChanges ON DATABASE;
GO
```

Enable (or disable) a trigger using SSMS

1. Open SSMS and connect to a server.

2. Open Object Explorer if it is not already open.

3. Expand the server node, and then expand the Databases folder.

4. Expand the AdventureWorks2012 database.

5. Expand the Programmability folder.

6. Expand the Database Triggers folder.

7. Right-click the trAuditTableChanges trigger and select Disable from the context menu.

8. Right-click the trigger again and select Enable.

 Note To disable a trigger, simply select Disable in step 8 of this procedure.

Dropping triggers

In some cases, you may decide that a trigger is not needed, or you may realize that the additional work is adversely affecting the performance of your application or server. To mitigate these problems, you must remove the trigger. You can drop triggers using either T-SQL or SSMS.

Drop a trigger using T-SQL

1. To drop a trigger using T-SQL, execute the following code:

```
USE AdventureWorks2012
GO
DROP TRIGGER trAuditTableChanges ON DATABASE;
```

1. Open SSMS and connect to a server.

2. Open Object Explorer if it is not already open.

3. Expand the server node, and then expand the Databases folder.

4. Expand the AdventureWorks2012 database.

5. Expand the Programmability folder.

6. Expand the Database Triggers folder.

7. Right-click trAuditTableChanges and select Delete from the context menu.

   The trigger is removed from the table.

Summary

In this chapter, you learned about data definition triggers, which can be scoped at the database or server level. In the event of a data definition operation, the trigger will execute, performing an action. In addition, you learned how to create, drop, enable, disable, and view data definition triggers.

Dynamic management objects

After completing this chapter, you will be able to

- Use dynamic management objects to gain insights into SQL Server.

- Query valuable passively collected server-performance statistics.

- Query valuable passively collected indexing statistics.

Entire books have been written on the subject of dynamic management objects (DMOs). Large wall-posters are available at your local SQL Server User Group detailing each DMO in small font sizes. With each version of Microsoft SQL Server since 2005, more and more information has become available in the massive collection of passive SQL Server statistics, accessible via dynamic management views (DMVs) and dynamic management functions (DMFs). This data is passively collected by SQL Server, which means DMOs do not need to be turned on; they're happily collecting valuable data from the time the SQL Server service starts.

In this chapter, you will be introduced to several DMOs available in SQL Server 2012. You will learn how to use these objects to gain insights into an instance of SQL Server.

Retrieving SQL Server metadata from DMOs

The deep insights available via DMOs don't need to be turned on or activated. They're already running on your SQL Server instance, though most of them reset when your SQL Server service is started. They've been collecting valuable data all along to help you improve performance, tune maintenance plans, and troubleshoot server slowdowns in the short and long term.

DMOs require that your database is in SQL Server 2005 compatibility mode or above for the most part, although some newer DMOs will require SQL Server 2008 or SQL Server 2012 compatibility mode. For the purposes of this exercise, your AdventureWorks2012 database is already in (11.0) mode for SQL Server 2012, so this isn't an issue. Other databases in your production environment need to be in SQL Server 2005 (9.0) mode or higher for you to benefit from this chapter.

The DMOs you're going to learn about in this chapter are the foundation of countless third-party SQL Server monitoring applications. These tools have no magical access to hidden secrets inside SQL Server—they do little more than archive and present the same information you can query yourself, with nothing more than VIEW SERVER STATE or VIEW DATABASE STATE permissions. That's right, you do not even have to be a sysadmin to query many DMOs.

Let's get right to it and review a "best of" list of DMOs found in any veteran DBA's tool belt.

Querying server performance statistics

Entire software packages are for sale by third-party companies based on two DMVs: *sys.dm_os_wait_stats* and *sys.dm_os_waiting_tasks*. As these are DMVs, not DMFs, they can be queried and joined like any other view object. (You'll see some sample scripts later in this chapter.)

Wait statistics are an important short-term and long-term metric that you should be aware of on SQL Server. At any time, regardless of the workload, SQL Server is incurring and recording at least several wait types. There are over 600 wait stats in SQL Server 2012, but most you will never see, and many can be ignored as they indicate an idle status.

Among the remaining wait types are the most common ones to look out for. It is not an indication of a problem if you see these as the most common waits on your server, but a sudden increase in a wait type or a correlation of poor performance with spikes in waits is a clue to the smart DBA. Here are the most common wait types you'll encounter on your production SQL Server instance:

- **LCK_M_*** Spiking values in lock wait types indicate transaction contention.

- **PAGEIOLATCH_*** Spiking values in page I/O latch wait types indicate that requests are overwhelming the physical I/O subsystem (the server's hard disk storage).

- **CXPACKET** A tricky wait indicates excessive parallelism in execution plans. More efficient queries always help, but investigating the Max Degree of Parallelism setting is prudent.

- **SOS_SCHEDULER_YIELD** Spiking values in this wait type indicate CPU pressure—too many runnable tasks for the server's processors to handle.

- **ASYNC_NETWORK_IO** Spiking values in the asynchronous network I/O wait type indicate a time spent waiting for external resources, perhaps a remote client or linked server.

The two wait DMVs show wait type statistics differently:

- *sys.dm_os_wait_stats* This wait DMV shows aggregated wait times since the last time the SQL Server service was restarted, or if it was manually reset. The wait_time_ms for each of wait type will continue to grow until the counter is reset.

- *sys.dm_os_waiting_tasks* This wait DMV shows waits happening right now on the server. The wait_duration_ms will grow only until the request causing the wait ends.

Determine which waits are most common

1. Open SSMS and connect to a server.

2. Open Object Explorer and right-click the Server Name row. Choose New Query.

3. Execute the following query:

```
select top 10      wait_type
,      wait_time_ms
,      Percentage      =      100. * wait_time_ms/sum(wait_time_ms) OVER()
from sys.dm_os_wait_stats wt
where wt.wait_type NOT LIKE '%SLEEP%'
order by Percentage desc
```

> **Note** The preceding query ignores several wait types with the word "SLEEP" in the name. These wait types and many others are not a cause for concern and can be filtered out of queries on wait type DMVs.

This query returns the top 10 wait types, with a percentage of time. The wait types returned will be vastly different from your production to development boxes. Observe this data over time; you should be on the lookout for a type creeping up the top 10.

Determine which waits are happening right now

1. Open SSMS and connect to a server.

2. Open Object Explorer, right-click the Server Name row, and then choose New Query.

3. Execute the following query:

```
SELECT       wt.session_id
,      wt.wait_type
,      er.wait_resource
,      wt.wait_duration_ms
,      st.text
,      er.start_time
FROM      sys.dm_os_waiting_tasks wt
INNER JOIN sys.dm_exec_requests er
on wt.waiting_task_address = er.task_address
OUTER APPLY      sys.dm_exec_sql_text(er.sql_handle) st
where      wt.wait_type NOT LIKE '%SLEEP%'
and      wt.session_id >= 50
ORDER BY wt.wait_duration_ms desc
```

The preceding query ignores session IDs less than 50, which are system connections. Usually these are not a concern for wait type performance tuning.

Note The use of two other DMVs, *sys.dm_exec_requests* and *sys.dm_exec_sql_text*, will be explained later in this chapter.

The results of this query are probably going to be empty for you. If so, that's a good thing! Remember that this query returns data for queries currently incurring a SQL Server wait. On a production server, you will see your heaviest-hitting queries showing up here.

4. Comment out the line of T-SQL code that filters out session_ids less than 50. Place two hyphens before the text in the line to comment it out—this should turn that text green in SSMS.

```
where    wt.wait_type NOT LIKE '%SLEEP%'
--and        wt.session_id >= 50
ORDER BY wt.wait_duration_ms desc
```

5. Execute the query again to see wait types being incurred by system processes.

The results of this query contain a number of wait types that can be safely ignored, as they indicate a harmless wait. Remember, SQL Server is always recording a wait, even if it is "I'm idle." Wait types you'll likely see here are *ONDEMAND_TASK_QUEUE*, *BROKER_TRANSMITTER*, and *KSOURCE_WAKEUP*, among others.

Querying server information

In this section, you'll quickly review a few helpful DMVs that expose server information.

sys.dm_server_services

The following query exposes help information about the SQL Server instance, requiring only the VIEW SERVER STATE permission. You can retrieve the service account information, the service status, and much more without launching SQL Server Configuration Manager.

```
SELECT    *
FROM    sys.dm_server_services;
```

sys.dm_os_volume_stats

This DMV, when correlated with the system view *sys.database_files*, will display all files in the current database, along with information about the volume they exist on. Most important, this DMV returns the size of the drive and the available space on the drive, which in this example is converted from bytes to megabytes. Prior to the introduction of this DMV in SQL Server 2008 R2, it was not easy to query this data from inside SQL Server.

```
use AdventureWorks2012;
select df.physical_name
,      vs.file_id
,      vs.file_system_type
,      total_mb          =      vs.total_bytes / 1024. / 1024.
,      available_mb      =      vs.available_bytes / 1024. / 1024.
from sys.database_files df
cross apply  sys.dm_os_volume_stats (db_id(),df.file_id) vs;
```

sys.dm_os_sys_memory

This DMV conveniently allows the current host server's total and available memory to be queried from inside SQL Server. Available columns in this DMV also return information on the Windows page file and the system cache.

```
select     total_physical_memory_gb            =      total_physical_memory_kb / 1024. / 1024.
,      available_physical_memory_gb    =      available_physical_memory_kb / 1024. / 1024.
from sys.dm_os_sys_memory;
```

sys.dm_exec_requests and sys.dm_exec_sessions

These two DMVs provide queryable data on current sessions (connections) and requests (active queries) against the SQL Server database, along with much more information about the nature of the current request.

Because the sample query is a *LEFT OUTER JOIN*, the result set will include all sessions, but blank data for the right half of the result set when no request is active. To show only currently executing requests, change the join to *INNER JOIN*.

If you are familiar with the system stored procedure *sp_who2*, these two DMVs provide a query-able, richer, and more flexible look at server sessions and requests, and they are frequently used by DBAs to examine current activity.

```
select     s.*, r.*
from sys.dm_exec_sessions s
left outer join sys.dm_exec_requests r on r.session_id = s.session_id
where s.session_id >= 50 --retrieve only user spids
```

sys.dm_exec_sql_text

You saw how this DMF was used in conjunction with the *sys.dm_os_waiting_tasks* DMV to pull actual statement text for the request that was generating the wait.

Any DMO that references *sql_handle* in its result set can be used to identify the actual statement text using *sys.dm_exec_sql_text*. Let's take a look at *sys.dm_exec_sql_text*, *sys.dm_exec_requests*, and *sys.dm_exec_sessions* used together to return the statement text of current requests:

```
SELECT s.*, r.*
, offsettext = CASE      WHEN r.statement_start_offset = 0 and r.statement_end_offset= 0 THEN
NULL
                ELSE      SUBSTRING (            est.[text], r.statement_start_offset/2 + 1,
                CASE WHEN r.statement_end_offset = -1
                THEN LEN (CONVERT(nvarchar(max), est.[text]))
                ELSE r.statement_end_offset/2 - r.statement_start_offset/2 + 1      END)
                END
FROM sys.dm_exec_sessions s
INNER JOIN sys.dm_exec_requests r on r.session_id = s.session_id
OUTER APPLY sys.dm_exec_sql_text (r.sql_handle) est
```

Using this query, you should be able to see your own request in this query, made from the host name, made from the login_name. You'll recognize the query in the offsettext column: *SELECT s.*, r.*, offsettext = ...*

Querying performance information

SQL Server caches the execution plans of queries and then reveals a wealth of information about these plans via DMVs. This information helps a DBA identify the most "expensive" queries that have run recently against SQL Server, in terms of CPU cost, duration, disk operations, or frequency. Given realistic activity against the SQL Server instance that has been running for, say, a month, this information can help direct query-tuning efforts by DBAs and developers.

sys.dm_exec_query_stats

The result set ranks the queries by their relative amount of total_worker_time (CPU time), physical reads, and execution duration. When dissecting this query, you'll recognize no fewer than five DMVs or DMFs in use that *sys.dm_exec_query_stats* brings together. Note the usage of *sys.dm_exec_sql_text*, which is used to return the actual query text from the statement that used the execution plan. By using the offset values in *sys.dm_exec_query_stats*, it is possible to determine—even inside of a lengthy stored procedure—which statement out of many is the problem code. This query may take over a minute to complete, but it will present an invaluable list of the highest cost queries that have recently executed on your SQL Server instance.

```
SELECT TOP 50
stmt_text        =      REPLACE (REPLACE (SUBSTRING (sql.[text], PlanStats.statement_start_
offset/2 + 1, CASE WHEN PlanStats.statement_end_offset = -1 THEN LEN (CONVERT(nvarchar(max),
sql.[text])) ELSE PlanStats.statement_end_offset/2 - PlanStats.statement_start_offset/2 + 1
END), CHAR(13), ' '), CHAR(10), ' ')
,    qp.query_plan
,      PlanStats.total_physical_reads
,      PlanStats.total_logical_writes
,      PlanStats.execution_count
```

```
,       tot_cpu_ms         =        PlanStats.total_worker_time/1000.
,       tot_duration_ms        =        PlanStats.total_elapsed_time/1000.
,       PlanStats.total_rows
,       dbname = db_name( convert(int, pa.value) )
,   sql.objectid
,   planstats.last_execution_time
FROM ( SELECT *,
    ROW_NUMBER() OVER (ORDER BY stat.total_worker_time DESC) AS CpuRank,
    ROW_NUMBER() OVER (ORDER BY stat.total_physical_reads DESC) AS PhysicalReadsRank,
    ROW_NUMBER() OVER (ORDER BY stat.total_elapsed_time DESC) AS DurationRank
  FROM sys.dm_exec_query_stats stat ) AS PlanStats
INNER JOIN sys.dm_exec_cached_plans p ON p.plan_handle = PlanStats.plan_handle
OUTER APPLY sys.dm_exec_plan_attributes (p.plan_handle) pa
OUTER APPLY sys.dm_exec_sql_text (p.plan_handle) AS sql
OUTER APPLY sys.dm_exec_query_plan (p.plan_handle) qp
WHERE pa.attribute = 'dbid'
ORDER BY PlanStats.CpuRank + PlanStats.PhysicalReadsRank + PlanStats.DurationRank asc;
```

Querying indexing statistics

Since SQL Server 2005, the database engine has provided a passive "wish list" feature for nonclustered indexes, known as the *missing indexes* DMVs, a set of DMVs that collect information that guides DBAs toward creating well-crafted nonclustered indexes. As you learned in Chapter 6, "Building and maintaining indexes," nonclustered indexes are crucial to good read performance from tables.

The missing index feature of SQL Server generates data that suggests only new nonclustered indexes, and it will not guide the creation or alteration of a clustered index on a table.

Like other DMOs, the missing index feature is already running on SQL Server since SQL Server 2005. It does not need to be turned on. The missing index DMVs reset when the SQL Server service is restarted, just like other DMOs. So viewing the missing index DMVs for suggested indexes should occur only after a solid period of actual usage in your environment.

Unlike other DMOs, the missing index DMVs clear out data for a table when that table's schema is changed. Old index suggestions may no longer be valid or helpful for a table that has its columns or indexes changed.

Let's demonstrate the missing index feature inside the AdventureWorks2012 database:

- *sys.dm_db_missing_index_groups*

- *sys.dm_db_missing_index_group_stats*

- *sys.dm_db_missing_index_details*

Identify missing indexes

1. Open SSMS and connect to a server.

2. Open Object Explorer, right-click the Server Name row, and then choose New Query.

3. Execute the following two queries. Execute this batch a total of three times.

```
use AdventureWorks2012;
SELECT    SalesOrderID, CarrierTrackingNumber, OrderQty, LineTotal
FROM Sales.SalesOrderDetail d
where     d.UnitPrice < 200 and d.OrderQty > 1;
SELECT    SalesOrderID, CarrierTrackingNumber, OrderQty, LineTotal
FROM Sales.SalesOrderDetail d
where     d.OrderQty > 1;
```

4. Type the following query to reference the missing index DMVs and then execute it.

```
SELECT      mid.statement,       unique_compiles, migs.user_seeks, migs.user_scans,
last_user_seek, migs.avg_total_user_cost, avg_user_impact, mid.equality_columns,
mid.inequality_columns, mid.included_columns
FROM sys.dm_db_missing_index_groups mig
INNER JOIN sys.dm_db_missing_index_group_stats migs
ON migs.group_handle = mig.index_group_handle
INNER JOIN sys.dm_db_missing_index_details mid
ON mig.index_handle = mid.index_handle
order by avg_user_impact + avg_total_user_cost desc
```

In step 3, you executed queries that could have run more efficiently with new nonclustered indexes. Review the result sets from step 4, and note that two index suggestions are listed. Each of these suggested, nonexistent indexes would have been seeked as part of an execution plan three times (user_seeks). The last time the generating query executed is also listed (last_user_seek), along with the cost of the operation that generated it (avg_total_user_cost). The avg_user_impact column is SQL Server's estimate of how much the avg_total_user_cost would have been reduced by, had the suggested index been in place. The equality_columns, inequality_columns, and included_columns data inform the DBA on how the suggested index should be created.

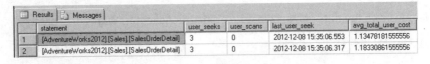

	statement	user_seeks	user_scans	last_user_seek	avg_total_user_cost
1	[AdventureWorks2012].[Sales].[SalesOrderDetail]	3	0	2012-12-08 15:35:06.553	1.13478181555556
2	[AdventureWorks2012].[Sales].[SalesOrderDetail]	3	0	2012-12-08 15:35:06.317	1.18330861555556

avg_user_impact	equality_columns	inequality_columns	included_columns
76.88	NULL	[OrderQty]	[SalesOrderID], [CarrierTrackingNumber], [LineTotal]
74.88	NULL	[OrderQty], [UnitPrice]	[SalesOrderID], [CarrierTrackingNumber], [LineTotal]

5. Create the suggested indexes by opening a new query window and executing the following code:

```
CREATE NONCLUSTERED INDEX IDX_NC_SalesOrderDetail_OrderQty_UnitPrice
ON
[AdventureWorks2012].[Sales].[SalesOrderDetail] ([OrderQty], [UnitPrice])
INCLUDE
([SalesOrderID], [CarrierTrackingNumber], [LineTotal]);
```

Note that you have created only one index. Why? This is to demonstrate a crucial concept in the SQL Server missing index feature: SQL Server will suggest that overlapping indexes be created, based on the queries that have been provided. The skillful, mindful DBA will always consider all index suggestions on a table and combine them when the column orders are compatible.

In this simple demonstration, as shown in the previous image, the data in row 1 suggests that you create an index keyed on the OrderQty column. The data in row 2 suggests that you create an index on the same table, keyed on the OrderQty and UnitPrice columns. Index key order does matter, and in this case, the index suggested by the data in row 2 would also improve the query that generated the suggestion in row 1.

To prove this point, you'll make sure that index suggestions for your original queries no longer appear.

6. Execute the T-SQL query from step 4 again.

Note that no more suggestions appear for that table because the table changed. A new non-clustered index was added in step 5.

7. Execute the T-SQL queries in step 3 three times.

8. Execute the T-SQL query in step 4 again.

The queries that previously generated missing index suggestions are no longer generating suggested index data.

sys.dm_db_index_usage_stats

Creating new indexes with the missing index DMVs is one thing, but what about gauging the effectiveness of existing indexes?

All nonclustered indexes should provide a large positive impact to *SELECT* statements in order to offset their penalty to the performance of *INSERT, UPDATE,* and *DELETE* statements. The *sys.dm_db_index_usage_stats* DMV provides information on the usage of existing indexes by tracking the number of times user queries have been used and maintained. Four columns are key, as they weigh the benefits (user_seeks, user_scans, user_lookups) against the cost (user_updates) of a nonclustered index.

Low numbers of seeks, scans, and lookups versus a high number of user updates means this index is being maintained but rarely used. Consider dropping the index; it isn't pulling its weight.

Like the missing index DMVs, you should consider using *sys.dm_db_index_usage_stats* only after a lengthy period of typical business usage since the last server restart. The duration of this period of observation should be equal to a typical business cycle (for SQL Server–based reports, for example).

sys.dm_db_index_physical_stats

This DMF allows you to determine the fragmentation level of an object. An example of usage appears in Chapter 21, "Managing and maintaining indexes and statistics," as this DMF is crucial to a custom strategy for index maintenance.

Summary

This chapter reviewed the basics of dynamic management objects (DMOs). You learned about several DMOs that provide useful information to a database administrator or developer. You also walked through steps to demonstrate how to query vital diagnostic information about SQL Server using DMOs.

CHAPTER 31

AlwaysOn

After completing this chapter, you will be able to

- Understand the improvements in failover cluster instances.

- Create AlwaysOn Availability Groups.

- Administer AlwaysOn Availability Groups.

- Read secondary database copies.

With high availability and disaster recovery becoming priorities in corporate IT departments, there has been a need for a more robust set of solutions compared to the built-in solutions in previous versions of SQL Server prior to Microsoft SQL Server 2012. Oftentimes, one or more technologies had to be combined to satisfy requirements for true high availability as well as disaster recovery. In SQL Server 2012, Microsoft released a set of solutions under the AlwaysOn umbrella. This solution combines improvements made to failover clustering as well as a new concept known as *availability groups*, which is built on top of the mirroring code base that was introduced in SQL Server 2005.

Failover clustering has several improvements that SQL Server 2012 can take advantage of. Some of the highlights are as follows:

- Up to 64 nodes

- Flexible failover policy

- Multisite failover clusters

- tempdb on the local disk

Availability groups are new to SQL Server 2012 and provide the following benefits:

- Databases can be grouped together and failover as a group.

- Availability groups support multiple replicas.

- Replicas can be used for read activity—the long-awaited "warm readable spare."

- A mix of synchronous and asynchronous modes can be used between replicas.

- Backup activity can be offloaded to replicas.

- There is no shared storage requirement.

- Availability groups use Windows Server Failover Clustering (WSFC) for health detection and to manage failover.

Failover clustering provides instance-level protection as it does with previous versions, but the improvements just listed have made this technology more robust, scalable, and manageable. Failover clustering is commonly used for high availability within the data center, but with the improvements made in SQL Server 2012, it can easily provide high availability and disaster recovery across data centers.

Availability groups provide database-level protection typically used in disaster recovery scenarios. With availability groups, users have more options when designing a disaster recovery plan by placing replicas in both the same data center and remote data centers since multiple replicas are supported. You will learn more about availability groups later in this chapter.

Failover cluster instance improvements

SQL Server clustering, also known as *failover cluster instance* (FCI), provides a framework within the operating system for a SQL Server instance to be compatible and capable to run on one of several servers that make up the cluster. Clustering is a function of the operating system, and the SQL Server software is compatible with this operating system function.

Clustering provides the ability for a service and its associated resources to be grouped together and run on any nodes, or servers, that make up the cluster. As a best practice, it is recommended for all nodes to be similar hardware and for SQL Server to be the same version and build number. Although clustering is not a new concept in SQL Server, the new improvements with SQL Server 2012 make this technology more scalable and robust.

 Note For more information on AlwaysOn Failover Cluster Instances, visit *http://msdn.microsoft.com/en-us/library/ms189134(SQL.110).aspx.*

With clustering being an existing technology supported by SQL Server, there are a few major improvements made with the release of SQL Server 2012. Some of the highlights are detailed in the sections that follow.

Multisubnet clustering

SQL Server 2012 supports cluster nodes that reside in more than one subnet. This is achieved in the way SQL Server binds the IP addresses for the cluster resources—it now uses the OR algorithm instead of the AND algorithm for IP binding. This means a SQL Server instance can start if just one of the network interfaces is available.

Robust failure detection

The older method of IsAlive has been replaced with a system stored procedure call to *sp_server_diagnostics*, which now performs health detection. The administrator can control the level of failure to initiate a cluster resource failover, known as a *flexible failover policy*.

tempdb on local drive

tempdb can be located on a local disk on each node within the cluster. You can expect significant performance improvements when using the local disk as opposed to a shared SAN disk. Since the location of tempdb files is in the master database, which fails between nodes, the path and permissions to the directory housing the tempdb files should be the same on all nodes to prevent the SQL Server service from starting.

Creating AlwaysOn Availability Groups

Prior to creating AlwaysOn Availability Groups, you must install WSFC on each node in the topology. Next, you must create a Windows cluster that includes each node. Finally, you must enable AlwaysOn on each SQL Server instance.

Windows Server Failover Clustering

Microsoft received feedback from the previous technologies used for high availability and took those suggestions seriously when it created the new AlwaysOn Availability Groups technology. When SQL Server 2005 Service Pack 1 was released, it included a new feature: database mirroring. The major downfall to database mirroring was that you could have only one mirror, and that mirror could not be used for anything unless a database snapshot was created. In addition to database mirroring, SQL Server 2005 included log shipping and clustering. Log shipping allows you to read the secondary database; however, connections must be dropped when the shipped logs are periodically restored. Clustering, on the other hand, can be configured with several topologies that include several servers; however, only one copy of each database is available for any activity. This made it hard to justify to upper management the cost of secondary inactive servers.

 Note Log shipping is discussed in Chapter 32, "Log shipping."

With the release of SQL Server 2012, Microsoft introduced AlwaysOn, which includes availability groups. Availability groups require that all servers you want to include in the topology be part of a WSFC, not to be confused with a SQL Server FCI. There is no shared disk requirement for the WSFC, and the availability group framework uses this for health detection and to initiate and manage failover. When setting up the WSFC, please be sure to configure the quorum appropriately. Once the WSFC has been set up, there will be no storage and no cluster resources—only nodes should exist.

Figure 31-1 shows that no storage or services are part of this WSFC; the figure depicts a cluster that has been created and includes three servers.

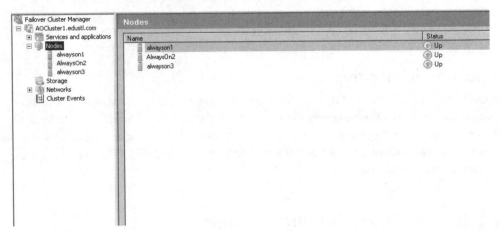

FIGURE 31-1 The Windows Server Failover Cluster Manager.

 Note For more information on quorum settings for WSFC, please see *http://msdn.microsoft.com/en-us/library/hh270280.aspx*. While the steps needed to configure a WSFC cluster are not provided in this chapter, note that Microsoft provides a very intuitive wizard to assist in building the cluster.

When installing SQL Server for participation in an availability group, you'll need to perform a stand-alone install, not a cluster install. Although an FCI can exist as a participant in an availability group, only manual failover is supported, and an FCI is not a requirement for availability groups.

Enabling AlwaysOn

To enable AlwaysOn for an instance of SQL Server, you must use the SQL Server Configuration Manager. Once AlwaysOn is enabled, that instance must be restarted before you can actually create an availability group.

Enable AlwaysOn using SSMS

1. Click Start | All Programs | Microsoft SQL Server 2012 | Configuration Tools | SQL Server Configuration Manager.

2. Click SQL Server Services in the left navigation pane.

3. Right-click the instance of SQL Server that needs AlwaysOn enabled and select Properties from the menu.

4. In the SQL Server Properties dialog box, click the AlwaysOn High Availability tab.

5. If you have not included the server in a WSFC cluster, the check box will be disabled. However, if you have included the server in a WSFC cluster, select the Enable AlwaysOn Availability Groups check box.

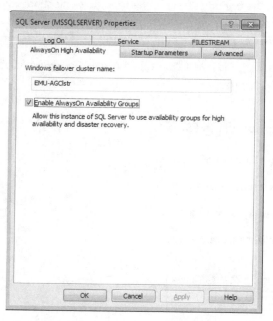

6. Click OK and restart the instance of SQL Server.

Remember, this procedure must be done for each replica or instance of SQL Server that will participate in the availability group.

Creating availability groups

At this point, you are ready to start creating an availability group. The following is a list of rules to remember when you are designing an architecture consisting of availability groups:

- You can have up to four secondary replicas, for five total replicas.

- Up to three total replicas can be synchronous data movement.

- Up to two total replicas can be automatic failover.

- An FCI can be a replica in an availability group, but only manual failover is supported.

In addition to these server topology rules, there are a few restrictions on the database. First, the database recovery model must be set to Full. This is similar to database mirroring and log shipping, and you should implement it as a best practice if your organization requires point-in-time recovery of data. In addition, you must take a full backup prior to including a database as part of an availability group. More than one database can be included in a single availability group, meaning they fail as a group. This is a huge improvement over mirroring and log shipping, as those technologies were database by database and required increased management during a failover to make sure all databases that made up an application were running together on the same hardware.

Finally, you need to create a share on the primary server in the topology. This share will be used during availability group creation to store a backup of the database or databases that have been included in the availability group. Each server must have permission to access this directory.

In SQL Server Management Studio (SSMS), the new folder called AlwaysOn High Availability is the starting point for creating a new availability group.

Create a SQL Server availability group using SSMS

1. Open SSMS and connect to an instance of SQL Server.

2. Open Object Explorer if it is not already open.

3. Right-click the AlwaysOn High Availability folder.

4. Select New Availability Group Wizard from the menu.

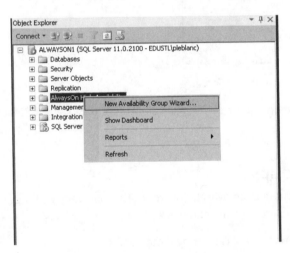

5. Click Next on the Introduction page.

6. On the Specify Availability Group Name page, enter **SBSAGroup** in the Availability Group Name text box.

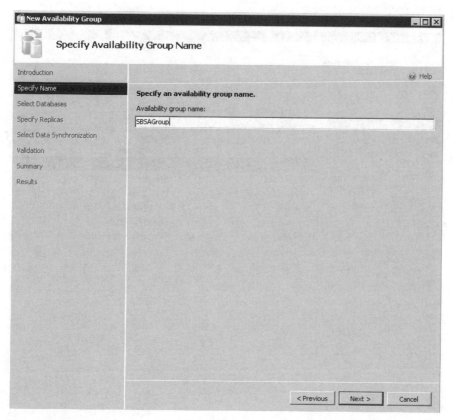

7. Click Next.

On the Select Databases page, you can choose to add several databases as part of your availability group. SQL Server will let you know which databases meet the requirements and will provide a short status explanation of any problems.

8. Select the check box to the left of the AdventureWorks2012 database. You can see additional information about database prerequisites by clicking the hyperlink in the Status column for a given database.

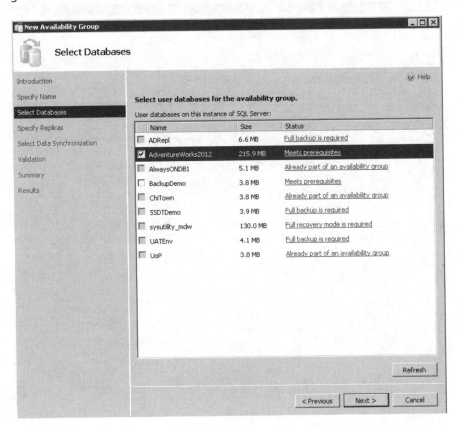

9. Click Next.

10. The Specify Replicas page is used for many purposes. The first is to add all the servers that will be part of your topology. To do so, click the Add button located in the middle section of the page.

11. On the Connect to Server page, enter the name of the server that you want to include and click Connect.

12. Repeat steps 10 and 11 for every server that will participate in the availability group.

13. In the Automatic Failover (Up to 2) column, select the boxes that correspond to the servers that will serve as your high-availability pair. Note that you can select a maximum of two.

14. In the Synchronous Commit (Up to 3) column, select the boxes that correspond to the servers that require synchronous mirroring. Typically, servers that are part of the high-availability pair and those on which backups will be performed are configured for synchronous movement.

> **Note** Synchronous data movement is required for automatic failover, as it guarantees no data loss. The way synchronous data movement works is that when a transaction is committed on the primary, it is sent to the replica and has to wait for acknowledgment back from the replica before a response is sent to the client. This ensures no data loss, as the transaction is hardened to the transaction log on both the primary and all synchronous replicas before the commit is sent back to the calling program. This procedure is not recommended for replicas in remote data centers because the latency involved in this process can cause a performance degradation to the application. Asynchronous data movement sends the transaction to all the asynchronous replicas but does not wait for acknowledgment back before sending the response to the calling application.

15. In the next column, Readable Secondary, you have three choices:

- **No** When the server's role is secondary, you cannot read from it.

- **Yes** If the server's role is secondary, you can read from it, regardless of the application intent.

- **Read-intent only** If the server's role is secondary, you can read from it only if the application intent is set to read-only in the connection string. For example, when accessing a database using SSMS, the intent is read/write. If Readable Secondary is set to read-intent, a connection cannot be made.

Your choice depends on your organization's requirements. If you intend to offload read-only workloads, you should select either Yes or Read-Intent Only. In the following image, one is set to No, one to Yes, and one to Read-Intent Only.

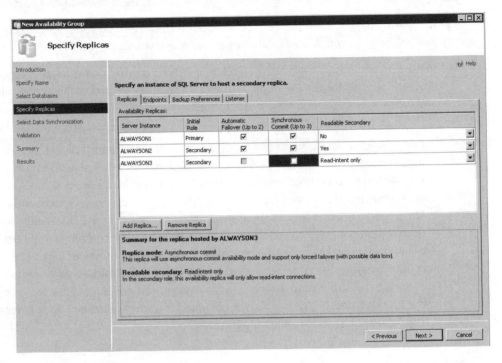

16. Click the Endpoints tab.

SQL Server will create these endpoints if they do not already exist. Notice the endpoint name is Hadr_endpoint; this naming convention is new to SQL Server 2012. The administrator has the ability to set the port and encryption settings. Leave the default settings as they are.

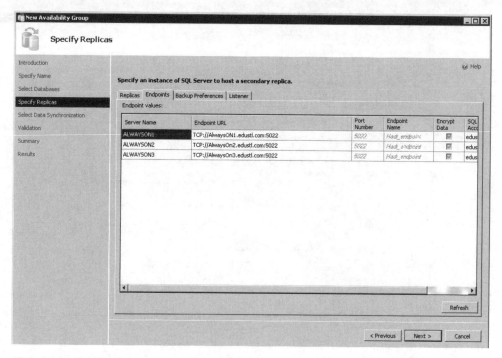

17. Click the Backup Preferences tab.

This tab is where you set the backup preferences. You can exclude replicas as shown here, and you can set preferred settings for automated backup jobs. You can prioritize backup replica preferences by specifying a higher number for a given replica.

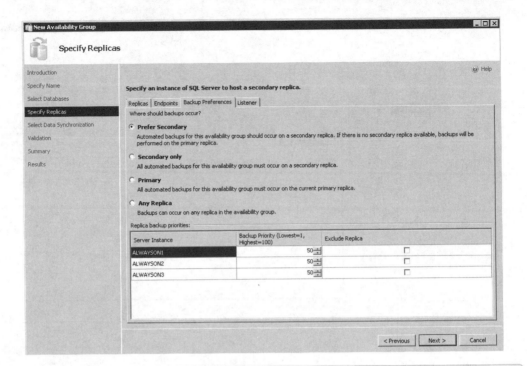

 Note Only FULL backups with COPY_ONLY as well as transaction log backups on replicas are available at this time.

18. Click the Listener tab.

    The listener is a virtual network name that can be used to access the availability group. When applications and end users connect, they should connect using a listener rather than the physical network name. In the event of a failover, the listener is moved to the current primary server. As a result, any role change would be transparent to applications.

19. Select the Create an Availability Group Listener option.

20. Enter **SBS_List** in the Listener DNS Name text box.

21. Enter **1433** in the Port text box, unless you change the SQL Server port.

22. Select Static IP from the Network Mode drop-down list. This is strongly recommended over the DHCP option, which may lead to client time-outs upon lease expirations and will not work across subnets.

23. Click Add and enter an available and valid IP address in the IPv4 Address text box.

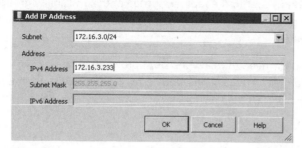

24. Click OK.

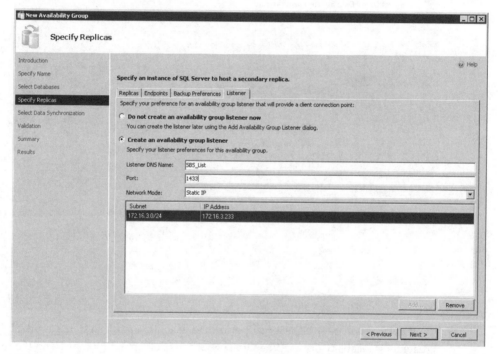

25. Click Next.

On the Select Initial Data Synchronization page, you are presented with three choices:

- The default, Full, will perform a backup at the time the availability group is created and restore that backup to all the replicas using the shared UNC path that is provided in the Specify a Shared Network Location Accessible by All Replicas text box. All servers must have access to this path for this option to work successfully.

- The second, Join Only, is typically for large databases. In this case, the DBA should copy full and transaction log backups over to the replicas outside of the availability group creation process and restore them with NORECOVERY so the replicas are already seeded before the availability group is created.

- In the final scenario, you will need to follow the steps provided at *http://msdn.microsoft.com/en-us/library/hh272568.aspx*. You'll typically use this option when you want to manually start data movement.

26. For now, accept the default and click Next.

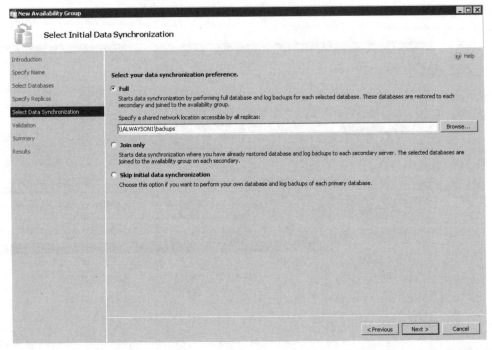

27. On the Validation page, SQL Server performs a validation to make sure everything is ready to create the availability group. When you choose the Full option for initializing the replicas, the databases cannot exist on the replicas or validation will fail. Click Next.

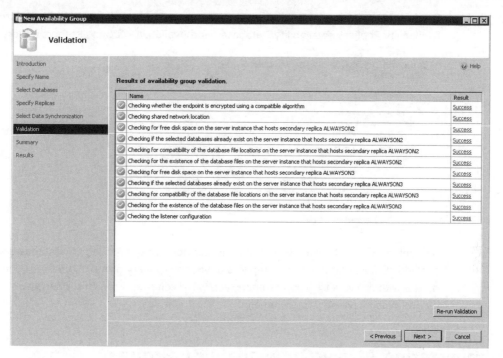

28. On the Summary page, a complete listing of all the configurations is displayed. You can also decide to script all the steps using the Script button located in the bottom-right corner of the page.

Click Finish and the availability group creation process will begin.

29. If you click the arrow next to More Details, SQL Server provides a comprehensive list of all the steps that will be performed when creating the availability group.

When everything has completed successfully, you can expend the AlwaysOn High Availability folder and then expand Availability Groups, where you will find the new group.

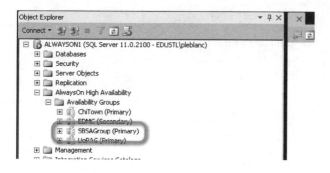

In addition to viewing the availability groups, you can expand Availability Groups to view the Availability Replicas, Availability Databases, and Availability Group Listeners folders.

By right-clicking either the Availability Replicas node or the Availability Databases node, you can add additional databases or replicas to your availability group. Note that if you attempt to do this with availability group listeners, you will receive an error. This is because each availability group can have only one listener.

Administering AlwaysOn Availability Groups

Now that you have created an availability group, you can view its state with the dashboard available in SSMS. As an administrator, you have the ability to view state, latency, and other information vital to the health of your availability groups.

Monitor availability groups using SSMS

1. Open SSMS and connect to the instance of SQL Server that is currently the primary server in your AlwaysOn topology.

2. Open Object Explorer if it is not already open.

3. Expand the AlwaysOn High Availability folder.

4. Expand the Availability Groups folder.

5. Right-click SBSAGroup and select Show Dashboard from the menu.

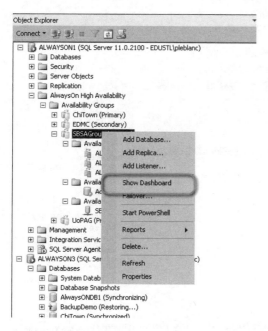

On the dashboard, you can see who the primary or secondary replicas are. You can also view the synchronization state and determine if there are currently any issues.

6. If you want to add addition columns, click one of the gray bars and a menu will appear that lists all available columns.

7. Click the gray bar directly below Availability Replica and select Availability Mode.

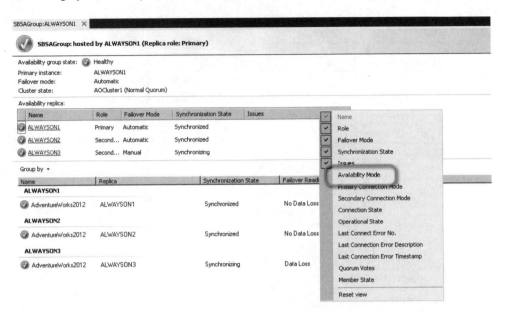

8. This column will be added, showing the availability mode for each replica.

You can use this extensive list of items to monitor, maintain, and administer your AlwaysOn configurations. Unlike clustering, where most of the administration was handled by the Cluster Administrator, AlwaysOn provides DBAs with a means of management from inside the familiar SSMS tool. In addition, DBAs can manually fail an availability group over to another instance of SQL Server using the dashboard included in SSMS.

Perform a manual failover using SSMS

1. Connect to the primary instance of SQL Server for the availability group you created earlier.

2. Open the availability group dashboard.

3. In the top-right corner, click the Start Failover Wizard hyperlink.

4. Click Next on the Introduction page.

5. On the Select New Primary Replica page, select the box next to the replica that will be the new primary server. Note that SQL Server provides a warning about potential data loss for any replicas that are using an asynchronous commit mode.

 Note This warning may create a new step in the wizard called Confirm Potential Data Loss, which will require you to select a check box acknowledging the risk. Proceed from there only if you are OK with data loss.

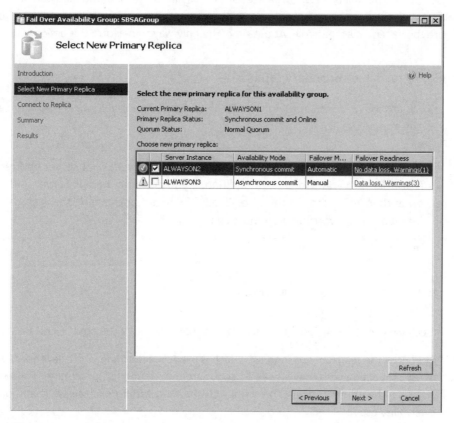

6. Click Next.

7. On the Connect to Replica page, click the Connect button.

8. On the Connect to Server page, choose your authentication method and click Connect.

9. Click Next.

10. Review the Summary page and click Finish.

The failover process begins. If you click the arrow next to More Details, you can see each step of the process.

If you connect to the new primary server and open the dashboard, you can view the current state of the availability group. Also, if you connect to one of the secondary servers, you can view only that secondary server.

Reading secondary database copies

As mentioned previously, one of the main features of AlwaysOn is the ability to read the secondary database copies. This ability allows organizations to fully leverage all of the hardware in their high-availability and disaster recovery topology. However, prior to accessing these databases, you need to configure the instances as readable. At this time, the only way to perform this action is using T-SQL.

Configure readable secondary replicas

1. Configure the read-only routing URL. To do this, execute the following T-SQL for each replica on the primary replica.

> **Note** In the following script, replace *SERVER NAME* with your server and replace *DOMAIN* with your domain. In addition, if you are running SQL Server under a port other than 1433, change this also. Finally, if you are performing these steps for a different availability group, you must change the name.

```
USE master
GO
ALTER AVAILABILITY GROUP [SBSAGroup]
 MODIFY REPLICA ON
N'<SERVER NAME>' WITH
(SECONDARY_ROLE (READ_ONLY_ROUTING_URL = N'TCP://SERVER NAME.DOMAIN.com:1433'));
```

2. Configure the read-only routing list, which is used to determine which secondary to use when connecting with the listener. To configure the routing list, execute the following T-SQL on the primary server. This script must be executed for each server that is part of the availability group:

```
ALTER AVAILABILITY GROUP [SBSAGroup]
MODIFY REPLICA ON
N'<SERVER NAME>' WITH
(PRIMARY_ROLE (READ_ONLY_ROUTING_LIST=('<SERVER NAME>','<SERVER NAME>', '<SERVER
NAME>')));
```

In the routing list, you should provide a list of servers in the order of read access. In other words, assume you have three servers in your topology, Server1, Server2, and Server3, where Server1 is the primary server, and Server2 and Server3 are readable secondary servers. The routing list would resemble the following:

```
ALTER AVAILABILITY GROUP [SBSAGroup]
MODIFY REPLICA ON
N'SERVER1' WITH
(PRIMARY_ROLE (READ_ONLY_ROUTING_LIST=('SERVER2','SERVER3□, 'SERVER1□)));
```

3. For this to work correctly, you must add an additional property to your connection string. This property is *Application_Intent*, which must be set to *ReadOnly*. A sample connection string is as follows:

```
Server=tcp:SBSAGroup,1433;Database=AdventureWorks2102;IntegratedSecurity=SSPI;
ApplicationIntent=ReadOnly
```

With everything configured, if you connect to the listener using the preceding connection string, the application will be redirected to Server2. If Server2 is not available, it will be redirected to Server3, and so on until the list is exhausted.

Summary

This chapter covered a new feature of Microsoft SQL Server: AlwaysOn Availability Groups. A brief discussion of Windows Server Failover Clustering (WSFC) was provided. Next, you were introduced to availability groups, and you walked through the steps required to create an availability group. You learned how to use the dashboard to monitor your availability group and how to use the dashboard to manually failover. Finally, you saw how to configure the replicas for read-only access.

Log shipping

After completing this chapter, you will be able to

- Understand when and why to use log shipping.

- Understand the components that play a role in log shipping.

- Configure log shipping.

Log shipping is a low-cost, straightforward, and resilient solution you can use to achieve high availability and/or to offload reporting. It is used to automatically synchronize two databases at a chosen time interval. It accomplishes this by backing up, copying, and restoring transaction logs on a scheduled basis. With log shipping, failover is a manual process and is not automated. This is a primary drawback to log shipping when compared to a more robust technology such as AlwaysOn Availability Groups. The secondary database can be made available for read-only access between transaction log backup restores.

Log shipping offers the following benefits:

- The hardware cost is low. Your secondary server does not have to be as robust as your primary server, and it can even be a shared environment to help justify the expense. Many companies use their old hardware for the secondary server, while others combine instances and share space with development.

- The software cost is low. Log shipping is free and is part of every edition of SQL Server 2012 Express and above.

- It is relatively easy to set up and maintain.

- It is generally very reliable and rarely breaks.

- With practice and documentation, manual failover can be done fairly quickly (in less than 15 minutes).

- Depending upon the interval chosen and the reason for failover, the amount of data lost may be as long as the backup interval.

- It is useful in speeding up recovery from user or application error (queries that are accidentally damaged or deleted data).

The following are some of the downsides of the log shipping solution:

- Failover is not automatic—it requires practice, documentation, manual intervention, and time.

- Log shipping is incremental and not "real time." Depending upon the intervals chosen and the reason for failure, it is possible for some data to get lost between transaction log backup intervals.

- While a log-shipped database on a secondary server can be accessed for reporting, it will be read-only and it cannot be updated.

- Prior to each transaction log restore, any user connections to the database on the secondary server must be severed for the job to succeed.

- After each restore, the procedure cache and the data cache on the restored database are cold. SQL Server plans must be re-created and data reloaded into memory as queries are presented.

Now that you have an understanding of the pros and cons of log shipping, you'll move on to cover the different log shipping components. You'll learn about log shipping prerequisites, and then you'll work through the steps involved in configuring log shipping.

Log shipping components

To implement log shipping, you will need the following components:

- **Primary server** The instance of SQL Server that is your production environment.

- **Primary database** The database on the primary server that will be synchronized to the secondary server.

- **Secondary server** The instance of SQL Server that will receive and host the synchronized database from the primary server. There can be one or more secondary servers.

- **Secondary database** The database on the secondary server that started out as a copy of the primary database and is being periodically kept in sync through log shipping. There can be one or more secondary databases.

- **Monitor server** An optional instance of SQL Server that tracks the success or failure of the three pieces (jobs) that tie log shipping together across the primary and secondary server: backups, file copies, and restores.

In addition to these components, several SQL Server Agent jobs are created:

- **Transaction log backup job** Created on the primary server. See Job A1 in Figure 32-1.

- **Transaction log file copy job** Created on the secondary server. See Job B2 in Figure 32-1. The original transaction log backup file remains on the primary server. Each secondary server is responsible for acquiring its own copy of the source transaction log backup files.

- **Transaction log restore job** Created on the secondary server. Each secondary server will have its own log restore job. See Job B3 in Figure 32-1.

- **Alert job** Both the primary and secondary server have alert jobs created to detect if a backup or restore operation does not complete successfully within a chosen threshold of time.

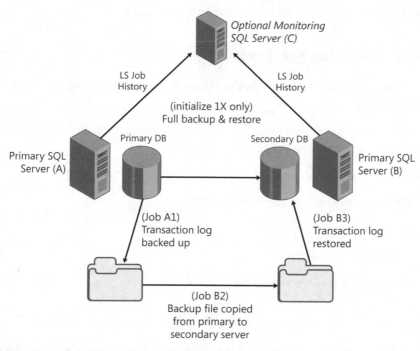

FIGURE 32-1 A sample topology of a log shipping architecture.

Log shipping prerequisites

Before you can configure log shipping, you must complete a few steps to ensure that everything meets the minimum requirements. First, you must ensure that the individual configuring log shipping is a member of the sysadmin fixed server role. Next, you must create a share that allows the secondary SQL Server instance to access the location where the transaction logs are initially backed up by the primary SQL Server instance. For example, if the primary server backs up the logs to C:\LSDemo, this same folder would need to be accessible by the secondary server as a UNC path, similar to \\PrimarySQLServerName\LSDemo. Security for the shared folder and the network share is usually the hang-up for transaction log shipping. To mitigate any challenges or potential security issues, ensure that the SQL Server Agent service account for both servers has been granted access to this folder.

Finally, you must ensure that the primary database uses either the full or bulk-logged recovery model, and a full database backup must be performed on the same database. The restore must be done in either No Recovery or Standby mode to allow future transaction log backups to be applied.

As the name "log shipping" suggests, logs are shipped from one server to another. Specifically, transaction logs are copied from the primary server to a secondary server. As stated earlier, when log shipping is configured, a SQL Server Agent job is created that backs up the transaction log. As a result, you must ensure that other mechanisms outside of the transaction log backup job created by log shipping are not also performing transaction log backups. For example, you must disable any maintenance plans that may be currently backing up the transaction log.

Prepare the database for log shipping

Prior to executing the steps, you need to create a share on the primary server and grant the secondary server access to it.

1. Open SQL Server Management Studio (SSMS) and connect to the server that will act as the primary in your log shipping topology.

2. Open a new query in SSMS.

3. In the query editor, execute the following T-SQL code:

    ```
    USE master
    GO
    CREATE DATABASE [LSDemo]
    GO
    ALTER DATABASE [LSDemo] SET RECOVERY FULL
    GO
    ```

    This query creates a database and then changes the recovery mode to FULL.

4. Create a folder on your C drive named LSDemo. Use Windows permissions to share the folder publically for the purposes of this exercise.

5. Open a new query window and execute the following T-SQL code:

    ```
    USE master
    GO
    BACKUP DATABASE LSDemo
    TO DISK = 'C:\LSDemo\LSDemo.bak'
    ```

6. Open SSMS and connect to the server that will act as the secondary in your log shipping topology.

7. Open a new query window and execute the following T-SQL.

 Note In the following script, *alwayson1* is the name of the primary server and *lsdemo* is the name of the share for the C:\LSDemo folder.

```
USE master
GO
RESTORE DATABASE LSDemo
FROM DISK = '\\alwayson1\lsdemo\lsdemo.bak'
WITH NORECOVERY
```

The last line in the statement, *WITH NORECOVERY*, ensures that additional transaction logs can be restored to this database. If you open Object Explorer on the secondary server and expand the Database folder, you will see the database in the list with Restoring in parentheses.

Configuring log shipping

With all the pieces in place, you can now configure log shipping between the two servers. SSMS provides an intuitive user interface for configuring log shipping.

Configure log shipping using SSMS

1. Open SSMS and connect to the primary server.

2. Expand the server in Object Explorer.

3. Expand the Databases folder.

4. Right-click the LSDemo database and select Properties from the menu.

5. In the Select a Page pane, select Transaction Log Shipping.

6. In the right pane, select the Enable This as a Primary Database in a Log Shipping Configuration option.

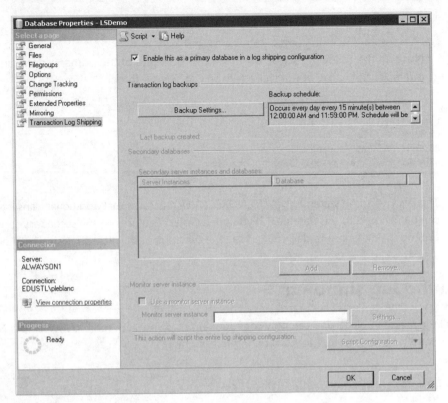

7. Click the Backup Settings button in the Transaction Log Backups section.

8. In the Network Path to Backup Folder text box, enter the UNC path to the share that will be used by the secondary server to access the local backups on the primary server—for example, \\PrimarySQLServerName\LSDemo.

9. In the If the Backup Folder Is Located on the Primary Server text box, type in the local path to the transaction log backup location on the primary server—for example, C:\LSDemo.

10. Review the Delete Files Older Than setting. This setting controls how many days of transaction log backup files to keep on the primary server. SQL Server will automatically delete any files older than the set value each time the backup job runs. In this sense, it is similar to the maintenance cleanup task in a maintenance plan. The default is 72 hours (3 days).

11. Review the Alert If No Backup Occurs Within setting. The default is 1 hour.

12. Choose how often you would like to have the transaction log backup occur. The default is every 15 minutes, beginning at the top of the hour. To adjust this time, click the Schedule button and use the scheduling wizard that appears. The schedule for backups is separate from the schedule used for either the copy or restore portions of log shipping. In other words, you can choose to back up the log every 15 minutes and copy and/or restore less often (say, hourly), if that better suits your needs.

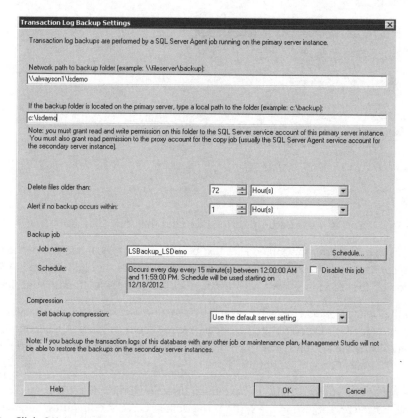

13. Click OK. You are returned to the previous Database Properties dialog box.

14. Click the Add button under the Secondary Server Instances and Databases grid.

15. Click the Connect button at the top right to choose the secondary SQL Server instance.

16. In the Secondary Database text box, choose (if it exists) or type (if it is new) the secondary database name.

17. On the Initialize Secondary Database tab, choose the first option to create a Full Backup of the Primary Database and restore it to the secondary server.

18. Click the Restore Options button. In the Restore Options dialog box, you can specify the location of the secondary database data and log files on the secondary server. The location of these files may differ from their named location on the primary server. Enter the desired locations.

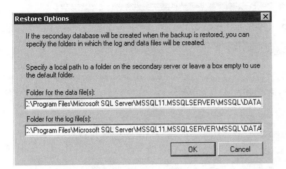

19. Click OK.

20. On the Secondary Database Settings dialog box, click the Copy Files tab.

21. In the Destination Folder for Copied Files text box, type in the local path (from the perspective of the secondary server) to which the transaction log backups should be copied. A SQL Server Agent job on the secondary server will be copying files from the UNC path specified in step 8.

22. Review the Delete Copied Files After setting. This setting controls how many days of transaction log backup files to keep on the secondary server. The secondary SQL Server Agent will automatically delete any files older than the set value each time the file copy job runs. The default is 72 hours (3 days). Accept the default.

23. Choose how often you would like to have the transaction log copy to occur by clicking the Schedule button and adjusting the setting. The default is every 15 minutes, beginning at the top of the hour. It often makes sense to stagger this slightly from the backup job in step 9. In this example, accept the default setting.

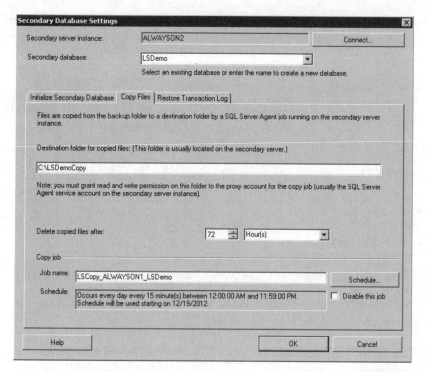

24. Click the Restore Transaction Log tab.

25. You have two choices in the Database State When Restoring Backups section:

- No Recovery Mode leaves the secondary database in a recovering state in which users cannot connect and the database is not available for read-only connectivity. Further transaction logs can be restored.

- Standby Mode allows processes to connect to the secondary database in read-only mode. When this option is selected, a check box option is enabled that dictates whether to disconnect users in the database when restoring backups. If this option is not selected, transaction log restores will be blocked by the existence of any connections to the secondary database.

Select the No Recovery Mode option.

26. If you would like to delay the transaction log restore process on the secondary server, choose a delay time under the Delay Restoring Backups at Least section. The delay controls how recent the logs being applied should be.

For example, a delay of 0 minutes (the default) would cause a restore to apply all transaction log backups found in the copied folder. A delay of 15 minutes would restore only those transaction log backups present in the copied folder that are more than 15 minutes old. Accept the default. Table 32-1 provides a sample backup, copy, and restore schedule that you may use when implementing log shipping.

TABLE 32-1 Example backup/copy/restore schedule

	Backup job	Copy job	Restore job
Interval	Every 15 minutes	Every 15 minutes	Every 15 minutes
Start time	Top of the hour	2 minutes past the hour	Top of the hour
Example run times	12:00, 12:15, 12:30	12:02, 12:17, 12:32	12:00, 12:15, 12:30 . . .
Delay			30 minutes
Restoring logs before and equal to timestamp			11:30, 11:45, 12:00 . . .
Quantity of unapplied backups			2

27. Review the Alert If No Restore Occurs Within setting. The default is 45 minutes.

28. Click the Schedule button to access a dialog box where you can control when and how often the restore job runs on the secondary server.

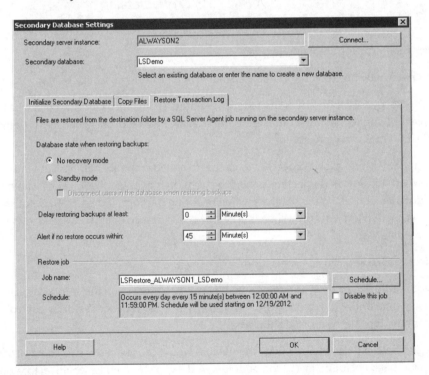

29. Click OK.

30. If you choose to use a monitoring SQL Server (optional) instance, select the Use a Monitor Server Instance check box toward the bottom of the Database Properties dialog box. Click the Settings button to designate the monitor server. Then perform the following steps:

   a. Click the Connect button and select the instance of SQL Server that will be used to monitor log shipping.

   b. Specify the means of authentication.

   c. Choose how long to keep history (the default is 96 hours) on the monitor server.

   d. Click OK.

31. Prior to completing the wizard, you may want to script the log shipping configuration to T-SQL for easier reimplementation. To do so, simply click the Script Configuration button and choose the clipboard, a file, or a new query window.

32. On the Database Properties dialog box, click OK to begin log shipping. The wizard will perform all of the tasks requested and set up the log shipping jobs on the servers participating in your log shipping architecture.

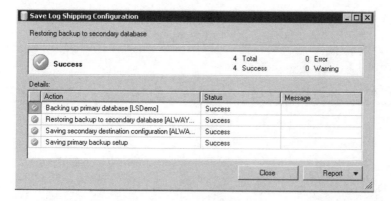

Log shipping is now configured. Any changes made to the database on the primary database will be shipped and synchronized via the log shipping process.

Summary

This chapter provided an overview of the log shipping components and prerequisites, and you learned how to configure log shipping. Log shipping is a relatively low-cost, hardy, and easy-to-implement mechanism that can be used for multiple purposes: achieving high availability with manual failover, moving reporting activity away from the production database, and recovery from user or application error that damages or deletes data.

With the wizard provided in Microsoft SQL Server 2012, setting up and supporting log shipping is easier and more foolproof than ever before.

Index

Symbols

A

About the Author

PATRICK LEBLANC is a Microsoft SQL Server and Business Intelligence Technical Solution Professional. He has written several blogs and articles on his blog at *http://patrickdleblanc.com*, *www.sqlservercentral.com*, and *www.bidn.com*. Along with his 10 plus years of experience, he holds a Master of Science degree from Louisiana State University. He is the author and co-author of four SQL Server books. His past work experience includes senior consultant at Pragmatic Works and database architect at several companies. Prior to joining Microsoft, he was awarded the Microsoft MVP award for his contributions to the community.

What do you think of this book?

We want to hear from you!
To participate in a brief online survey, please visit:

microsoft.com/learning/booksurvey

Tell us how well this book meets your needs—what works effectively, and what we can do better. Your feedback will help us continually improve our books and learning resources for you.

Thank you in advance for your input!

How To Download Your eBook

To download your eBook, go to
http://go.microsoft.com/FWLink/?Linkid=224345
and follow the instructions.

Please note: You will be asked to create a free online account and enter the access code below.

Your access code:

> JXLRBDG

Microsoft® SQL Server® 2012 Step by Step

Your PDF eBook allows you to:

- Search the full text
- Print
- Copy and paste

Best yet, you will be notified about free updates to your eBook.

If you ever lose your eBook file, you can download it again just by logging in to your account.

Need help? Please contact:
mspinput@microsoft.com